Global Ireland

"*Global Ireland* is quite simply a masterpiece. Tom Inglis has set out to connect the small personal worlds of family, community, tradition and place, with the large-scale processes of globalization. His canvas is the modern history of Ireland, and the challenge is to explain how a small country with a robust sense of its own cultural distinctiveness has nonetheless been transformed into one of the most globalized countries in the world. Clearly written and well-informed, subtle and sensitive to paradox, this book will have a wide readership among all those interested in Ireland, globalization and the Irish diaspora, and will become a reference point for years to come."

Bob Holton, Sociology, Trinity College, Dublin

"Among sociologists working on Ireland in the nineteenth and twentieth centuries, Tom Inglis stands at the very top of the class. With his latest book he helps us all to much better understand how Ireland has been swept up and transformed in the wave of globalization at the end of the twentieth century and the beginning of this one. *Global Ireland* is a work to be savored!"

James S. Donnelly, Department of History,
University of Wisconsin–Madison

Global Ireland offers a concise synthesis of globalization's dramatic impact on Ireland. In the past fifteen years, Ireland has transformed from a sleepy and depressed European backwater to the "Celtic Tiger," a country with a booming economy based on knowledge and high-tech industries. Using a number of case studies of Ireland's transition, Tom Inglis explains what this means for traditional Irish culture and society and offers an incisive social portrait of globalizing Ireland.

Tom Inglis is Associate Professor of Sociology at University College Dublin. He is the author of three books on Ireland: *Moral Monopoly, Lessons in Irish Sexuality* and *Truth, Power and Lies*.

Globalizing Regions

Globalizing Regions offers concise accounts of how the nations and regions of the world are experiencing the effects of globalization. Richly descriptive yet theoretically informed, each volume shows how individual places are navigating the tension between age-old traditions and the new forces generated by globalization.

Global Ireland

Same Difference

TOM INGLIS

Routledge
Taylor & Francis Group

NEW YORK AND LONDON

First published 2008
by Routledge
270 Madison Avenue,
New York, NY 10016

Simultaneously published in the UK
by Routledge
2 Park Square, Milton Park, Abingdon,
Oxon OX14 4RN

Routledge is an imprint of the Taylor & Francis Group, an informa business

© 2008 Taylor & Francis

Typeset in 11/14pt Joanna by RefineCatch Limited, Bungay, Suffolk
Printed and bound in the United States on acid-free paper by Sheridan Books, Inc., MI

Library of Congress Cataloging in Publication Data
A catalog record for this book has been requested

ISBN10: 0–415–94422–8 (hbk)
ISBN10: 0–415–94423–6 (pbk)
ISBN10: 0–203–93400–8 (ebk)

ISBN13: 978–0–415–94422–9 (hbk)
ISBN13: 978–0–415–94423–6 (pbk)
ISBN13: 978–0–203–93400–5 (ebk)

Contents

In memory of
Aileen
(1952–2005)

Acknowledgments

This book has been a long time coming. It began more than five years ago with an invitation from my old friend, and former PhD supervisor, Charles Lemert to write the book on Ireland that was part of a new series of national studies of globalization called *Globalizing Regions* that he and Dave McBride were putting together. As with everything else, he sold the idea very easily to me. I knew very little about globalization but knew that I wanted to write about cultural rather than economic or political issues, and that I wanted to integrate not just the national, but the local and the personal. I had decided to focus on a village and had chosen Ballivor because of the presence of NEC, a Japanese transnational corporation which had a factory in the town. I remember meeting Tom Malone in June 2002. Everything was going well. Ireland was in the final of the World Cup. I was on a high.

Then my world fell apart. The morning after Ireland beat Saudi Arabia 3–0, my wife Aileen told me she had breast cancer. After a desperate fight to stay alive, she died in May, 2005. She was the love of my life. I am very grateful to everyone who gave me the time and space to help me deal with such a loss.

In between Aileen's diagnosis and death, I was fortunate to be awarded a Senior Research Fellowship in 2004 from the Irish Research Council for the Humanities and Social Sciences. The Fellowship was crucial to the completion of this book.

There are numerous people who have helped me bring the book to fruition. I would like, in particular, to thank everyone in Ballivor who allowed me to interview them, particularly M.J. McGearty, and in NEC Ireland, especially Tom Malone. Jim Dalton from the Central Statistics Office and Karen Andersen and Freddie Muldoon helped me gather the data. Martin Dowling, Alice Feldman, Steve Loyal, Donal McAnaney and Iarfhlaith Watson read and commented on various sections of the book. My son Arron, again, came up with a wonderful image for the cover design.

I am grateful to the comments of the referees who provided some excellent insights and advice about an earlier draft of the manuscript. Steve Rutter has been a wonderful editor to work with, enormously encouraging and supportive.

However, above all, I owe an enormous debt of gratitude to Carol MacKeogh. She read and reread the chapters as I wrote and rewrote them, and was wonderful in her criticisms, comments, and determination to help me finish.

In times of great emotional turmoil, my son Arron and daughter Olwen have been a rich source of love, beauty, comfort and consolation. And so I come to the end of these brief acknowledgments which, on previous occasions, always referred to my love for Aileen. Much of what I wrote was for her. She was always the first to read and comment on my work. I loved her intensely. She made my world so beautiful.

Foreword

I have written this book primarily for people who are intrigued by what is happening in Ireland. The central question is simple: what have been the effects for Ireland of having moved so rapidly from being a very traditional, insular, Catholic society to becoming one of the most open, globalized societies in the world? I concentrate on the Republic of Ireland—the North has unfortunately been a different place for far too long—and I focus particularly on culture. There are already numerous studies that have examined the growth and development of the "Celtic Tiger" economy. I concentrate on the impact of social and economic transformations on popular culture and everyday life. Most of all, I try to find out what makes the Irish different and to what extent this national cultural difference is significant. Have the social and economic transformations resulted in the Irish adopting a lifestyle and way of being in the world which is little different from the rest of Western society? I write about the transformation in the Irish sense of self, particularly the emergence of a new individualism in Ireland. I have written the book in a way that would appeal to a general reader. I have tried to avoid being either too empirical or too theoretical.

The book is written from a sociological perspective, mainly because I believe that sociology provides the best explanation for how human society has come to be the way it is and, consequently, how the Irish have come to be the way they are. It is mostly a reading of Irish history and, in particular, the transformations that have taken place in Ireland over the last fifty years. I rely on secondary sources, previous research, the internet, newspapers and so forth. I also rely on some of my own experiences during this time as well as research I have conducted on transformations in Ballivor, a village in the east of Ireland. I have tried to place these transformations in the context of cultural globalization and the rapid increase in the flow of media messages, ideas, knowledge, people and beliefs around the world.

The book hangs together on a theoretical framework of sameness and difference. This opens up a can of philosophical and sociological worms. I have deliberately avoided trying to develop some abstract general theory of sameness and difference. But sameness and difference are central to understanding identity and social life. They have to do with the way individuals present themselves to others. They are the masks of social life. Individuals emphasise and play out their sameness and difference according to the social context. I am the same but different from other members of my family. My family is different but the same as other Irish families. What happens in Irish families is central to what makes the Irish different. But Irish families and Irish culture have been opened up to global influences that make the Irish the same as many others around the world.

To help reveal these complexities, I sometimes write about myself. Sometimes I refer to the Irish as "they" as if I was not the same. At other times I refer to "we", as if I recognize and accept my sameness. The reason is simply that depending on the context, I feel as if I am like no other Irish person. But, then, at other times I feel I am like every other Irish person. And, then, to make matters worse, there are times when I feel like every other human being.

One

My mother didn't hug me as a child. I have no memory of sitting on her lap, being held and cuddled. She was a generous, kind woman but, physically and emotionally, a cold fish. She was afraid of touch. All the time I was growing up, I craved to be touched. I knew I was loved, but I wanted to feel it.

When I look back over my early adult life, I can see how this lack of physical affection manifested itself later. When I first met Aileen, I struggled to hug, caress and make love to her. It took time and patience to develop the physical and emotional bond that held us together. I still have difficulty hugging; just standing in the middle of the day, in the middle of my home, in the middle of my life and hugging the ones I love. There is a link between bonding and how we come to be the way we are. My personality and emotional way of being in the world were shaped by my parents, my family and the way we bonded. But the way our family came to be the way it was, the way my parents brought me up, the way I came to be the way I am, were shaped by social structures, discourses and long-term historical processes that stretched way beyond my family and home in the suburbs of Dublin. It was the particular way in which these structures and processes came together in my family that made me different. But, at a higher level, these structures and processes had their origin outside of Ireland. It is the way in which the Irish adapted to these structures and processes that made them different. I am interested in what makes me the same as but different from other people. But to answer that question I have to find out what makes the Irish the same as but different from other people. The desire to be the same as but different from others is, like the desire to bond and belong, a universal feature of human society. It has always manifested itself at the level of families, clans and tribes. More recently, with globalization, it has operated at the level of nations. What interests me is the way globalization has influenced the nature of social bonds and the way people struggle to be the same but different.

There has been much that has been written about globalization, about how the world is becoming one place and how, more and more, Western culture is seeping into the everyday lives of more and more people.[1] This book is an attempt to explore this process. However, rather than attempt a comparative study of global culture, I will look at what is happening in Ireland and the extent to which culture and everyday life in Ireland are becoming the same as or remaining different from the rest of the West.[2] To understand this process I think it is necessary to go below the level of national culture and to examine to what extent local everyday life is becoming global.[3] Consequently, towards the end of the book I will look at the impact of globalization on the culture and everyday life of Ballivor, a small village in the east of Ireland.

What makes Irish people different are cultural practices that have been developed over centuries and inherited through socialization. Irish people have developed different ways of bonding and relating to each other. It is these practices, derived from a particular habitus or unquestioned pre-disposed way of being in the world, that produce a collective identity and sense of belonging.[4] The more Ireland became globalized during the latter half of the twentieth century, the more it entered into the global flow of culture, the more it moved from a Catholic culture based on practices of chastity, humility, piety and self-denial to a liberal-individualist consumer culture of self-indulgence.[5]

We grow up and become who we are in circumstances not of our own choosing. I grew up in a strong Catholic family. My mother went to Mass and Holy Communion every day. Everyone told me she was a saint. Certainly she was an extraordinarily holy, Catholic, self-sacrificing woman. The problem with saints is that they are closer to heaven than earth. They are lofty creatures who strive to escape from their bodies, from this mortal coil, and reach higher spiritual plains. Maybe saints cannot hug because being physical is literally beneath them? I wish my mother had not been a saint. When I was fourteen, I asked her why she never hugged me. She told me that she wanted me to be strong and independent. I told her to fuck off.

We never talked about that incident. It was the beginning of a long struggle of resistance against the culture into which I had been born and which had molded my soul, my sense of self. I know I hurt my mother with all my questioning. She lived in the depth of her Catholic faith. She did not like to reflect about herself or her religion. "A little bit of knowledge," she used to say, "does an awful lot of harm."

My father was a religious man, but no saint. He went to Mass once a week and he read the Bible most nights in bed. I don't know what it was like for him to be married to a saint. I never saw him kiss or hug my mother. I never saw them exchange a caress or an embrace or, indeed, any basic signs of love and affection. The idea that they kissed or made love seems weird, like some gross pornographic film. I never saw them naked. They slept in separate beds.

The particular social bond that made me different emerged from cultural practices that made the Irish the same and that, in turn, made them different from the rest of the West. This physical and emotional way of being in the world became so embodied through socialization that it became second nature. It was something that was so taken for granted that it was rarely thought of or questioned.[6] It is like the air we breathe; we notice it most when it is not there. When we are in it we are like fish in water.[7]

As I grew older I realized I was not alone. I came from a long line of emotionally and sexually repressed Catholics. I was just another guy who had been subjected to a child-rearing practice that involved physical and emotional distance.[8] Children were not to be indulged. It would make them soft and selfish. It was part and parcel of growing up in Catholic Ireland in the 1950s.[9] There was a strange taboo about the body, sex and being physically affectionate.[10] There has always been a strong element of self-denial and penitential practice in Irish Catholicism.[11] It had a strong influence on Irish culture and the personalities to which it gave rise. Of course the Irish were not unique; elements of Victorian emotional detachment and prudery were to be found in other Western cultures. It is just that in Ireland they seemed to have survived much longer into the twentieth century and to have penetrated further into our bodies and souls.[12]

The absence of physical affection, an obsession with sex, and an emphasis on self-denial have been central to what makes the Irish different. It is the source of their imagination, their humor, self-presentation, conversation, literature, art, music.[13] It is part of the way they relate, work, engage and play with each other. It is a language of being in the world that became as rich and different as the Irish language itself. It is a surrender of the self to the wider group. It is this peculiar form of self-repression and surrender that is at the center of Irish *"craic"* (fun) which revolves around witty conversation, banter and repartee, laughing at life, drowning sorrows but, most of all, a relentless ruthless teasing and making fun of oneself and others. It is a way of being in the world that shuns and shows disdain for ambition, selfishness and materialism. It can be wonderful, but it can also be soul-destroying. In this world, if you get "above your station" or "too big for your boots," you could be crucified. They may not nail you to a cross, but the tongue-lashing could be a social death worse than flaying.

UNDERSTANDING SAMENESS AND DIFFERENCE

The question of sameness and difference lies at the heart of social life. Our knowledge of the world begins with classification systems and, as Durkheim pointed out, the most fundamental of these begins with seeing and understanding ourselves and other members of our family, clan, group, community or nation as similar, and others as different.[14] Everyday life revolves around individuals and their struggle to be seen, understood and appreciated as being members of the social groups to which they belong, of doing and saying things that identify them with the group. And yet, while the group strives to create and maintain a sense of sameness and belonging, there is within the membership a struggle for individual difference and recognition and acceptance of that difference.[15]

Classifying people as similar and different is embedded in social life, both in the micro-events and practices of everyday life and in the macro-strategies of organizations, institutions and nation-states. The problem with studying similarity, identification and belonging is that they can be relatively permanent as well as transitional if not momentary. It is said of the Irish that if there were three of them left on a desert island, two of them would be in a corner talking about the other. But the next day the combination might have changed.

Sameness and difference are so intertwined and co-dependent that it is difficult to separate them analytically. Any individual is both the same as and different from other members of the family, group, nation to which he or she belongs. While the struggle between being the same and being different is a universal feature of human society, the conditions in which this struggle takes place have changed. The way a member of a remote tribe in the Amazon jungle struggles to be the same but different is quite unlike the struggle for someone like me living in Dublin. There are different cultural symbols and practices. And yet there is the same sense of balancing difference with bonding and belonging. However, what is different is the nature and strength of the social bonds. Members of the Amazon tribe are more subsumed within their culture. They operate more within an unquestioned reality in which there is little or no critical self-reflection. The bonds that bind individuals to the tribe are so strong that they dominate their identity and sense of self. The social bonds in Catholic Ireland were never that strong, but they often came close. There was an attempt to cultivate a culture in which one lived without questioning.

There have been dramatic changes in Ireland over the last 50 years. Irish people are now part of a culture in which the emphasis is on self-realization. The culture of the world capitalist system is based on using mostly mass-produced, commodified consumer symbols to create personal identities and an individual sense of difference. What binds Irish people more together now—what creates a sense of bonding and belonging—is a commitment to self-realization through con-sumer choice. The Irish way of being in the world is now structured more by market and media forces which emphasize the importance of difference, self-realization and continual self-transformation and which rarely emphasize the importance of self-denial and self-surrender. The world capitalist system has changed the conditions in which we realize our sameness and difference. It has changed the nature of our social bonds.

One of my reasons for studying sociology was to try to understand how I came to be the way I am. Psychotherapy, counselors and therapists seem to have developed a monopoly over journeys of self-discovery. We are used to the idea of people delving deeper and deeper into their past, into their character, to bring to the surface the hidden feelings, ways of being and relating to others, that become part and parcel of who they are. I am interested in what makes me different. But to understand that difference I have to understand what makes Irish people different. Has the way in which the Irish have been brought up over generations, the way in which they have been socialized, given rise to a different way of being in the world? Is this related to our being an island people, to our Celtic heritage, to our colonization by Britain over centuries, to our remaining Catholic rather than becoming Protestant, to the Great Famine of the nineteenth century?

I am also interested in the extent to which Irish people are increasingly becoming the same as the rest of the West. In the last 50 years, Ireland changed from being a very isolated, insular, Catholic rural society revolving around agriculture, to a more open, liberal-individualist, secular urban society revolving around business, commerce and high-tech, transnational corporations. In the last 15 years, the pace of change became more dramatic and Ireland now is identified as one of the most globalized societies in the world. To what extent has this affected Irish culture, the way Irish people see and understand themselves? How have the global exigencies of being at the heart of the world capitalist system impacted on what it is to be Irish? Fortunately very few people buy into the stereotypical tourist image that the Irish live in small, isolated, rural cottages and travel around with donkeys and carts. However, there are many who still think of Ireland as a country of devout Catholics who like to live simple, humble lives. Few would see us as the most globalized society in the world.

When I was studying at university, I was told that one of the cardinal rules of sociology was that one should never generalize from the particular; any person, place or thing was representative of nothing other than itself. In recent years I have begun to realize the fallacy of this rule. I think it is possible to reveal how cultural globalization is taking place through a detailed examination of one particular society. The task is to look for pieces of evidence that reveal the interaction between global and local cultural elements. We need to look for clues that reveal to what extent the Irish have adopted elements from other cultures. But we also have to look for clues that reveal the extent to which it has remained different. In some respects, Irish culture is similar to Irish fauna. There are native elements, but there have always been elements that have been imported or blown in from abroad. The question is to what extent have imported cultural elements come to dominate indigenous ones. What is the balance between local Irish culture and what have become global aspects of Western culture?

This method of looking for similarities and differences can be applied at a more local level. As well as looking at Irish culture as a whole, it is revealing to look at one particular place, in this case Ballivor, to examine the extent to which local culture has been infiltrated by global culture, and the way in which the local and global have interacted. To what extent is everyday cultural life in a small village in Ireland the same as it was 50 years ago, the same structure, habitus and practices? To what extent has it become globalized? Again the argument is that a forensic sociological examination of one particular village can bring to the surface clues and pieces of evidence which, when properly analyzed, reveal the nature and structure of Irish culture and the changes that have taken place, particularly in terms of cultural globalization. The village I chose to study was an ideal case as NEC, a large Japanese transnational company, had established a factory there in the 1970s. How did the arrival of such a factory impact on the everyday cultural life of the village?

To understand how global cultural elements become enmeshed with national and local elements, it is necessary to appreciate how this process takes place at the level of particular individuals, in terms of their identities, how they see and understand themselves and the world in which they live. This requires what may be called deep sociological tissue work. The task is to discover how cultural representations from different parts of the world become embedded in Irish people's bodies and souls, how they become part of their habitus.

To understand Irish people, it is necessary to understand how we came to be the way we are. When I was at school I was reminded constantly that we were an island of saints and scholars. We were told that we were a spiritual people more interested in things of the mind rather than the body and the material world. Over the last 50 years, the relatively closed, insular Irish habitus was gradually forced open by global cultural flows. The result has been a mixture of the old and the new, of traditional Irish ways of being becoming mixed with new global cultural elements. Ireland has come out of its shell in the last 15 years. There is a new self-confidence, but there is also still a commitment to family, religion, and community. It may well be that this combination of old and new ways of being in the world means that the Irish have the best of both worlds. The Irish have become very well-off, they have become part of global culture, but they still have strong social bonds and sense of self.

IRISH PEOPLE

Looking at a globe of the world, Ireland is seen as a small island in the North Atlantic off the coast of Europe. The overall population of the island is around 5.5 million people. Its geography, climate, people and history have been dominated by the Atlantic. Given that it is so far north it should have a climate like Newfoundland, but the Gulf Stream which comes from the Caribbean brings mild winters and moist summers which keep the country green and fertile.

Most people in the world probably know little or nothing about Ireland. If they do know anything, it has most likely come through the media which has fed the world with sound-bites and images of Ireland being a place where for decades Catholics and Protestants were locked into a bitter conflict involving riots, bombings and shootings. Stereotypical images contain elements of truth. Certainly it would be wrong to see contemporary Ireland in terms of a bitter conflict, let alone a battleground, between Catholics and Protestants. There are many similarities in the habitus and lifestyles of Catholics and Protestants, but there is a cultural legacy, particularly in Northern Ireland, that still sees religious identity as the main social and cultural division between people. To understand Irish people and what makes them different, it is essential to understand the last 400 years and what made them so Catholic and so Protestant. And to understand this, it is necessary to appreciate how Ireland, although a minnow in economic and political terms, has always been a thorn in the side of Britain.

Throughout its history, Ireland has been dominated by Britain. When in the sixteenth century, Britain became a

Protestant state, Ireland remained Catholic. As the British economy grew in the eighteenth century with the industrial revolution, as its towns and cities grew, Ireland remained a predominantly rural, peasant society. It was then that the British state started to be concerned about its nearest neighbor. Ireland became the first colony in what was to become the biggest empire in the modern world. Throughout the seventeenth and eighteenth centuries, Britain sought to subdue, control and pacify the Catholic Irish, primarily by turning them into Protestants. When this failed, they turned Catholics off their land and out of their homes, which they gave to Protestant settlers brought in from Britain. This colonial strategy of "planting" Protestants in Ireland generally failed. The one success was in the North of Ireland. The legacy of that success has dominated Irish history. In 1922, the island was divided. The South, with 26 counties, was given political independence, the North, with 6 counties, remained part of Britain. This led to a double minority in the island. The Catholics who dominated the South were in a minority in the North; the Protestants who dominated the North were in a minority in the South.

During the nineteenth century, the economic gap between Ireland and Britain grew enormously. While Ireland stagnated, Britain began to dominate the world. The Irish economy had developed, largely as a spin-off from the industrial boom in Britain. The population had increased threefold to 8 million in less than 100 years. But it was an unstable and haphazard growth. To accommodate the growth in numbers, farms began to be subdivided or established on marginal land. A large proportion of the population, particularly in the West, became dependent on the potato crop. When that crop failed three years in a row from 1845, there was a devastating famine. Over a million people died. By 1851, the population declined by about 2.25 million through disease, starvation, and emigration. Emigration was to become the major fact of Irish life throughout the rest of the nineteenth and all of the twentieth century. People had been fleeing the island way before the Famine, and continued to do so long after. Between 1800 and 1845, up to 1.5 million emigrated. Between 1845 and 1870 up to 3 million left. Some went to Australia, Canada and Britain, but the majority went to the United States.[16] Ongoing emigration became the safety valve for Irish society. The Irish developed peculiar demographic characteristics. Fewer people married in Ireland and those who did marry tended to marry at a late age. However, even though they married late, the Irish tended to have more children than could be comfortably catered for on small farms. This necessitated ongoing emigration in each generation.

Ireland, then, grew up in the shadow of Britain. Although geographically next door neighbors, they were economically, socially and culturally far apart. The British were at the center of the new world capitalist order; the Irish were at the periphery. From the foundation of the new state in 1922, the new leaders of Catholic Ireland attempted to shun the new world order by imagining Ireland as a latter-day island of saints and scholars who delighted in a spiritual life based on frugal comforts. Ireland remained a predominantly agricultural economy based on small-scale production up until the 1960s. Whatever goods were exported—mostly agricultural—went to Britain. At the same time, as emigration to the United States became more difficult, Britain soaked up the surplus labor from Ireland. The Irish became the lumpenproletariat who helped build Britain's cities, roads and railways. The British set standards for civilized behavior, social order and parliamentary democracy. The Irish developed a reputation for fighting and drinking. The British media tended to see and depict the Irish as feckless savages. The Irish tended to see the British as cold, calculating, colonial masters who were responsible for all their social and economic ills.

Throughout the nineteenth and twentieth centuries, Ireland was mostly an impoverished society. With the exception of some parts of Northern Ireland, it never industrialized. It was a green, rain-soaked land with most people living as peasants on small farms. They were barely able to scratch together a decent living: they found consolation and compensation in the Catholic Church. It was only towards the end of the twentieth century that things began to change. The Irish state, and then the people, began to abandon the Church's model of a spiritual and moral life based on frugal comforts. They began to embrace a new lifestyle based on economic growth, the development of the European Union, and the pleasures of materialism and consumerism. The goals and ambitions of the Irish have changed, but much of the Catholic habitus lingers on, deeply embedded in people's identity and sense of self.

CATHOLIC CAPITALISM

To understand how Ireland is different, it is necessary to understand the way in which it modernized and became part of the world capitalist system. There are many reasons why, during the nineteenth and twentieth centuries while many parts of Europe became core regions of the capitalist system, Ireland remained very much on the periphery. Most of these reasons are economic and political. The British state and the capitalist class had no interest in Ireland other than its being a food and labor provider and, at the same time, becoming civilized and politically stable, and remaining militarily impotent. The Irish were seen and treated as different, as a bunch of uncouth, unsophisticated peasants who, if not dealt with properly, could pose a threat to the wealth and stability of the rest of the British Isles.

Most Irish Catholics wanted to become prosperous, modernized and civilized, but not in the same way as the Protestant English counterparts. Again for numerous reasons dating back to the Reformation and the refusal to become Protestants, the Irish became steadfast, loyal Catholics. It was primarily because Irish society modernized through the Catholic Church that Ireland became different. Throughout the twentieth century Ireland became increasingly capitalist but, compared to elsewhere, the rate of growth of capitalism was quelled by a deep commitment to Catholicism and the Catholic Church. The Church was adamant that Ireland should not become the same as the rest of the West.

The task of the Church was to create and maintain Ireland as different, a Catholic culture and society which would be an example to the rest of the world. At the center of this difference was the creation of a disdain for and detachment from materialism, that is, for seeking satisfaction through involvement in the world, particularly through material comforts, consumer products and sensuous pleasures. Irish Catholics had to be protected from anything that distracted them from their spiritual way of life. They had to be kept innocent and pure. Even the simplest of pleasures of tea and bread could ruin the most virtuous of Irish souls. This is how Dr. Thomas Gilmartin, Archbishop of Tuam, described the evils of the material world to the Mayo *Feis* in 1927:

> The cheap foreign products of machinery have taken the place of the solid and lasting work of the Irish hand. Instead of milk and porridge, we have repeated doses of strong tea and white bread. Instead of socks and stockings made of Irish wool, we have foreign importations of imitation silk to minister to the vanity of

our girls. Instead of visiting and story-telling, there are cinemas and night-walking, often with disaster to virtue. Instead of Irish dances we have sensuous contortions of the body timed to a semi-barbaric music. Instead of hard, honest work there is the tendency to do little for big wages.[17]

The deeply embedded desire to remain Catholic, combined with the Church's monopoly over education, health and social welfare, ensured that little or nothing was said or done that was contrary to the ethos and teachings of the Catholic Church. While Ireland did not become a theocratic state, it did become a very Catholic society in which a Catholic way of thinking permeated public opinion, the media and everyday social life.

Ireland still sees itself as a very Catholic society. When Pope John Paul II visited in 1979, over a million people came to greet him in Dublin. Given that he made visits to other parts of the country and that the total population of the republic at the time was just 3.5 million, this was a considerable indication of the depth of faith of the people. In 1974, over nine in ten people were Catholic and nine in ten of these went to Mass once a week. Although this level of devotion has waned in recent years, Ireland still has a comparatively high level of religious belief and practice. In 1999, a study of European values found that nine in ten Catholics believed in God and heaven, almost two-thirds went to Mass at least once a week, and almost half prayed every day.

The heyday of the Catholic devotionalism and the Church's monopoly over morality and social life may be in decline, but a Catholic habitus is still deeply engrained in the hearts and bodies of most Irish people. Over the past 50 years, but particularly in the last 10 years, Irish Catholics have combined their devotion to the Church with an equal devotion to indulging themselves in the material world. They have learnt to render unto the Church the things that belong to the Church and to the marketplace the things that belong to consuming. For most Irish Catholics, not to marry in church, not to send their children to Catholic schools, not to celebrate First Holy Communions and Confirmations, and not to have a Catholic funeral would be anathema. But it would also be anathema for them not to have a good time, own a nice home, travel in a stylish car, indulge themselves in new clothes, go on shopping sprees, eat and drink well, take foreign holidays and so forth. The poor Irish Catholic mice seem to have had little difficulty in becoming self-consumed capitalist rats.

CONSUMER CAPITALISM

The stereotypical image of Ireland—produced primarily for tourists but cherished by many Irish themselves—is of a rural retreat where people work to live rather than live to work, have time to meet, gossip and laugh at life, and have a Catholic sense of self that permeates their being. It is an image which is directly at odds with the disenchanted world of rational, bureaucratic life, cities, traffic, the daily routine of getting and spending, being always on the move but always "in touch" through a mobile phone. If the stereotypical image of Ireland was correct, then it would be the most insular, disconnected, non-globalized society in the West. And yet, for three years running (2002–2004) a survey by A.T. Kearney/*Foreign Policy* magazine ranked the Republic of Ireland as the most globalized country in the world. On a variety of different criteria, Ireland scored higher than Singapore (second), Switzerland (third), Canada (sixth) and the United States (seventh). Ireland had the most open economy, particularly in terms of foreign trade and investment. It also scored high on three other measures: use of modern technology, travel and communication outside Ireland, and involvement in global organizations and politics. Moreover, if the Economist Intelligence Unit (EIU) is correct—and there must be some concern for the type of questions asked to devise the indicators—Ireland is also the best country in the world to live in, in terms of the quality of life. Using a regression analysis of responses to life-satisfaction surveys from 74 countries the EIU identified nine indicators to determine quality of life: income, health, freedom, unemployment, family life, climate, political stability and security, gender equality, and family and community life. When these were all added together, Ireland comfortably topped the league with a score of 8.33; which was significantly higher than second-placed Switzerland with 8.07. The EIU said that Ireland came out on top because it "successfully combines elements of the new (the fourth-highest GDP in the world in 2005, low unemployment, political liberties) with the preservation of certain cosy elements of the old, such as stable family and community life."[18]

Globalization is the main reason why Ireland became so rich so quick. In the 1950s, Ireland was primarily a slow, insular economy that was oriented to protecting home industries and keeping out foreign competitors and products. Family farming was still the primary industry. Politicians and civil servants were mainly devout Catholics and, even if they had doubts, they portrayed a Catholic vision of Irish society which gave primacy to family and community and shunned materialism, consumerism and liberal individualism. It was a Catholic form of capitalism. In the 1950s, when most other European economies were thriving after the Second World War, Ireland was in the depths of economic depression.

Over the next 50 years, two things happened. Many politicians and civil servants started to realize that Ireland was being left behind. They began to shake off their Catholic view of capitalism and to embrace materialism, trade and economic growth. Ireland could be both fully Catholic and fully capitalist. Economic growth took off. Trade barriers were taken down, consumer goods began to flood into the country. The education system was radically overhauled. It was still dominated by the Catholic Church, but the state changed the curriculum away from a classical education towards a more scientific and technological one and, at the same time, made second-level education free for everyone.

At the same time, transnational companies began to take an interest in Ireland. It had the advantage of a young, relatively cheap, relatively well-educated labor force. More importantly, in 1973 Ireland gained entry to the European Union. The state engaged in a strategic policy of canvassing these companies and inviting them to come and set up factories in Ireland. Towards the end of the 1980s, and another decade of economic depression, the state became even more aggressive in attracting direct foreign investment. It provided various incentives to transnational corporations, the most important of which was a low level of corporation tax. But it also offered a young well-educated workforce, stable industrial relations and a form of corporate government in which programs of social and economic policy were agreed between the main social partners, particularly the state, employers and trade unions.

There are two different ways of examining Irish wealth. One way is to look at the income per head of population. When this is adjusted for price differences across countries, the level of Gross Domestic Product is obtained. Since the emergence and growth of the Celtic Tiger, particularly in the late 1990s, Ireland has been one of the richest countries in the world. In 2004, the GDP per head of population was $48,250. While less than Norway and Luxembourg, this was over $6,000 higher than the United States and almost

$10,000 higher than the United Kingdom. However, if one examines the amount of income accruing to people who reside in Ireland—Gross National Product—the picture is a bit different. This is because GNP accounts for only 82 percent of GDP. This gap is one of the biggest in the world. Using this measure, Ireland is only the 17th richest country.[19]

The reason for the difference is that transnational companies have been the source of the Celtic Tiger. The profits which they make are often exported out of the country. Thus while exported profits are included in GDP, they are not included in GNP figures. Moreover, because Ireland has a very low level of corporation tax, many transnational companies seek to have profits from their operations registered here, to avoid paying tax. Subsidiaries in low-tax countries like Ireland can also import components at artificially cheap prices, assemble them and sell them on at inflated prices, recording artificially high profit rates. Such practices are especially prevalent in sectors where components have no clear "open-market prices," like electronic components or patented preparations for pharmaceuticals and soft drinks.[20] It has been estimated that foreign firms employ one in 10 people in the Irish economy which, in turn, gives rise to other employment. They invest twice as much in staff training, account for nearly three-quarters of all private research and development and pay the state more than €2.5 billion in profit taxes.[21]

The emergence of the Celtic Tiger economy created major changes in Irish social and cultural life. Although there are still major gaps between the rich and the poor, particularly between a new cosmopolitan elite that is globally oriented and a local underclass that is dependent on social welfare, a large new middle class has emerged whose standard of living has increased dramatically. When I was growing up in the 1950s, Dundrum was the nearest village. It was about five miles from the city center. It had a small main street with the usual assortment of grocers, drapers, butchers, chemists, pubs and, a sign of the times, two bicycle shops. In March 2005, a new shopping mall opened in Dundrum. It is said to be one of the biggest in Europe. It covers 1.35 million square feet, has 3,400 car park spaces, employs over 4,000 people, and attracts over 50,000 customers each day. Over 75,000 people turned up on the first day. In order to create a link with the past, the designers of the new cathedral to consumerism decided to keep the old mill pond and two of the original trees, the only difference being that the mill pond was transformed into an illuminated water feature. The director of the center maintained that the center would "define the way we live today and offer a holistic experience to enrich, indulge and inspire every aspect of our lives." He went on: "It is our intention to ensure that our core values of quality, luxury and contemporary style are translated seamlessly into the Town Centre." On the morning the new center opened in Dundrum, there was a short ecumenical service. One of the prayers read: "God of Beauty, may we see in the magnificence of this centre a reflection of your beauty, variety, brightness and color, may it fill us with wonder and may it raise our hearts and spirits to you."[22]

There was a debate in Ireland towards the end of the last century as to whether Ireland was a priest-ridden society. It was argued that the Catholic Church had grown up almost like a parasite on Irish society. It had created a culture of fear—people believed that if they did not obey Church rules and regulations they would burn in hell for eternity. It had developed a monopoly over education, health and social welfare services on which people were dependent and which, therefore, kept them compliant. In reality, of course, the Irish people wanted to be good Catholics in order to increase their standard of living, to become civilized, and to be spiritually and morally superior to the English Protestants who had colonized them for centuries. Times have changed and having once blamed the priest for all their ills, there are those who now blame the capitalist; advertisers and market managers are deemed to create fantasies and desires and to entice people to buy goods and services that they don't need. The reality is that Irish people do not just want to consume, but love to do so. It may have been the capitalist entrepreneurs who built the Dundrum town center, but it was consumers who wanted if not demanded it. Owners and controllers of the means of consumption are constantly competing with one another to see who can be the most responsive to the demands of consumers.[23] Much as Irish Catholics did not see themselves as dominated and controlled, neither do contemporary Irish consumers. Consuming is time-consuming and risky, but it is something that consumers like doing. It is fantastic and exhilarating. It brings excitement into the treadmill of domesticity, commuting and working. A reporter for *The Irish Times* went to Dundrum shortly after it opened. She spotted a tiny, pink, Japanese-made, metal-finished cabin bag for €230. When she asked what would happen if it got scratched, the salesman announced that "You just buy next season's one."[24]

There are many complex reasons for this rapid transformation, many of which have been well covered elsewhere and some of which I will address. But I am interested in how these transformations have impacted on Irish cultural life, on how Irish people live their everyday lives, how they see and understand themselves and the world in which they live. I am interested in the cultural diet of the Irish. How much of it is Irish, how much comes from other parts of the world, how do the two mix together? The idea that the Irish have been overrun by American fast food and entertainment is ludicrous. However, the idea of the Irish becoming more rational, predictable, efficient and calculable—what Ritzer calls the McDonaldization of social life—is less so.[25] We have been swept into a hyperactive, new world of getting and spending, and of being constantly stimulated and entertained. Irish people see and understand themselves less in terms of their ethnicity, nationality and religion and more in terms of personal tastes, identities and lifestyles. But although the balance between these two cultural dimensions may have changed, the question that needs to be investigated is how the two mix, how strong and resilient are the more native cultural elements, and to what extent do they contribute to the global cultural flows that sweep over other people around the world.

THE LOCAL AND THE GLOBAL

It was early Sunday morning in June 2002. I was in Ring in County Waterford. It is the only *Gaeltacht* area in the south-east of Ireland. These are designated areas where the Irish language is the official language of everyday life. There are a number of other *Gaeltachts* in the country, most of them along the western seaboard. They are parts of Ireland where for various reasons, mostly economic (they tend to be isolated, impoverished rural areas), the infiltration of the English language was prevented. Despite substantial state subventions, the success of the *Gaeltachts* is slowly being eroded. It is not just the influence of the English language. It is the media and Western culture.

In the local shop, locals still greeted and spoke to each other in Irish, but all the goods on sale were described and promoted in English. More importantly, the vast majority of newspapers were in English. The Irish language is not sinking. It is holding its own. But its survival has perhaps more to do with national cultural identification processes outside the *Gaeltachts* than inside them. Being proud to be Irish, speaking Irish and, in particular, sending children to schools where they are taught through Irish, are becoming strong badges of identity, particularly among the new educated urban bourgeoisie.

I was thinking of a swim before breakfast and had gone down to a small pier. On the grey stone walls of the pier was a white hand-painted piece of graffiti: "Leeds Utd", a reference to the English soccer team Leeds United. Many Irish people are keen followers of English soccer. They watch matches on television. Reports of the big matches are given wide coverage in Irish newspapers and there is considerable discussion about teams, players, and analysis of matches on Irish radio. At that time, the manager of Leeds United was David O'Leary, well-known former international player: three of the Leeds team were members of the Irish soccer team.

What made these events in the Ring *Gaeltacht* intriguing is that there is deep antipathy among many people in Ireland, particularly cultural nationalists, to soccer. It is seen as a foreign sport and not part of traditional Irish culture. Until 1973, the Gaelic Athletic Association—the largest sports organization in the country with over 750,000 members and supporters—did not permit members to play what it deemed to be foreign sports. For the most part, this referred to soccer and rugby. It promoted *gaelic* football and hurling. These are games which attain enormous support and following throughout the country and are unique to Ireland. However, the antipathy to soccer is so strong that until 2007 the GAA refused to allow soccer to be played in Croke Park—the biggest stadium in Ireland, which holds over 80,000 spectators. The irony is that the GAA did allow American Football matches to be played. American sport may have been seen as less likely to contaminate the minds and hearts of GAA supporters. There is nothing strange about this. For many Irish people, particularly nationalists, there is a close affinity with America. For over

200 years it has been seen as a source of hope and consolation. More important, America never colonized Ireland. Unlike the English state, it never attempted to eradicate Catholics from social life through the Penal Laws of the eighteenth century. It never took land from Catholics and planted it with Protestants. It never attempted deliberately to undermine the Irish language.

That Sunday in June 2002 was a key day in Irish sport and Irish cultural life. Ireland had qualified for the second round of the Soccer World Cup. They were playing Spain. In previous World Cups, the country had almost gone silent and come to a halt as people gathered in front of televisions to watch the match. The hotel in which I was staying was already over-flowing by midday with a mixture of families enjoying a traditional Sunday lunch out, and people gathering to watch the match in the bar. As the adults watched the match, the children chased and played with each other in the hotel lobby. They were part of a new middle class in Ireland who had grown wealthy on the back of the success of the Celtic Tiger economy. They had the money and they were not afraid to go out and enjoy themselves. In the past there was difficulty in being openly self-indulgent. It was a bit like sex. It was something best done quietly behind closed doors. Now Irish Catholics can be self-indulgent and hedonistic as well as religious. They have the best of both worlds.

We Irish have a reputation for being great hypocrites, for saying one thing and doing another. People would talk about the curse of drink perhaps even when drunk. They would curse about the power of the priest and then fawn over him the second he appeared. I suspect that despite the commentary being in English, many of the people from the Ring *Gaeltacht* watched the World Cup match that Sunday afternoon, that despite soccer being a foreign game, many GAA supporters and officials, were also watching, and that although it was a sin, many Catholics were over-indulging themselves in drink and not giving a thought about the teachings of the Catholic Church to which they belonged. I used to think that hypocrisy was a means the oppressed Irish devised for dealing with power. When they were asked to account for themselves by their masters—landlords or priests—they gave them the answer they thought the masters wanted to hear. In recent years, we have learnt that some of our political leaders were the real hypocrites, telling us we all had to tighten our belts while they themselves were living corruptly and in the lap of luxury. Similarly, we used to think that all our priests and bishops were paragons of virtue, exemplars of the good spiritual and moral life, and yet some of them were having sex *and* children while others were having sex *with* children. Of course, hypocrisy does not belong just to the Irish, it is just that as with many other things in life, we are better at it than others. It is perhaps our success at hypocrisy that makes us different.

Four years later I was on a boat to France and I was watching England play Portugal in the quarter-final of the World Cup. Ireland had not qualified. The bar was packed. The match went to extra time and then to penalties. Every time a Portuguese player scored there was a roar of delight. Every time an English player missed there was another roar of delight. When the Portuguese player scored the winning penalty, the bar erupted. What is this thing the Irish have against the English? In some ways it is simple: for hundreds of years they were our colonial masters. For centuries, the English were the other against whom the Irish understood and realized their difference. Whatever else we were, we were not English. But is this an indication of a wider social phenomenon? Is it just the Irish who have a dislike of the English, or is it something that permeates the rest of Europe? To what extent have the English become the global "baddies" and the Irish, because they have no colonial baggage, become the global "goodies"?

THE SAMENESS OF SELF-CONSUMPTION

There are many practices and processes that make the Irish different. I will explore these in more detail in Chapter Four. But the reality is that while continuing to retain a sense of difference, most Irish people are beginning to act like the rest of the West. This is particularly the case in the fields of work and consumption, but it also pertains to housing, travel, communication, leisure, sexuality, identity and sense of self. We have been sucked into the center of a world capitalist system in which we expect things to get bigger, better and faster, where life becomes increasingly rationalized, monitored and evaluated, where there is a continual drive to find the one best way of doing everything. This is what drives business, global competition and globalization. What makes people the same around the world is that when it comes to earning a living they are increasingly playing the same game on the same pitch. The same terminology is being used all over the world to find the cheapest, fastest, most reliable, predictable, rational way of producing goods and services. No matter how much I try to detach myself from this insidious system I fail. Life becomes an endless task of perfection, of increasing production and efficiency. It invades not just one's work and private life, but one's very sense of self.

I find myself talking about the best way to drive from Dublin to Cork, the best time of day to leave, the best route to take, the best place to stop for coffee. Even though I enjoy cycling up the mountains around Dublin as a means of escaping from the relentless colonization of my mind, of being able to be in the world and be mindless rather than mindful, I find myself becoming obsessed with time, frustrated by the inadequacies of my machine, wanting to get a new bike, with a better gearing, better wheels. It seems impossible to slow down. And yet, more and more, I feel like a lemming rushing to the end of my life, unable to stop. Even if I was told that I had cancer and was sure to die, I wonder if I would be able to stop. I fear, in this respect, that I am no different from many other Irish people who, in turn, are no different from the rest of the West. I have become part of the malaise of modernity. I would love to find an ethical and spiritual cure, but I have no idea where to begin looking. What makes matters worse is that I live in such bad faith, actively doing little to remedy the poverty and injustices in Ireland and the world, standing idly by as millions die from AIDS and hunger throughout the world, sitting comfortably in my car as I pollute the atmosphere.

What is happening to me is happening around the rest of the world. In effect, there is a global habitus which has begun to grow on the pond of Irish cultural life. This habitus is what helps individuals around the world feel connected, the same as each other. It is an almost automatic, predisposed way of literally being in the world into which we have been socialized and which becomes taken for granted, which becomes second nature to us and which is reproduced within everyday life. There is a similar way of working and living, presenting oneself, operating within public and organizational spaces, communicating, working, traveling, eating and so forth. This global habitus is structured by a discourse which is developed and promoted by corporations through advertising and marketing. At the center of this habitus is a belief in liberal-individualism and the freedom to choose. Happiness is an individual right and an individual pursuit. Morality is an individual responsibility. There is no society, just rational individual actors who realize themselves as individuals through market choice. The development of a global habitus is closely allied to the spread and development of the world capitalist system and the spiral of ever-increasing production and consumption, getting and spending. Consumerism is the cocaine of the people.

What is the nature of social bonding in a world where people increasingly see and understand themselves and relate to each other in terms of consumption and similar/different tastes, preferences and lifestyles? What does this do to families, groups and communities? Moreover, if the contemporary phase of globalization is about increasing interconnectedness between individuals around the world, what is the nature of the bonding that takes place?

Shortly after I began to look at Ireland from a detached global perspective, I saw a documentary on television about AIDS in Rwanda. There was a woman lying in her bed. She was dying. She had, beside her bed, photographs of her children. I remember the happy smiling faces of the children, some of them in their First Holy Communion regalia. They were such a strong contrast to the forlorn look of the woman who looked into the camera and asked if the world would remember her. I felt a huge compassion for this woman somewhere on the far side of the world. It was an identification with another human being. Robertson is right. Globalization not only involves the shrinking of time and space, of the world becoming one place, it also involves an increasing awareness of humankind, of all of us belonging to the human family.[26]

But how does this imagining of the world work in practice? Is it possible to have lasting effective social bonds with an abstract, general universal other? I was aware of this woman, and while I sympathized with her, could I connect with her and develop a social bond without meeting, communicating and interrelating? Is it possible to develop a sense of care and moral responsibility for someone without developing a social relationship?

Love, sex and death are universal features of human life. There are quintessential features of human bonding. It is increasingly possible to fall for someone through the Internet who is distant and whom you may never have met. But can you love them without ever meeting them? Are they more a figment of your imagination? It is also increasingly possible through the phone calls, video links and straightforward pornography, to have sex with someone whom you have never met. You can even be with someone who is dying whom you have never met. But what is the nature of these social bonds? Love, sex and death, while universal features of human life, will remain for most people most of the time, a very local activity. Social bonds are mostly maintained physically and emotionally. They take place within spaces, homes and communities that generate a sense of identity and belonging. So when we are talking about the local, it is imperative that we talk about the nature of social bonding. Death, like social bonds, is a universal feature of life, but it has most meaning and significance when local and personal.

In some respects this brings me back to where I began. What makes me different is not just my relationship with my mother and father, but also, in more global terms, that I was brought up in the 1950s on an island off the coast of Europe which although it had been swept by the winds and tides of globalization, had become predominantly white, Catholic and English-speaking. We were nearly all the same. And because most of us grew up in the same Catholic families, went to the same Catholic schools and ended up living the same Catholic lives—and defined ourselves as different from our English Protestant colonial masters—there was a very strong sense of bonding. We knew who we were. We knew where we belonged. We did not have to go looking for our roots. We grew up not just in the same world, but the same habitus, the same sense of living and being in the world. Of course we were not all the same. We were all brought up that bit differently. Some parents hugged their children most of the time, others some of the time, and some none of the time. And as we grew up in this same world, we struggled to realize ourselves as individuals, as different. What was crucial during the second half of the twentieth century was how, for some people, that sense of difference moved from a predominantly Catholic culture to one of commodity capitalism. Instead of realizing ourselves as different through the language of the Church and its teachings and practices, we gradually switched to realizing ourselves through the language of the market and its teachings and practices. Besides the weather and the landscape, what makes Ireland different is that we still manage to live in these two different worlds. We still have a very strong sense of difference, belonging and bonding, and it is perhaps this strong sense of self and identity which has enabled the Irish to enter the global marketplace, the world of liberal-individualism, of getting and spending without the same emotional costs.

In writing about the Irish and what makes us the same, there is a tendency to generalize or, indeed, "essentialize"—to suggest that there are some features that are culturally or bio-logically inherited. I think that what makes most Irish people the same is that they feel that they have strong common social bonds, they were brought up as Catholics within similarly structured homes and schools involving similar discourses and practices. Trying to identify and describe these similarities is not to deny differences between rural and urban areas, social classes and, in particular, between the North and the

South. Indeed it is because Northern Ireland was deliberately sent down a different track by our English colonizers that I have tended to see it as another country where they do things differently, even the Catholics.

What is happening in Ireland is no different from what is happening in the rest of the world. In some respects, everyday life is becoming the same, in others it is different. There is an ongoing mix of the global with the local. At a macro level, this process of glocalization can be understood as the way the global flows of money, goods, people, ideas and practices change the local, adapt to the local and, then, are changed by the local.[27] But to understand globalization and, more specifically, glocalization, it is necessary to go beyond an analysis of macro-transformations and understand how these processes are lived out in particular places by particular individuals. The process of globalization is local, personal and particular. The task of understanding Ireland globally, necessitates discovering how Irish people mix and match elements of Irish culture with other cultural elements from around the world. We have to develop an image of people as artists or bricoleurs who in their everyday lives strategically combine the local with the global, how some emphasize the importance of local and others the global, and how some are more cosmopolitan than others. But although it is important to bring people into the analysis of globalization, we will never understand it properly unless we understand their moods, motivations, and struggle for meaning, identity and sense of belonging.[28]

But everyday life in the modern world capitalist system is as much, if not more, about the struggle for position and power as it is about bonding and belonging. To understand this struggle, it is necessary to understand the struggle for distinction and, in particular, the struggle for cultural capital and how this relates to the acquisition of other forms of capital. Following Bourdieu we can say that class position is not just a function of income or wealth. It is also related to culture, particularly education, but also religion, art, sport, music, literature, food and so forth.[29] The acquisition of cultural capital is closely linked to the acquisition of other forms of capital, particularly economic. It used to be that the dominant classes in Ireland relied on being good Catholics and accumulating religious capital as a means of attaining other forms of capital, economic (wealth), political (power), social (connections) and symbolic (honor). It used to be that the main sources of cultural capital and to a lesser extent economic capital came from within Ireland. What has changed dramatically over the last 40 years, particularly with the development of the Celtic Tiger economy, is that the main sources of economic capital are outside of Ireland. The Celtic Tiger also meant that to obtain cultural capital, Irish people were no longer dependent on local and national sources. The market provided a wide range of consumer choices: travel enabled people to go to exotic places, develop new tastes, collect souvenirs and, thereby, accumulate not just alternative but respected forms of cultural capital. Those who could afford it were able to develop global as well as local forms of cultural capital. These new cosmopolitans were able to distinguish themselves from those who had to rely solely on local cultural capital. However, as I shall argue, while the significance of cosmopolitan cultural capital has increased enormously, it has not displaced local cultural capital. Indeed it could be argued that through a combination of increased wealth and better promotion and marketing, as well as increased competition for cosmopolitan sources, local cultural capital has thrived in the new global cultural environment.

The questions behind this book are simple. Are the Irish different? What makes them different? How are these differences manifested in everyday life? Are the differences really significant or have the Irish effectively become the same as the rest of the West? A central thesis is that there is a link between the struggle for the Irish to be the same and therefore different and the struggle by individuals to be the same, to have a sense of bonding and belonging, but also to have their individual difference recognized and accepted. There is a struggle to be seen as the same, to be liked, loved, accepted and respected as well as a struggle to be different, to achieve position, power and distinction and to be deferred to. This is reflected in the transformation from Catholic to consumer capitalism, in the shift from a culture of self-denial and self-surrender to one of self-realization and self-indulgence. It is reflected in the greater importance given to cosmopolitan rather the local cultural capital, in the struggle between cultural entrepreneurs who import global culture and cultural guardians who seek to promote and develop local culture.

It is impossible to write a book that tries to capture the cultural complexity of contemporary Ireland, and to put it in a historical and global context, without being selective and personal. What has made Irish people different—their immersion in Catholic culture which emphasized sameness—is being eroded by their immersion in a consumer culture which emphasizes individual difference. This is what makes the global personal. I believe that to understand globalization it is necessary to understand the personal. I do not claim to be representative: I am a sample from male, middle-aged, middle-class, urban Ireland. But in the same way that a description of what is happening to Ireland through globalization provides an understanding of what is happening elsewhere in the world, so too does a description of the process by which I became globalized provide some understanding of what happened to other people in Ireland.

Before continuing this journey, it is necessary to develop some of the theory and concepts that I have outlined in this introduction. I want to tease out how, while I consider material economic forces to be the main influence behind the changes in Irish society, there are important cultural factors. The development of the world capitalist system derives from a material economic interest. The pursuit of a decent standard of living and the avoidance of poverty are perhaps universal interests. But individuals also have an interest in leading meaningful, well-balanced, responsible, ethical lives. The pursuit of economic wealth is generally balanced by an interest in living a good moral life. As well as making the global personal, it is also necessary to develop a sense of agency. The development and penetration of the media and the market created new choices, tastes and opportunities for Irish people, but it is individuals who make choices. I was one of those individuals who made choices. The question for me, as for many other people in Ireland, is whether in moving from living the life of a pious, humble, but poor, Catholic Church mouse, I have become an over-stimulated, consumption-driven rat. Or am I, like many other Irish people, living in a twilight culture; one still dominated by a Catholic habitus but one that has been steadily infiltrated by desires to consume new products and develop new tastes and lifestyles?

But issues of the self, personal identity and agency link back to the Irish identity and what makes Irish people different. The incoming flow of global products and media messages and the promotion of alternative ideas, tastes and lifestyles did not emerge willy-nilly. They were imported into Ireland through the agency of cultural entrepreneurs. They were the force that has led Irish culture to become commercialized and commodified. This is what is being resisted by cultural guardians who seek to maintain and develop traditional indigenous Irish culture.

Having described the forces behind globalization and the way it has taken place in Ireland in Chapter Two, I will then, in Chapter Three, go on to examine how and why such a small country like Ireland has developed a global reputation. Over the centuries the Irish have made significant contributions to the global flow of people. Members of the Irish diaspora have become well established around the world, particularly in North America, Britain and Australia. In Chapter Four, I try to unravel what the cultural practices and processes are that make the Irish different, focusing particularly on language, music, sport and religion. In the next chapter, I look at how everyday life in Ireland has become similar to other Western societies and how this links to producing and consuming more and a new form of individualism that revolves around continual self-transformation. In Chapter Six, I look at how these changes are reflected in the transformations in Ballivor.

Many people who come to Ireland take a guided tour in which they are introduced to well-known places and people. In some respects, what I have written is a kind of guidebook. It is a selected way of reading and interpreting Irish people and culture and the transformations that have taken place, particularly in the last 50 years. I suggest that to understand how Ireland has changed, it is necessary to put it into a global perspective. To develop this perspective, I will introduce some concepts and theories that I use in the rest of the book which, I think, help bring together the different pieces of evidence in a more coherent way.

The central pillar on which this book is based is that individuals, like nations, are both similar to and different from each other. Everyday life in Ireland is similar to and different from life in other societies and cultures. Individuals in Ireland are similar to and different from other individuals both in Ireland and abroad. I am interested in the forces that have helped constitute the Irish as different from other people. I think these forces relate to the particular type of social bonds and sense of belonging that developed in families and communities around Ireland during the nineteenth and twentieth centuries. I think that those bonds were so tight that they stifled individualism. This changed dramatically with the opening of Irish society and culture during the latter part of the twentieth century. I believe the main force of change in

Irish people, in the way they live their lives and the way they see and understand themselves, has been globalization.

I begin this chapter, then, by outlining in more detail some of the ways in which the Irish are both similar to and different from other people. I argue that while there have always been differences between individuals and groups within Ireland, what has changed is the nature, pervasiveness and intensity of these differences. Globalization has dramatically increased the consumer and lifestyle choices through which Irish people develop new identities and realize themselves as individuals. It is this new emphasis on choice and individual self-realization that has diminished Irish difference and made us more like the rest of the West.

But how are we to understand globalization? I think it is mainly about economics: the spread of capitalist modes of production and consumption has led to globalized lifestyles and, literally, a similar way of being in the world. But the process of globalization is more complicated. It is also about knowledge and information. The global flow of ideas and images has changed the way the Irish think of themselves. There has also been an increase in the frequency and level of contact with other people. The flow of ideas and the flow of people have created new ways of being Irish, a new breed of Irish people. While there have always been global elements in Irish culture, the pace and intensity of global flows have increased the number of ideas and people in the cultural melting pot. Quite suddenly Ireland went from a homogeneous type of white, English-speaking, Catholic society to one with a mix of race, ethnicities and religions. There has been an explosion in the varieties of Irishness. If the concept of globalization helps us understand how Irish people and culture have become open to global flows, the concept of glocalization helps us understand how these flows became integrated and adapted to Irish conditions. But glocalization also helps us understand how elements of Irish culture became swept up in these global flows to be deposited, grow and develop elsewhere around the world.

However, as I have already argued, global culture does not become embedded in Ireland and elements of Irish culture do prosper and become disseminated without the agency of individuals, particularly cultural entrepreneurs who introduce, mix and match global with local Irish culture and cultural guardians who work at maintaining local and national difference. But the extent to which global culture becomes embedded and the extent to which local and national culture survives, depends on the extent to which individuals attach value to them and see them as an important addition to their accumulation of cultural capital. There can be benefits to being cosmopolitan and familiar with other cultures. But there can also be material advantages and symbolic capital—not just in Ireland but among cosmopolitans around the world—in developing a knowledge and appreciation of Irish culture.

This relates back to the struggle by individuals to be accepted, to be seen and recognized as the same, as belonging to a group and, at the same time, as being unique, individual and different. The main cultural transformation in Ireland over the past 50 years is that individuals have increasingly sought to create and establish difference through the consumption of globally produced cultural goods and services. Ironically it is this pursuit of difference through consumption which made the Irish more like the rest of the West and which has led to a diminution of the cultural elements that made them different.

It is this drive towards self-realization and self-transformation through consumption which has the capacity to undermine the strong social bonds and sense of belonging that come from a dominant religious culture of self-deprecation and denial. It is this self-transformation, the creation of a radical new type of individualism, that makes the global personal. This leads to a paradox. At one level, globalization is directly linked to increased individualism but, at another level, the spread and development of global communications seem to have created a heightened sense of global human bonding and belonging. But it may well be that in comparison to local families and communities revolving around face-to-face interaction, the bonds that create a sense of identity and belonging to other human beings is based on media images and messages which produce a sense of bonding and belonging that is transitory, shallow and weak. This brings us back to the question of agency and how the inexorable immersion in capitalist consumer culture might be resisted and, in particular, how local bonds and sense of belonging can be sustained in a global culture that has become saturated with messages advocating self-fullfilment and indulgence.

EXPLORING IRISH DIFFERENCE

Are Irish people different? In many respects we are different from Americans, Japanese and English. We have a different way of being in the world that comes from living on an island with a different history and culture. This is more than just a different language, art, music and sport. We have developed characteristics, ways of doing and saying things, a sense of humor and, most importantly, a different sense of self.

On the other hand, Irish people are the same as other people, particularly those living at the heart of modern consumer capitalist culture. We live similar lives. We live in similar spaces, work in similar conditions, commute in similar traffic, use the same machines, watch the same television screens, and so forth. Most people reading this book will live in democratic societies, be part of an expanding middle class, and have reasonably comfortable lifestyles. We have become rational social actors. We shop around for the best prices. We look for the political party that best represents our needs and interests. Many people in Western society live similar lives but there is little in that similarity that binds them together. The large middle classes of the West have become a social category that exists in itself rather than for each other and, more importantly, for the rest of the world.

There seems to be a symbiotic relationship between social sameness and difference. The more social wholes become bigger and the more social life becomes the same, the more individuals strive to be different.[1] The insistence on Irish difference grew with globalization. The national cultural movement that emerged in Ireland in the late nineteenth century was similar to what was happening elsewhere in Europe. The more that cultural life in Ireland became the same as the rest of the West, the greater was the demand to revive traditional customs.[2] What makes Irish people the same—what binds them together at a national level—is what makes them different globally. The more everyday life in the West becomes the same, the more tourists, travelers and cosmopolitans go in search of authentic difference. People travel to the ends of the earth frantically searching for what is new and different.

There has never been a unique, essential way of being Irish. But this has not stopped people—and the groups and organizations to which they belong—from trying to make out that there are core characteristics to being Irish. These range from being born in Ireland, to having Irish ancestors, speaking the Irish language, listening to Irish music, playing *gaelic* sports, supporting the nationalist struggle in the North and so forth. Over the last 50 years, during the period in which I have lived, the influence of these people, groups and organizations has waned. There is increasing acceptance that there are many different ways of being Irish. There are many people around the world who were not born in Ireland, who have no Irish blood, who might never have been to Ireland, and yet they may speak the language, listen to and play Irish music, and, generally, have developed a deep appreciation of being Irish. There are also many migrants who have embodied Irish customs, pastimes and habits. Many have become more Irish than the Irish themselves.

There are also many different varieties of Irishness. As I mentioned in the previous chapter, I grew up in a very Catholic family, but it was also an Anglo-Irish family. There was not the same dislike or antipathy towards the English found among strong nationalists. In the 1950s, I grew accustomed to listening to English radio stations and, particularly on Sunday, reading English newspapers. I had aunts and uncles who had gone to live and work in England. I followed English politics and sports. As I child I watched English television. I aped the habits and customs of the English. I grew up with a distaste of all things Irish, particularly music, dance and sport. At school, I detested having to learn the Irish language. It was, then, the way I came to be Irish, the way I was brought up, that makes me different from other Irish people. I am—in different ways at different times—like no other Irish person, like some other Irish people, like every other Irish person.

More than anything else, exposure to the world has led to an increasing acceptance of the diversified ways of being Irish. The more Irish people were exposed to alternative forms of values, beliefs, knowledge, ideas, media messages and life-styles, the more they began to travel and to meet other people, the more they began to import new strands and dimensions to being Irish. The arrival of television in the 1960s meant that

Irish people became exposed on a regular basis to American and British ways of being in the world. They began to identify with and embody different tastes and lifestyles, music and fashion, attitudes and beliefs. It became cool, particularly among the urban bourgeoisie, to be cosmopolitan. Everyday life in Ireland became more Western. Irish culture became a vibrant mixture of the local, national and global.

One might expect that the exposure to global, particularly Western, culture, might have led to a decline in Irish culture, in Irish difference. In fact, the opposite seems to have happened. Irish culture, especially Irish sport, language, music and dance, is surviving if not thriving in a global cultural environment. In some respects, then, the more Irish culture has become global, the stronger the importance of maintaining Irish difference has become. The greater the level of contact with other people, the greater the need to develop a different sense of identity and belonging. The question, however, is whether the new cosmopolitan Irish culture can produce the level of bonding and belonging necessary to create new varieties that will last over generations.

To understand globalization, it is necessary to understand the often conflicting imperatives to be the same and to be different. During the last half of the twentieth century the forces that brought Irish people together—religion, family and community—began to be weakened by a consumer culture that emphasized liberal-individualism. People were similar in the way they entered into and became consumed by the market and the media. However, unlike religion, family and community, the media and the market are not based on building and maintaining social bonds. The media and the market generate transitory feelings of identity and belonging—such as occur at a rock concert or sport event. But there is little or no collective belief. There is no long-term commitment to the wider group. There is little self-surrender, there are no lasting, significant social bonds. However, the lure of difference, pleasure, excitement and self-indulgence can be very powerful. This is why to fully understand globalization it is necessary to understand the appeal of difference, of becoming cosmopolitan, of breaking free from social bonds and being able to pursue personal pleasures.

As a teenager in the 1960s I began to make my own way in the world. I was desperate to be different, to shake off my Irish roots and become cosmopolitan. I was envious of my friends who had American jeans and T-shirts, bought the latest pop records, worked in factories in England, went to rock concerts, smoked French cigarettes, traveled in Europe and came home tanned. I was not aware of it at the time, but I was realizing myself as an individual in conditions not of my own choosing. I was caught up in long-term processes of social change. Ireland was becoming globalized and I was becoming immersed in consumer culture. There was a whole new marketplace of ideas and goods in which I could realize myself as an individual, realize my difference. I could shake off cold Catholic Ireland, discover my body, give in to my desires and sensual pleasures, and become not just cool, but hot and sexy.

What were the forces working through me that led me to want to become a cosmopolitan, a man of the world? It seems that my opening up to the world was part and parcel of Ireland opening up to the world. It was all part of globalization. But what exactly is globalization or, more precisely, what do I understand by globalization?

GLOBALIZATION

Rather than try to provide an exact definition of globalization, it may be better, following Holton, to describe what it involves.[3] First, and perhaps most importantly, it involves interconnection: "the intensified movement of goods, money, technology, information, ideas and cultural practices across political and cultural boundaries." While this has been going on since the beginning of time, it intensified with the development of the world capitalist system from the sixteenth century. An event on one side of the globe can have major lasting consequences for Irish people thousands of miles away. These interconnections are happening so frequently and so fast that there is, as Giddens describes it, a disembedding or lifting out of social relations from local contexts and their immersion into global time and space.[4] More people are more connected through time and space than ever before. Time and distance no longer pose the same problems they did even 50 years ago. The flow of money, ideas, people, goods and services around the world is probably faster now than it was around Ireland 50 years ago.

The intensification of movement brings an increase in interdependence. More and more of what happens in Ireland depends on the actions of other people around the world. Increased interconnection and interdependence lead to increased global consciousness and an identification of the world as one place.

I grew up with a small globe in my bedroom. When someone mentioned a country, I was able to spin the globe and locate it. My tin globe was no more than a round tin map. I really only knew the world in terms of where other countries were in relation to Ireland. It was more of an "inter-national" than a global perspective—of where Ireland was in relation to other countries. Then, with space travel, I started to see the world differently. I began to see and understand it as I had formerly seen and understood the island of Ireland, as one place, one quite small and fragile place. This increasing consciousness of planet Earth and, to a lesser extent, of human beings being one people, changed the way I understood the world, my place in the world, and the process of globalization.

Such is the speed and intensity of globalization that, according to Friedman, the world is now flat. For Friedman, the miracle of the technological revolution is increased global equality: "Everywhere you turn, hierarchies are being challenged from below or transforming themselves from top-down structures into more horizontal and collaborative ones."[5] From this optimistic perspective, the invisible hand of technology will bring us to a new flat world where social inequality, class divisions and all other elites and hierarchies will disappear. People will be linked by a new sense of communality, of being members of the one human family.[6] People will no longer be selfish and greedy, but will develop a global sense of care and responsibility for each other, other species and the planet. There will be a new ethic of global responsibility. The world will become not just some imagined community, like nations are at present, but a real live community. But will everyone have the same shared values and beliefs in this community, or will they be different? And if the values, beliefs and practices are different, what will be the nature of this difference? Will it be the same difference around the world?

But it seems to me that while globalization involves the shrinking of time and space and of the world increasingly becoming one, what really drives globalization is economics. I may not have realized it at the time, but what was happening to me back in the 1960s was a slow but subtle form of penetration. What characterizes globalization, what characterizes all the changes that have taken place in Ireland, is the all-pervasive, deeper penetration of the world capitalist system into everyday life and people's knowledge and understanding of themselves and the world in which they live.[7] Capitalism is not just a form of economic life. It is not just about processes of production and consumption, state regulation of markets, different social classes, and different forms of exploitation. Life in the world capitalist system involves a whole way of being in the world. It has become the way of the world. It has colonized the way people lead their lives, their very under-standing of themselves. We take it completely for granted. It has become the unquestioned *doxa*.[8] Marx was wrong. It is not religion that is the opium of the people, it is producing and consuming.

Capitalism is primarily about exploitation, greed and self-ishness. People who believe in globalization and the world capitalist system seem to believe that it is possible for everyone to get rich, to have ever-increasing economic growth, for everything to go on getting bigger and better. I am not so sure. If there is a global culture it seems to be a shared belief in the cult of the individual, of liberal-individualism, and the general right of the individual to pursue life, liberty and happiness with as little interference as possible. Liberal-individualism is the way the rich justify being rich. It is the symbolic domination that lies behind economic domination. It is the collective belief of the globally rich that keeps working classes localized, isolated and dependent.[9] Of course there is a rhetoric of sharing and caring, but is it just a rhetoric? How often does it get turned into practice? Don't the rich give to the poor to legitimate themselves and assuage their guilty consciences?

There seems to be no alternative. We have become driven and consumed by fulfilling our pleasures and desires, by having more excitement and more comfort, by greed and pure self-interest. The world capitalist system sells us difference. In the cult of capitalism the realization of self is sacred. It is becoming the meaning of salvation. We adorn ourselves with commodities. We pamper ourselves with services. We seek anything that provides distinction, that confirms our individual difference. The world capitalist system brings with it a common way of being in the world.

Sometimes when it comes to understanding globalization I get confused. I find it hard to stand outside, to be detached and objective, to see what is exactly going on in the world. Even when I think I am being objective, I realize that I am easily swayed. One day I am optimistic, and the prophets of boom like Friedman carry me away to a bright new world. The next day, the prophets of doom have their way, and I think we are on the road to perdition. When it is hard to figure what is going on in the world, it is best to narrow the gaze and focus in on what is going on around you, in your own backyard. In other words, instead of trying to define and capture the essence of globalization, it is better to concentrate on finding out how it works empirically and specifically.[10] Recently in sociological analyses of globalization there has been a move away from abstract general theorizing and a greater emphasis on empirical studies.[11] There is a concentration on developing more middle-range theories and concepts that focus on how globalization is taking place in particular countries. This approach ties in with an understanding of glocalization as a process through which local people adapt and contribute to different global flows.[12] It also connects with a more anthropological approach to understanding glocalization.[13]

THE IRISH WAKENING

For generations, the Catholic Church tried to stem the tide of rampant consumer capitalism by persuading people to avoid the evils of materialism and self-indulgence. During the first half of the twentieth century its attempts to keep Ireland different were quite successful. The level of cultural contamination was quite small. Most of those who traveled out of the country did not come back. There were very few radios or televisions. People did read books and go to the cinema, but censorship was very strict. The Church regularly railed against the evils of materialism and modernity, particularly fashion, music and dance. Anything that aroused the senses and stimulated desire, particularly anything that was sensual or erotic, was eliminated from social life.

The Catholic Church had a strong influence on the political thinking of Catholic politicians, their vision of Irish society and the policies of the state. It was not until the 1960s that the state began to abandon deference to Catholic Church teaching and rigorously pursue its own vision of Irish society. It was instrumental in developing trade and economic growth, opening up the consumer market and, later, attracting the foreign investment and the transnational corporations, particularly from America, that gave birth eventually to the Celtic Tiger. Whatever the desire and interest of the Irish people and the Irish state to become modernized, westernized and globalized, Ireland and its Celtic Tiger economy have become dependent on transnational corporations. It is they, more than anything else, that have pushed the Irish into becoming the same as the rest of the West.

Once the Irish went from living in rural communities and surviving off the land, to living in ever-expanding towns and cities and participating in global production and consumption, there was no need for the Catholic habitus and practices which had been central to the control of individuals, their desires and pleasures. This repression and sacrifice of self—the antithesis of the self in consumer society—had been crucial to controlling population, increasing the size of farms, improving the standard of living and, generally, modernizing Irish society. However, once the basis of the Irish economy changed during the last half of the twentieth century, there was a change in culture. The Irish stopped tarring themselves with the same brush of self-denial and self-repression.

But economic transformations do not explain sufficiently the passion the Irish had to remain Catholic, to maintain and develop their own language, sport and history, to realize an ancient historical difference: They, unlike the English, were Celts. Again it seems there are two viewpoints, one optimistic and one pessimistic. The optimistic view is that the Irish people have always been a people on the path to self-realization. We have always had our own religion, language, sport, music, dance, literature and, generally, our own way of being in the world. If it wasn't for years of colonial oppression by Britain we would have realized this difference centuries ago.

The pessimistic view is that all this emphasis on natural national difference is an illusion, an invented tradition fostered by states.[14] This suggests that left on their own, Irish and English people would get on with each other, that any cultural differences are artificial and have been constructed by both states primarily through the education system and the media in order to maintain social and political control. What Irish people understand as national and local customs and traditions, are really forms of political and social domination. The perceived differences between Irish and English people are deliberately constructed and arbitrary. National culture becomes reduced to nation-states attempting to hide the inherent contradictions, inequalities and limitations to freedom which are endemic to capitalism by creating and maintaining differences between groups—the Irish and the English—and within groups.

Being a cultural nationalist had its rewards. Many people who succeeded in Irish life in the twentieth century, particularly in politics, tended to be strong Catholics and cultural nationalists.[15] The notion of culture is, then, the outcome of collective historical attempts to come to terms with the contradictions, the ambiguities, the complexities of the socio-political realities of the world capitalist system.[16] All culture is part and parcel of a system that reproduces differences, hierarchies and inequalities. For this reason, from this perspective, there will never be cultural homogenization or global culture. The only value of local collective identities is that they help generate opposition and resistance to existing forms of domination and exploitation.[17]

The penetration of the world capitalist system into everyday life is, then, central to understanding globalization and, specifically, to what happened in Ireland. The question is whether this penetration has created more sameness or difference. The Irish may have struggled to create and maintain a sense of cultural difference from their colonial masters, but the reality is that along with uneven economic development there was uneven cultural development. The amount that Ireland contributed to English culture was nothing compared to the influence of English science, technology, law and language on the Irish way of life. During the twentieth century, as part of its emergence as the core region of the world capitalist system, the influence shifted more to the United States. But despite the influence of American, British and Western culture generally, the Irish have never become fully Anglicized or Americanized. They have remained different. They have developed a culture, a way of being in the world that is different. But again the question is how significant is this difference. How long will it last and how can it be maintained and developed without being commercialized?

But culture is not just a means to an end of maintaining economic and political dominance, it is also an end in itself:

it is about meaning, identity, bonding and belonging. The more that people bond together in different groups, the more they will see, read and interpret the world differently. As well as wanting freedom and power, people want to be accepted, honored and loved. It is the way Irish people come together in families, groups and communities, it is the way they bond and develop a sense of belonging, that makes them and Irish culture different. This sense of bonding and belonging emerged from the peculiar historical conditions through which Irish society modernized, the way the Catholic Church became so powerful, and the way self-denial became rooted in Irish social life. However, it may be that the more Irish people became connected with other people around the world, the greater the need to be the same as them, to become cosmopolitan. This is not to say that the Irish were not different and that they often made their cultural difference work for them but, as with all cosmopolitans, that they had to learn to present their difference in the same way. The reality of course is that the more time people spend being cosmopolitan—being of the world but not in it—the less time they spend in the small groups, families and communities that generate meaning, identity and belonging (the local) which are, effectively, the base for generating significant cultural difference.

Culture is also about the inheritance of ideas. Beliefs, values and ideas are crucial to understanding the serendipity nature of globalization. Robertson claims that it is the way beliefs and values come together at certain times that can push the development not just of a particular society but globality down a different line. For example, he asks, why did Japan develop the way it did? What were the internal sources of and resources for Japan's high degree of careful selectivity concerning what is to be accepted or rejected from without? How did a society which was, in some respects, the epitome of insularity and post-primitive mechanical solidarity, become a society whose elites were almost obsessed with Japan becoming an international, or a global, society?[18] His answers are obviously important as they may help shed some light as to why Ireland went from being such an insular, homogeneous, rural, agricultural society into becoming the world's most globalized society with one of its most successful economies.

Robertson's answer is that in the same way that an individual constructs his or her individual identity from the cultural system in which he or she grows up, so too does a society within the global economic, political and cultural system. There is a "strong element of choice involved as to the direction(s) of societal change and the form(s) of global involvement." He argues that the reason for Japanese economic success lay in Japanese culture, particularly its "proclivity for adopting and adapting externally generated ideas for its own specific purposes" and that this cultural openness was rooted in the "particular nature of Japanese *syncretism*." Japanese religion is, he says, "a calibrated syncretic mixture of interpenetrating religions of Indian, Chinese, Korean and, to a much smaller degree, Christian origins." It is not surprising, then, that the Japanese frequently adhere to more than one religious orientation. "Japanese people are not merely free to partake of what seems to suit their religious 'fancy' according to their particular life circumstances, but there is a diffuse ethos which indicates that the individual *should* regard different components of overall Japanese religion as catering to different needs."[19]

But if it was a syncretistic religion that gave rise to a syncretistic culture and, thus, to a successful economy and society, how is it that such a highly homogeneous, insular Catholic culture gave birth to the Celtic Tiger economy? If one was to follow Robertson's theory, one would have to argue that there were different cultural factors operating in Ireland and that the reason for Ireland's economic success was caused by an urban bourgeoisie abandoning the restrictive vision of Irish society engendered by Catholic culture. But when, where and how did the habitus of this bourgeoisie change? What was it that led them to abandon the Catholic worldview into which they had been socialized and to which they still gave such deference? Were they contaminated by "foreign" ways of thinking, or were they just dying to have some of the materialist pleasures and comforts which they had been denied—and which they had denied to themselves? To help answer these questions we need to have a bigger, broader understanding of how globalization works.

GLOBAL FLOWS

Instead of thinking in terms of Ireland's being constituted primarily by either economic or cultural forces, it is better to follow Appadurai and think of its being influenced by different types of global flows.[20] These may be understood as economic, cultural, social, political and technological movements that sweep across the planet gathering up and depositing monies, products, companies, services, knowledge, ideas, people, systems of communications, wars and other forms of political and domination. The concept of flows suggests fluidity: the way knowledge, goods and services become incorporated into people's lives is never the same everywhere. The concept of flows allows for different forms of adaptation initiated through the agency of organizations, groups and individuals. It is useful, then, to think of Ireland as being subject to different types of global flow that have swept over the island in the past and continue to sweep through people and society on a daily basis. The way these flows are received, the way in which they become embedded in our thinking and everyday life, is a matter of empirical investigation.

The first flow concerns the movement of people in and out of the country: those who go out to learn, work, for holidays, business, education, and those who come in as tourists, immigrants, refugees, asylum seekers. As Appadurai points out it is not just the physical movement, but it is the ever-increasing cognitive acceptance of the reality that we live in an age where people are constantly moving around the world to work, travel, holiday, visit friends and family.[21] Furthermore, even for those people in Ireland who may never have been abroad, the contact with tourists, with returned exiles, with those who have been abroad on holidays, means that the world is increasingly seen and imagined as one place.

The second flow is about the movement of technology which can be understood as the ongoing development of more rational, efficient, productive ways of mastering and controlling people and the environment. Every day there is a constant flow in and out of Ireland of new and better machines, new scientific knowledge, and new and better ways of doing things. This flow of technology comes through people, the mass media and the internet. It is perhaps best evident in the confidence and familiarity that young people have in using new forms of information technology and the influence this has not just on the way they communicate with each other but on their sense of self.

The third flow has to do with finance and pertains to the amount of money, goods, shares and services that move in, around and out of Ireland to and from centers all over the world, not just on a daily basis, but every hour and minute. Indeed if globalization revolves around thinking of the world as one place and involves the compression of time and space, then those who work in the financial field are probably the most globalized. In the world of finance an appreciation of place is closely linked to an appreciation of time: a loss of minutes can translate into a loss of millions.

The fourth flow is concerned with mediated messages, the reception and dissemination of knowledge, information and images of the world through mass media which is dominated by transnational companies that own film studios, television companies, newspapers, magazines and so forth. Increasingly Irish people are seen and understood by other people around the world in the way they are represented in news reports, documentaries, films, television programs. As Appadurai points out, what is crucially important is how, in this representation, the gap between what is real and what is fantasized or imagined is becoming blurred.[22] The traditional image of the Irishman in the pub swigging pints of Guinness while his wife and 10 children are at home may have disappeared into the mists of time. But by what has it been replaced? Perhaps the new image of Ireland is of a young urban, sophisticated woman leaving a theater? Who creates these images? Where are they to be found? For the most part, they are produced by companies marketing and advertising Ireland.

The final flow has more to do with the dissemination of religious, philosophical and political ideas about ways of living in the world, of organizing and regulating society, and of developing the controls, freedoms and rights that are central to democracy and the creation and maintenance of peace and prosperity in the world. In Ireland, the ongoing debates concerning civil society, the power of the state, individual freedoms and responsibilities, are reflected through knowledge and information about what is happening in other parts of the world. For example, the ideas and practices of the civil rights movements in the United States in the 1960s were an important catalyst to the Catholics in Northern Ireland developing their own movement.

The flow of knowledge, ideas, beliefs and values—new ways of understanding and being in the world—was to have a central role in shaping the world and for the intensification of globalization. While much attention has been given to the spread of scientific knowledge and technologies, spiritual and ethical ways of being in the world have also had a profound impact. How people make sense of their lives and the world they live in and how they struggle to be ethical and live a good life have had, over the course of history, as much influence on social life as economics, science and technology. Indeed it may well be that the greatest influence Ireland has had on the flow of global culture and on making the world what it has become today, took place centuries ago. The ideas developed by monks in Ireland back in the fifth and sixth centuries about how to live a good life—how to be ethical, rational, efficient and predictable—were exported throughout the Western world. The penitentials of the Irish monks became a central element in the construction of an other-worldly ascetic way of life which, with the Protestant Reformation, became the basis for an inner-worldly asceticism which was central to the rise of the world capitalist system. Inner-worldly asceticism eventually gave rise to inner-worldly salvation, liberal individualism, narcissism and hedonism—all central to consumer society—which has become embedded in work, family and social life and in people's knowledge and understanding of themselves.[23]

These cultural flows are occurring throughout the world on a daily basis. They have been speeded up spectacularly through the internet. However, they operate unevenly and inconsistently, producing disjunctures within and between countries. While their impact on different societies, particularly Ireland, depends on the context and conditions in which they operate, they generally contribute towards increasing deterritorialization in which the daily life—whether it has to do with money, technology, knowledge, people or pleasure—is less and less confined to the boundaries of particular nation-states. And, of course, it is important to remember that the flow is not one way. These flows have their origins in various parts of the world, and Ireland contributes to them in various different ways. For centuries now, Irish people have migrated all over the world. Traditional Irish music has become part of world music. It is hard to find a major city in the world without an Irish pub.

The concept of cultural flows enables us to think of lifestyles, products, ideas and practices being assimilated differently into Irish society and culture depending on local culture, lifestyles and practices. Young Irish people may embody American individualism, dress in the latest American fashion, drink Coca-Cola and eat hamburgers but do so while watching a local GAA match, swapping local gossip, telling Irish jokes and stories. The way global cultural flows are integrated into Irish culture depends on the strength and depth of existing local and national culture. Secondly, the concept of global flows captures the dynamic nature of cultural transfers; that as well as elements of Western and global culture being deposited in Ireland, there are parts of Irish culture that are gathered up by cultural entrepreneurs, become part of the global flow, and are deposited in various other parts of the world.

To understand how these flows become embedded in local life—and at the same time how local culture becomes part of global flows—it is necessary to focus on action and strategic agents. It is this notion of strategic agents which is central to understanding hybridization. This is where two different cultural traditions become deliberately grafted together to create a "third" culture. An example of this is the bringing together of Australian Rules Football with *Gaelic* Football to create International Rules Football played between Australia and Ireland. Creolization is another concept that is used to capture the way two or more cultural forms become mixed together, sometimes slowly as part of a long-term historical process, and sometimes as a deliberate act, such as the creation of *Riverdance* (see Chapter Four).[24] In other words, the mixing of cultural forms and traditions can come about as a result of the deliberate decisions made by cultural entrepreneurs who do the grafting, mixing and matching, but it can also come about more slowly through the way people have since the beginning of history moved around the world.

GLOCALIZATION

Robertson points out that the concept of glocalization—blending the notion of global and local—is originally Japanese and related to the practice of adapting farming techniques to local conditions. It was then adopted by the Japanese as a business principle of tailoring and advertising goods and services on a global basis to increasingly differentiated local and particular markets.[25] In relation to culture, glocalization can involve the deliberate tailoring and advertising of global cultural products, but it can also refer to the slower, more symbiotic way in which elements of the global cultural system are deposited locally and how indigenous people use and adapt these elements to the local culture.[26] The question then is how are we to distinguish the local from the global. Hannerz characterizes the local in terms of "everyday life," "face-to-face," "home," "immediacy," "immersion," "real," "sensual" and "bodily" experiences. In contrasting the local and the global, he argues that "local tradition seems to be just forever there, in limitless supply. The global is shallow, the local deep."[27]

Appadurai takes a different perspective. He argues that people now live in "imagined worlds" as much as "imagined communities."[28] The "communities of sentiment" to which they are attached stretch beyond the local and the nation-state. This suggests local distanciation and disembeddedness. People may live locally but think globally: their hearts and minds are literally elsewhere. However, there is increasing evidence that despite the influence of global cultural flows in terms of a search for difference and distinction, people's sense of self, place and belonging is still within specific geographical localities.[29] In the same way that nationalism and nation-states were part of an international process to create and sustain difference, there will always be a need for a center or haven in a globalized world in which a local habitus generates a sense of difference and belonging. The shrinking of time and space means increasing connections between local areas which, in turn, leads to and feeds the maintenance and development of local traditions.[30]

It is this combination of global and Irish culture that makes Irish people the same but different. Anyone who takes a journey through Ireland may notice how in terms of the force of law, the rational organization of life, civilized behavior, consumer products and services, Ireland has become like the rest of the West. But he or she will also be impressed by the strength of religious commitment and parish life, the vibrancy of traditional Irish sports, music and dance, the interest in local history, and the plethora of local festivals and celebrations that take place throughout the year.

But local culture no longer has an automatic existence in an increasingly globalized culture. It requires work to be maintained and recreated, often undertaken by cultural guardians.

Locals know their own habitus. They are like fish in water. But with increased global cultural flows people, particularly cultural guardians, have to work at reproducing the local water. For villages, parishes and neighborhoods to survive they have to be, as Appadurai points out, "simultaneously practical, valued, and taken-for-granted." But globalization has forced local cultures to be adaptive and critically reflective. They have to move from being local cultures in themselves, to becoming local cultures for themselves. This is done, primarily, by continually comparing and contrasting themselves with global culture.[31] Irish culture depends on people consciously being Irish, embodying the local and national habitus, history and culture, engaging in local events and practices. But it is also done by maintaining a high value for local cultural capital. This can only be achieved through its value in obtaining other forms of capital.

CULTURAL ENTREPRENEURS AND GUARDIANS

As mentioned above, the notion of strategic agents is central to understanding hybridization and creolization. They are dependent on cultural entrepreneurs who, as Hannerz puts it, "carve out their own niche, find their own market segment, by developing a product more specifically attuned to the characteristics of their local consumers."[32] Cultural entrepreneurs are the apostles of global culture.

In Ireland, the task of these cultural entrepreneurs has been to mix the messages of consumerism, liberal individualism and self-fulfillment with those of the traditional Catholic habitus of humility, piety and self-denial.[33] Throughout the twentieth century, there were many local cultural entrepreneurs around Ireland who opened cinemas and dancehalls, who organized shows and cabarets, who used global cultural products to stimulate pleasures and desires. These were the cultural sifters, the *bricoleurs* who successfully mixed and matched the global and the local. They read, listened and watched. They developed global knowledge and a new world-view. Through this they gained global cultural capital. They traveled and developed social networks outside of Ireland. They attained global social capital. They were able to trade these capitals for economic capital. Their geographic mobility matched their social mobility. Through embodying and developing a global habitus and incorporating this into Ireland, they became the new social elite.

It is important to put these cultural entrepreneurs in context. They were mainly confined to the field of entertainment and popular culture. There were, of course, intellectuals, academics, artists and others from the field of high culture who contributed to the glocalization of Irish culture. But the cultural entrepreneurs who had the greatest influence in spreading consumerism and liberal individualism were those involved in the media, marketing and advertising. Many of the entrepreneurs who opened people's tastes to new places, pleasures, music, food, drink and so forth, had engaged with the people and culture from which they emanated. There was, as Hannerz suggests, a willingness to develop a knowledge and competence in different cultures as part of a wider project of self-discovery and realization.[34] In some respects, the history of Ireland during the last half of the twentieth century can be seen as the emergence and dominance of a new elite of urban, cosmopolitan cultural entrepreneurs who facilitated the transfer from an isolated, insular island people, into a global culture and society.

Cultural entrepreneurs do not operate in an uncontested field. They face stern opposition from cultural guardians. Cultural guardians seek to essentialize what is local and national and protect it from global cultural contamination.

They seek to create and maintain pedigrees, lines of cultural lineage that can be traced back over generations if not millennia. Cultural guardians have played an enormous role in Irish social history. They came to prominence towards the end of the nineteenth century when the Irish were struggling for religious, economic and political freedom. They argued that there had always been something unique and different about the Irish, that they were originally and have always been a Celtic and Christian people. They point to the uniqueness not just of Irish language, music, dance and sport, but also of Irish art, literature, theater and poetry. There are thousands of cultural guardians throughout the country who work assiduously, often voluntarily, and mostly at local level, organizing local events and festivals, writing local social histories, maintaining the chains of collective memory. They are determined to maintain local and national difference. But it is important to realize that cultural guardians operate at all levels of social life, from private families to the ordinary man in the street. As we shall see when we come to look at Ballivor, Jamsie McKeown, a local bachelor farmer, strove to protect his own rights, but also the culture of Ballivor, by insisting on driving his cattle up and down the main street every day.

It would be wrong, however, to see cultural entrepreneurs and guardians as binary opposites. There are many Irish cultural guardians who have turned entrepreneurs and who have brought in elements of global culture and mixed them with Irish culture. We shall see this in the next chapter in relation to Irish music and dance. However, there are many cultural guardians who see the mixing of the global with the local as a form of foreign contamination that will eventually destroy traditional Irish culture. The same is true of Irish music. There are organizations and individuals who strongly resist the incorporation of "foreign" methods of playing traditional music or the use of "modern" instruments such as the guitar or piano.[35]

COSMOPOLITANS AND LOCALS

Cultural entrepreneurs and guardians can be seen as part of broader differentiation between cosmopolitans and locals.[36] Flusty suggests cosmopolitans are "continuously in transit, emancipated from space, and subject to experiences of disjuncture, in-betweenness, and de-essentialization."[37] Cosmopolitans are in favor of diversity. They are willing to engage with the "other." There is an openness towards divergent cultural experiences. There is a willingness to become a competent actor in the other culture by embodying the habitus, by speaking the language. Cosmopolitans feel at home in other cultures.[38] However, it is important to recognize that despite regular travel, most cosmopolitans live locally and, moreover, with the global flow of cultural goods, people can be cosmopolitan without traveling. On the other hand, there are some locals who rarely travel outside their geographical area, and whose involvement in global culture is perhaps restricted to contact with tourists and visitors, global products and media messages.

People who visit and live in other cultures for business or pleasure are not necessarily cosmopolitan. There are many Irish who have become part of the Irish diaspora and have gone to live and work abroad, but have effectively remained in an Irish bubble, living at home away from home. They still trade on Irish cultural capital. Similarly there are many holidaymakers, business people and, indeed, academics who travel around the world living in a Western bubble, enjoying all the comforts and security of home plus the benefits of a different climate and environment. There may well be some controlled exposure to some local cultural exotica, but without any real or meaningful engagement with the local people.[39]

While Hannerz is very good at describing cosmopolitans, he is not so good at describing locals and their social position vis-à-vis cosmopolitans. Following Merton, Hannerz argues that the position of locals relates not so much to what they know as to whom they know.[40] For example, allied to their involvement in more community networks and alliances, locals will tend to have a considerable knowledge of local history, people and events. They will be able to speak the language, tell the stories, and play the music and games that visiting cosmopolitans appreciate, like to consume, and add to the cultural capital accumulation. They are like fish in a local pond. One of the limitations of Hannerz is that he tends to suggest that cosmopolitans are always distinct from locals. The reality is that there are many cosmopolitans in Ireland who live locally and are well attuned to the local habitus.

Many of the issues surrounding locals and cosmopolitans relate to sameness and difference. The struggle to maintain local and national culture is part of a struggle to be different. The national project entails not only imagining but continually creating and maintaining a discourse and practice of being different which become embodied in everyday life in Irish villages, towns and counties. But the pride in being local and national, in being different, takes place in the context of a struggle to have the same lifestyle as the rest of the West. The local and national struggle to be similar but different reflects a similar struggle by individuals operating within the market of the world capitalist system. Indeed local and national cultures cannot survive unless they are consumed both by locals and cosmopolitans as part of the struggle to be different, to attain cultural and symbolic capital, to be seen and appreciated as morally superior. It is better, then, to conceptualize the division between cosmopolitan and local not so much in terms of binary opposite people, but as two ends of a continuum with cosmopolitans being oriented toward global culture and locals towards local culture.

The more locals become oriented towards global culture, towards consuming difference, and spend less time and effort creating and maintaining local culture, the more local culture is in danger of being colonized. Time and effort revolves around attending local functions. Local culture depends on people taking an interest, engaging in conversation, swapping stories and information about what has happened in the locality to whom, when, where, how and with whom. It thrives on gossip. It builds up what Peace calls the "cognitive map" to what is happening in a locality. Without this map it is impossible to interpret the meaning and significance of incidents and happenings. Gossip is at the heart of social bonds. If gossip is strong, committed locals will strive to avoid bad gossip about themselves. Concern about gossip is an indication of the strength of local social bonds. Cosmopolitans are less dependent on the local for social position, honor and respect. They travel more, are involved in different social fields and are less dependent on the local for identity and belonging. The less time cosmopolitans spend in the locale, the more they become the same as blow-ins. And so, as Peace argues, "even if they access conversational encounters between locals, in a shop or bar for instance, the meaning of the gossip they hear escapes them, the distance between themselves and those who are established in the place is reinforced."[41]

The maintenance of local social bonds is also dependent on local heroes and saints, people who are oriented towards achieving honor and respect locally, who make regular self-sacrifices for the good of the community. The hero is the person who achieves adulation either intentionally or unintentionally because he or she has brought rewards or distinction to the community through work as a local politician, a community activist, a sports-player or an entertainer. The saint is the person who does not achieve adulation but is nonetheless recognized for the quiet, unassuming sacrifices she or he makes for others and the community generally. Of course, it is often possible for cosmopolitans who live locally to become local heroes but it depends on their having local supporters and spending time courting them.

CULTURAL CAPITAL

We are used to understanding capital as being purely economic, a form of wealth that is accumulated. However, as Bourdieu reminded us, it is also useful to think of people accumulating other forms of power or capital.[42] We can, then, see people who are involved in a number of different social networks and who have a large number of contacts as having social capital. We can also see having access to resources and authority as a form of political capital, and being able to attain the honor and respect of other people as a form of symbolic capital. But the most important form of capital in terms of the present discussion is cultural capital. This results primarily from the accumulation of educational degrees and awards, but it is also related to, on the one hand, people being civilized, polite, artistic, sporty, religious and so forth and, on the other, to embodying a shared outlook, sense of self and humour and, generally, a way of being in the world.

There are two important things to remember about cultural capital. The first is that it is crucial to obtaining other forms of capital. It is difficult these days to get a good job and income without having a good education. Secondly, and this is something Bourdieu did not draw attention to very much, cultural capital can be global or local. If we follow this line of thought, then we can see that the survival of local and national culture depends on its becoming an important form of culture capital: If people accumulate local and national culture, it can lead to the accumulation of economic, social, political, symbolic and other forms of capital. It is difficult for local and national culture to survive when it is not an important form of cultural capital. While the struggle to maintain the value of local culture is undertaken by cultural guardians, it is only when it becomes part of the individual's struggle for capital that it will survive. Thus, in Ireland, unless having Irish cultural products, speaking the Irish language, listening to Irish music, being knowledgeable about Irish history, and so forth are seen as important forms of cultural capital—that is, they can be traded for other forms of capital—Irish culture will decline.

On the other hand, local and national culture can sometimes thrive when it becomes a part of global culture. We see this around the world in terms of the increase in value of embracing Irish culture. In other words, for cosmopolitans around the world, accumulating Irish cultural capital is not just hip, it can be important in terms of accumulating other forms of capital. The advantage of global cultural capital is that it can be used to attain economic, social and symbolic capital in different social fields in different societies. It can also be used locally to attain symbolic as well as other forms of capital. Global cultural capital increases the volume and variety of cultural capital. It brings diversity into the local cultural pool.

SAMENESS AND DIFFERENCE

The question of sameness and difference lies at the heart not just of this study, but of social life in general. As Durkheim reminded us, the origins of religion and human society lie in the way people classified themselves as belonging to different clans or tribes.[43] But to maintain a distinction between us and them, whether it is at the level of family, group, or nation, we have to develop and maintain a sense of sameness and belonging—what Durkheim referred to as a collective consciousness. We have to maintain and develop collective representations that engender social bonds, unity and a sense of sameness. But, and this is a central question for globalization, while people around the world may increasingly have the same liberal-individualist beliefs and values—the importance and the right of individuals to do their own thing—and while more and more people live similar lives, the question is whether they develop the same collective consciousness, the same sense of bonding and belonging that comes from, for example, living in families and communities.[44] We have become used to the idea that nations are imagined communities, created and sustained not by people physically coming together but by becoming consciously united through collective representations generated by the state and the mass media.[45] Do people have the same sense of bonding and belonging when they enter a modern cathedral of consumption? Moreover, can people effectively come together when their orientation is more towards individual sensations and pleasures rather than a surrender to the group?[46] The group is strong when individual success or salvation is tied to the success or salvation of the group.

More importantly, perhaps, how can individuals bind together if they keep doing their own thing? Now it may not be necessary to be part of a religious community or family—Durkheim recognized that people may develop a sense of bonding and belonging through participation in games—but what is important is that there is a coming together and that there is a surrender of self within the collective.[47] Can people bond together without an element of self-surrender? If so, what is the nature and strength of these bonds?

The other important legacy of Durkheim was that he reminded us that a family, group or society cannot maintain its sense of identity and belonging if it does not distinguish itself from other families, groups and societies.[48] A sense of sameness is dependent not just on people coming together and bonding, but on creating and maintaining identity boundaries with others. We are the same: they are different. The sense of sameness, and consequently of difference, is created through what are effectively arbitrary signs and representations brought together to create meaning and belonging but which, over time, take on a sacredness that has real consequences.[49] A good example of this is the division between Protestants and Catholics in Ireland over the meaning of Holy Communion. For Protestants Holy Communion is more of a symbol, but for Catholics in Holy Communion the bread and wine are substantially or literally transformed into the body and blood of Christ. The difference is so great that it literally prevents Catholics and Protestants from coming together to share Holy Communion.[50]

There is a correspondence between the way we see individuals carving out a distinct identity from others who operate within the same cultural system and the way we see nations, or rather nation-states, carving out difference within global culture. Although there will often be conflict between different identities there is agreement about the necessity of maintaining identity. It is the same at the level of global world culture; although the spatial and temporal compression of the world has led to increasing similarity in everyday life, there is an increasing emphasis on difference. In other words, while there is increasing penetration of local and national culture by "consumerist global capitalism" there is also a recognition and an acceptance of the importance of local cultures not only socially and culturally, but politically and economically. As

Robertson points out, "the contemporary capitalist creation of consumers frequently involves the tailoring of products to increasingly specialized regional, societal, ethnic, class and gender markets—so-called micro-marketing." The growing expectation of universality is matched by an equally growing expectation of particularity. With globalization "there is virtually no limit to particularity, to uniqueness, to difference, and to otherness."[51] The problem, however, as already mentioned, is to what extent this difference is based on a sense of sameness, of people having a sense of bonding and belonging that is strong and deep and stands in contrast to a globally commodified lifestyle that is weak and shallow.

Robertson insists that "globalization has involved and continues to involve the *institutionalized construction* of the individual." He refers to how much the state and non-governmental organizations promote individualism—education, human rights, women's rights. There is also the "celebration of subjective identity" and "minority" forms of personal and collective identification. He emphasizes that as well as there being a global economy, there is also a global culture. It revolves around the principle of people learning from each other and wanting to sustain a sense of identity.[52] Robertson invokes Smith's notion that at the end of the eighteenth century at the root of the national ideal was a vision of the world according to which humankind is "really" and "naturally" divided into distinct nations, each of which makes its own valuable contribution to the family of nations.[53] Indeed, the whole growth of nation-states and the ever-increasing demand for regional autonomy and the self-governance of ethnic groups is a result of the growth in globalization.

There is, then, for Robertson a link between the increasing size of social collectivities and the increase in individual and social differentiation. The more Irish society becomes the same as the rest of the West, the more the Irish need to continually create and maintain national difference. This balancing of sameness and difference is reflected at the level of the local: The perceived differences between counties in Ireland may have increased rather than diminished with globalization. Finally, the balance is reflected at the level of self and the struggle by individuals to realize their difference. But the more individuals insist on the need to be different, the greater the strains on social bonds. The more the variety in individual behavior, the greater the need for both individual self-constraint and law enforcement to maintain social order. There is, then, a base of sameness to the variety of difference found in Western social life. Before the world capitalist system and the present phase of globalization, there were greater contrasts in the way people lived their lives at local level, between beliefs and practices, between tribes, clans, ethnic groups, families and communities.[54] The difference was more at the level of the group than the individual. The individual was more subsumed by the group. There were more rigid external forms of self-restraint. There was a greater insistence on self-sacrifice.

What has happened in Ireland is that the contrast between the behavior of Irish people and the rest of the West has decreased. At the same time, there has been an increase in differences, in the varieties of beliefs, values, attitudes and practices and, generally, ways of being in the world. Irish people can now give more free rein to their impulses, pleasures and desires as long as they do this in a controlled manner that does not cause harm or offence to others. But the question is to what extent these differences, these varieties, are significantly different. Do they really mask an overall sameness to everyday life, in the sense of self, and the way of being in the world? Was the way of life in Ireland 50 years ago significantly different than from what it is today and, at that time, was it significantly different from life elsewhere in the world?

Again, following Robertson, the more optimistic view of globalization is that the more everyday life around the world becomes the same, the more do differences become shallow, and the more that people can identify with other human beings. In other words, the more people become aware of the world as one place and of "others" as being the same, the greater the feelings of love, care and responsibility for others thousands of miles away whom they have never met. Globalization, it is argued, has brought about a new collective consciousness, of everyone in the world being part of humankind.[55] In this way, it is not just that the world is being compressed into a single place through increased interdependence but that global consciousness develops a greater understanding, appreciation and receptiveness to cultures other than one's own.[56] Global consciousness is, then, similar to the way nations were created. It is a process through which people imagine they belong to a global community.[57] But again, we have to ask what is the sense of belonging and the strength of the social bonds within this global community. What characterizes Irish society—and indeed local communities—is that through shared experiences, narratives and traditions it has constituted a collective memory, albeit invented or imagined. But it is the absence of any shared collective memory or experience which undermines the notion of there being any global community. Smith puts this starkly:

> Unlike national cultures, a global culture is essentially
> memoryless. Where the "nation" can be constructed so as to

draw upon and receive latent popular experiences and needs, a "global culture" answers to no living needs, no identity-in-the-making. It has to be painfully put together, artificially, out of the many existing folk and national identities into which humanity has been so long divided. There are no "world memories" that can be used to *unite* humanity; the most global experiences to date—colonialism and the World Wars—can only serve to remind us of our historic cleavages.[58]

I think Smith is partially correct. Social bonds emerge through a collective chain of memory.[59] Children are told about people and events which socialize them into a family, neighborhood and society. Groups, organizations and institutions also have a collective memory. For social bonds to be created and maintained there has to be more than just an identification with the wider collectivity, there has to be an engagement in rituals and practices that generate a sense of belonging and recreate memory chains. The creation and development of a sense of Irish people belonging together came about through a renewed devotion to the Catholic Church, the revival of the Irish language, the development of *gaelic* sport, the promotion of Irish music and the rewriting of Irish history. And, as Mac Laughlin has argued, nations are not just imagined but are fostered and developed through people.[60] In Ireland, priests, schoolteachers, historians, antiquarians—what I have termed cultural guardians—were all central to the development of the notion of Ireland as a nation. They developed a chain of collective memory into which children were socialized and which was kept alive in stories, events and practices. This collective memory became part of what may be called "Irish-kind." The question is how the notion of humankind is created and maintained. What stories are told, what events take place, what practices are engaged in that develop a global consciousness of our all being human?

The global response to the tsunami in the Indian Ocean on 26 December 2004 would suggest that globalization is not just about money and markets, but about a greater appreciation and concern for humankind. It would suggest that although people are aware of religious and ethnic differences there is also an increasing identification with and concern for humankind in general. On 7 January 2005, less than two weeks after the event, there were 1.3 million responses to a search through Google using the words "tsunami appeal." By 26 January, the global search on Google revealed 4.5 million responses.

MEDIATED IDENTITY AND BELONGING

One of the key messages to come from the tsunami was that it confirmed McLuhan's argument that when it comes to understanding the influence of the media, it is the medium that is the message.[61] It is the way modern media technology is able to reach into the remotest parts of the world and send, so quickly, sounds and images from there all around the world, that not only shapes our knowledge and understanding of the world, not only creates the impression, but sustains the sense that the world is one place. Moreover, in the case of the tsunami, it was the immediate availability of live pictures of people involved in the tragedy which created a sense of global bonding. As there were thousands of holidaymakers in the region at the time, there was extensive video footage which enabled viewers around the world to witness what happened and to see and hear the victims. For example, within hours of the event, Irish news reports were conducting interviews with Irish tourists in the area using their mobile phones. Video footage from personal cameras was quickly made available to the world media.

Pictures and personal stories do more than anything else to develop a sense of humankind. Pictures make identification with other members of humankind easier. This is one of the reasons the tsunami was attractive to the media. In November 1970 there was a cyclone that hit Bangladesh (then East Pakistan) in which over 250,000 died. It received nothing like the same coverage as the tsunami, partly because there was little or no film footage. The following year there was a genocide in Bangladesh in which an estimated 3 million people died, mostly Hindus.[62] It may be the same as with the Rwandan woman to whom I referred in the previous chapter. Can we develop a common sense of humanity, a sense of belonging to humankind, through mediated messages? Or are lasting social bonds only developed through physical encounters with concrete individuals?

There were other factors that led to this spontaneous identification with humankind. It was an unusual cataclysmic event. The millions of people who die quietly from poverty, hunger and disease every day around the world do not have the same news factor and do not create the same shock and horror. It is also difficult to separate the global from the local. The local angle is also a key determination in deciding whether global stories get covered locally. An important Irish link to the tsunami story was that in 2004 over 40,000 Irish people had gone to Thailand, mainly on holiday. This suggests that there could be up to 100,000 people in Ireland who were familiar with Thailand and the other countries in the region affected. It was a global disaster but, in some respects, for many Irish cosmopolitans it was a local disaster.

The memory of the tsunami has faded in Ireland. It did not have the cultural guardians to keep it fresh in our minds in the same way as, for example, the Famine has been remembered. It is the ongoing reminders of events like the Famine and the rebellion of 1916 that have been central to maintaining a sense of Irish-kind. It is the absence of a critical mass of cultural guardians in Ireland to maintain the memory of the tsunami which is central to the inability to develop a more heightened and sustained sense of humankind.

BOURDIEU AND GLOBALIZATION

The pessimistic view about globalization is that far from creating a greater sense of humankind, it is undermining the social bonds that are central to creating stable sustainable societies and individuals. Throughout the latter part of his life, Pierre Bourdieu began to write—and indeed rage—about globalization, particularly in terms of what he saw as the imperialism of the universal, the rise of the logic of the market, the spread of neo-liberalism, the disappearance of civic virtue, the return of individualism, and the decline of the social welfare state.[63] He saw globalization as an economic policy aimed at creating a global economic field that would remove all obstacles in its way, particularly the nation-state. He argued that "globalization" had supplanted the earlier concept of "modernization" which was introduced by American social scientists and which measured all societies in terms of their distance from the United States which, he said, was not just "the most economically advanced society" but the "endpoint and end goal of all human history."[64] He railed against any notion that the state, operating on behalf of a free market, could ever deem to know how to make people happy.[65]

Bourdieu was right to talk about the inevitability of neo-liberalism, how it has become the unquestioned orthodoxy or *doxa* within the media, the intelligentsia, an public opinion generally. He was emphatic that globalization is "a myth in the strong sense of the word, a powerful discourse, an *idée force*, an idea which has social force, which obtains belief." This discourse is based on notions of unbridled radical capitalism, on flexible working—that is, working all hours in a 24/7 regime—and on the maximization of profit—the so-called law of the market. He predicted that the social costs of globalization would be an insecurity that would mainly afflict young people and would result in the type of riots that occurred in cities around France in 2005.[66]

There is a strong structural economic determinism in Bourdieu's thinking: the drive towards profit maximization brings with it a discourse based on the principle of the unfettered market that is constructed within neo-liberal economics. Adapted by the state and propagated by the media, neo-liberalism becomes an accepted orthodoxy among all classes. People are duped into a false sense of security and happiness. At the same time, workers are forced to be more efficient and productive. Those who do not or cannot, become labeled as misfits, free-riders, degenerates or simply stupid.[67] But similarly, young people are duped into a false sense of self-realization by corporate consumerism.

> By taking as their own chief targets children and adolescents, particularly those most shorn of specific immune defences, with the support of advertising and the media which are both constrained and complicit, the big cultural production and distribution companies gain an extraordinary, unprecedented hold over all contemporary societies—societies that, as a result, find themselves virtually infantalized.[68]

Bourdieu recognized what he saw as the insidious threat of the market and how easily people were seduced by figures such as the "international star of rock, pop or rap, presenting a lifestyle that is both chic and facile (for the first time in history, the seductions of snobbery have become attached to practices and products typical of mass consumption, such as denim, T-shirts and Coca-Cola)."[69] The pessimistic side of me tends to agree with Bourdieu. Economic policies promoting free markets, the maximization of profit, and the extraction of greater productivity have been the major determining influence in Western culture and social life. But there is still a need to describe and analyze how this happens. This is the importance of case studies and looking at how globalization operates in a particular society such as Ireland.

Another weakness in Bourdieu's theory of globalization is that he does not employ his own concepts of habitus, practice and capital to explain how globalization works.[70] I think it is important to develop a bottom-up approach to understanding globalization. There is a need to understand the logic of globalization in terms of the logic of consumption and how this operates at the level of the individual actor and then at the level of local community and national society. Bourdieu's concepts enable us to understand how the dominant Catholic habitus of self-denial was gradually transformed into a culture of self-realization and indulgence through a decline in the dominant position of the Catholic Church and the religious field and their replacement by the media and the market. However, the Irish were not manipulated or coerced into consumerism. Like everywhere else in the West, the Irish took to liberal-individualism with the ease of putting on a brand-new coat. As the habitus changed and the importance of the religious field declined, so too did the importance and significance of religious cultural capital. Being spiritual and moral, embodying religious teaching, engaging in religious practices, became less significant in obtaining other forms of capital, getting a good job, running a successful business, making social contacts, gaining people's honor and respect. Consumer cultural capital, such as having a new house and car, being dressed fashionably, going on exotic holidays, eating in good restaurants, began to have more cultural capital value. Individual identity and sense of self began to switch from being a good Catholic to being a good consumer. This is not to say that the switch has been complete. Ireland may be one of the most globalized societies in the world but it is still very small, local and Catholic.

Bourdieu was also not so good at describing and analyzing the logic of the practice of consumerism, the way getting and spending is attractive and meaningful to people. His great contribution was to show us how consumption was intrinsically linked to symbolic domination and the reproduction of class position. However, even in *Distinction* (1984), he rarely got beyond the structural imperative to maintain and improve class position, into the interest of people developing different tastes and lifestyles as part of an interest in being the same, in belonging. He raged against consumerism becoming the new religion, the new opium of the masses, without ever producing a hermeneutical description of the logical appeal that consumerism and new individualism have for people.[71] If we are to understand the transformation in Ireland from Catholic capitalism to consumer capitalism, we need to appreciate the transformation at the level of the individual and, specifically, the difference in the sense of self that emerges from being immersed in a discourse and practice of consumerism. How and why does consumption operate at the level of identity and sense of self? For example, this is how novelist Linda Grant described owning a new coat:

> You wait and wait for the weather to get cold enough to wear it
> and when, finally it does, you feel . . . and this where we get to the

point, which is nothing to do with price, labels or serviceability. Because how you feel when you have your new coat or wrap dress is something so mysterious, complex and potentially transformative that it is almost metaphysical. For a new coat can induce not only happiness but a radically revised sense of who you are. You can call this by some piece of jargon if you wish, you can invoke phrases such as "self-esteem", but they don't encompass the whole vast empire of the self. The new coat makes things possible. It casts you in a new light to yourself.[72]

THE GLOBAL BECOMES PERSONAL

One of the questions at the heart of this study is whether the inexorable drive to sameness at the center of the world capitalist system will undermine membership of families, groups and communities with strong social bonds. The task in understanding glocalization is to make links between long-term processes of social change such as the development of the world capitalist system and the micro-world of ordinary everyday life. At one level, glocalization can be understood in terms of how elements of culture from around the world become deposited in Ireland and how they become adapted to Irish conditions. If we are to understand this process of balancing sameness and difference then it is necessary to understand not just how globalization operates at the level of local and national culture, but also how it operates at the level of the individual.

As a young boy growing up in Ireland in the 1950s and 1960s I wanted to be the same as everyone else, to belong and be accepted, to attain honor and good standing in my extended family, my school and the wider community. This was done primarily through embodying the habitus of my family, religion and class. Saying and doing the right things provided me with a sense of identity and belonging. They also brought honor, respect and status. In effect I accumulated local cultural capital.

But I also had an interest in being different, in developing a personal identity. Increased difference led to increased status and deference. This was achieved through saying and doing things differently, by making different choices. These were reflected in my tastes and preferences, in how I dressed, what I liked to eat, the books I read, my favorite pop stars, films, television programs and so forth. Throughout the 1960s, as the flow of global culture increased, these tastes and preferences came from outside Ireland, primarily Britain and America. I was entering the world of consumer society, of attaining distinction through commodities, of accumulating cosmopolitan cultural capital. To be the same, to be accepted, I felt I had to be different. The quest for difference leads people to extend their choices, tastes and preferences from beyond the local culture. So I grew up desperate to talk about the hottest curry I had eaten, the amazing German beer I had drunk, the beach in Greece I had lain on. I wanted to be part of the same cosmopolitan peer culture which necessitated making different choices within the same lifestyle. I had moved seamlessly from being colonized by the Catholic Church, to being colonized by consumer culture.

Unless we understand how glocalization comes down to everyday life and the struggle to be the same but different, we cannot understand how the world capitalist system continues to grow and reach down to the smallest villages in the remotest parts of the world. It operates on an interest in status, stimulation, pleasure and excitement that works in the minds, hearts and bodies of us all.

Globalization is a complex, long-term historical process. The way in which the global flow of culture touches down in different parts of the world and the extent to which it reaches into the habitus of local people is something that is best studied through empirical case studies. Ireland is a good place to study globalization. It has moved from being a very homogeneous, insular, traditional society to becoming one of the most open, globalized societies in the world. The flow of global culture has become embedded in the Irish habitus and elements of Irish culture have become part of global culture. I have suggested that the survival and vibrancy of Irish cultural difference are dependent on maintaining a local habitus and that this, in turn, is dependent on the value of local cultural capital, particularly in relation to obtaining other forms of capital. The value of local cultural capital is partly dependent on cultural guardians who maintain and develop Irish culture at local and national level. However, local cultural capital is always under pressure from global cultural capital.

In many respects the everyday lives of Irish people revolve around the same habitus and practices that are endemic in the pattern of production and consumption that characterize the world capitalist system. They work to consume. They have become increasingly rational, predictable, punctual, reliable and efficient. The social bonds have become severely strained.

And yet Irish people still see and understand themselves as different. The seeds of Irish difference were sown long ago in the struggle to be different from the English colonizer, to be religious and moral but not to be Protestant, to be economically independent but not to become driven by materialism and consumption. The strategies and tactics instituted by church and state created a habitus in which frugal comfort, piety and humility reigned supreme. I will argue that it is this habitus that was central to making the Irish different.

But before examining the nature of Irish difference in more detail, it is first necessary to explore how the Irish have developed the global reputation that they have, particularly in the West. The history of Ireland, like many other societies, is characterized by the flow of people in and out of the island. However, what made Ireland different over the last 200 years, was that it was a major source of missionaries to the new world. They left a legacy everywhere they went, not just in religion, but in education, health and social welfare provision. More important, however, was the number of emigrants that left Ireland to go, particularly, to North America, Britain and Australia. It was this inordinate contribution to the global flow of people that has, perhaps more than anything else, created Ireland's global reputation.

The study of globalization centers on the daily flow of money, goods, services, media messages, knowledge and ideas around the world. This is nothing new. These flows have been part and parcel of the growth and development of human society. What is new, however, is the level, intensity and rapidity of these flows in recent decades. What is also new is the number of people involved in these flows. Through their engagement in everyday life, individuals become connected, directly and indirectly, with countless numbers of other individuals around the world, most of whom they have never met. Globalization is about the increase in the interconnectivity and interdependence of more and more people around the world. When I look at my desk, around my study, and at the rest of my house, most of the goods and items by which I am surrounded were designed, made and transported by people around the world who never met me or each other.

But globalization also involves the movement of people themselves. Again, there is nothing new in this. Migration is endemic to human being. What has changed, however, has been the number of people who move around the world each day, going on holiday, doing business, going home, returning to work and so forth. These commuters and travelers are different from migrants who go to another part of the world, to work and live, who stop, stay and put down roots. Migrants are the ones who intermix and intermarry and who contribute most to the processes of creolization and hybridization discussed in the last chapter.

In this chapter I look at the global flow of people in and out of Ireland over the centuries. In comparative terms, the island of Ireland is not that different from many other parts of the world: it has been as much subject to invasion and colonization—people coming to take whatever we had—as it has been to emigration, people wanting to, or having to, get out. The invaders and colonizers brought with them new ideas, knowledge and ways of being in the world which altered the way the Irish lived. At the same time, when the Irish emigrated, they too brought different customs, traditions, values and beliefs which eventually infiltrated into the local culture.

However, what is different about the Irish is that they became modern world leaders at emigration. During the nineteenth and twentieth centuries, for generation after generation, the Irish had the highest levels of emigration. They left to go and find a new life in Britain, America and the new world, as laborers, servants and missionaries. These migrants may be seen as having sown cultural seeds which, particularly in later generations, began to grow, develop and prosper. Many Irish emigrants worked their way to the top in the different social fields; they moved to the center of power. It became not just acceptable but desirable and rewarding to have Irish connections, to identify with being Irish. The descendants of the Irish diaspora have developed a global reputation.

But things have changed. Since the 1990s and the birth of the Celtic Tiger economy, the flow of people has been reversed. Instead of thousands upon thousands emigrating each year, there are now thousands, mainly from Eastern Europe, coming to live and work in Ireland. Ireland is rapidly becoming a multi-racial, multi-ethnic, multi-religious culture.

The early 1960s were a pivotal time in Ireland. In 1962, I was 11 years old, completely involved in my own world, when I learned that the world could come to an end. The Cuban missile crisis probably did more than any other single event to raise global consciousness.

John F. Kennedy was willing to bring us to the brink of nuclear annihilation and he was my hero. He was everything I wanted to be. He represented America which was everything Ireland wanted to be. But, like many other Irish people at the time, I believed he was Irish. His ancestors came from Co. Wexford. Like many other Irish they had emigrated to create a new world for themselves in the United States. He was the first Roman Catholic to be elected President. When he came to visit Ireland in June 1963, he said many nice things about us.

> Ireland has already set an example and a standard for other small nations to follow. This has never been a rich or powerful country, and yet, since earliest times, its influence on the world has been rich and powerful. No larger nation did more to keep Christianity and Western culture alive in their darkest centuries. No larger nation did more to spark the cause of independence in America, indeed, around the world. And no larger nation has ever provided the world with more literary and artistic genius.[1]

When, less than six months later, President Kennedy was assassinated I felt as if my own father had been murdered, as if my future had been taken away. The Irish adored John F. Kennedy. He was like a saint. When Kennedy died many people put up his picture on the mantelpiece, often alongside pictures of Jesus and that other great modern reformer, Pope John XXIII.

The Kennedys were probably the most famous of the emigrants who left Ireland. If Ireland has a global reputation it has less to do with the 6 million people who inhabit the island today and more to do with the influence of the Irish diaspora around the world. The millions of migrants who left Ireland over the past 200 years were a small part of the flow of people around the world that became a major characteristic of globalization. Like many other things, it is not that the Irish are unique in the way they emigrated. It is just that the Irish started early and lasted longer. Between 1801 and 1921, approximately 8 million people left Ireland. Although the flow of people from Europe was high—44 million migrated between 1821 and 1914—the contribution of the Irish to this flow was, relative to its size, larger than any other country's.[2]

The Irish became dispersed all over the new world, particularly in America. Many left because they were pushed. It was difficult for many parents to look after and provide a viable standard of living for all their children. Children were reared with the expectation that they would emigrate. Large families and emigration continued to be part of the Irish way of life through the nineteenth and most of the twentieth centuries. It was a sacrifice to which mothers and children became accustomed. Why did the Irish continue to have large families? The simple answer is that it was part of their Catholic culture; being good Catholics became central not just to maintaining a different identity from the Protestant English, but to improving the standard of living, becoming civilized, and developing a modern society.[3] And yet for generations a worldview developed both among the Irish diaspora and those at home that people were coerced into leaving their homes and families by forces beyond their own control, particularly by the British and landlord oppression. Emigration was seen as another form of eviction. It became part of the nationalist rhetoric, embraced on both sides of the Atlantic. Irish-Americans were homesick and alienated, they had a devotion to Mother Ireland, but they could never come home until she was completely free from her colonial oppressor.[4]

But the reality is that many young people were very anxious to get out of Ireland, pulled by the promise of a new life, steady work and a good standard of living. The most persuasive pressure came in the form of emigrant letters conveying news of relatives and neighbors abroad with very precise details of the cost of land, the wages of laborers and servants.[5] Even before the Famine years, successful migrants were sending back remittances to Ireland, a system that later developed into a huge traffic in pre-paid passage tickets to finance the great majority of voluntary migration.[6]

Before 1841, when mass migration had already seen an annual exodus of 50,000 from Ireland, Britain was the main destination, ahead of Canada and the United States. This began to change around the Famine. Between 1845 and 1855, 1.5 million sailed to the United States, another 340,000 embarked for British North America, and about 250,000 went to Britain. An entire Irish generation virtually disappeared from the land; only one out of three Irishmen born about 1831 died at home of old age.[7] Many of the Irish who went to Britain in the nineteenth century were the poorest of the poor. They were emigrants of despair, the unskilled, poor and without property who inhabited the slums and scrublands of the cities and countryside. They were distinguished from the "emigrants of hope" who could afford the fare to America.[8]

From the 1840s until the 1920s the United States received about 75 percent of the 5 million total of Irish migrants.[9] Those who were going to cross the Atlantic would never be seen or heard again. Unlike going to Britain, emigration to America was as final as death and those who went were given a wake similar to one for somebody who had died. The wake for emigrants leaving for America was a peculiarly Irish custom. Those gathered at an American wake lamented not only the emigration of a relative or friend but also the inexorable disintegration of old communities and the decline of traditional ways of life which emigration epitomized.[10]

Most of the nineteenth-century Irish migrants were constructed as non-white, the "black Irish," and encountered the same forms of denigration that they had suffered from their English colonial masters and which corresponded closely to the experiences of Native and African Americans.[11] The main struggle for these migrants was, literally, to be seen and treated as white and therefore for laborers to be able to compete for higher-order jobs and for those in business to operate outside of ethnic-Irish markets. They were very successful. In the era of the First World War, persons of Irish Catholic ethnicity already slightly exceeded the US national average on three major indices of occupational and social success: college attendance and graduation, professional careers, and white-collar careers.[12] By the 1970s the Irish had become the second most privileged ethnic group in the United States.[13]

Part of the nationalist myth is that most Irish migrants to America were Catholic. However, an analysis of demographic data showed that out of 44 million Americans claiming Irish heritage over half were descendants of Irish Protestants.[14] And so part of the success of Irish Catholics in America is that they managed to get descendants of Irish Protestant migrants written out of the history of the Irish diaspora and to convince most Americans that they were the Irish.[15]

But the Irish were equally successful in the other countries to which they emigrated, particularly Australia, New Zealand and South Africa. Irish-born descendants became the largest ethnic group in these countries and over generations were not only economically and politically successful themselves, but helped shape the character of those societies.[16] From 1921, Britain resumed its role as the major destination for Irish migrants and this pattern continued through to the end of the twentieth century.[17] Although emigration is still perhaps associated with the flow of Irish people to America, the reality is that the main flow during the twentieth century has been to Britain. In 1970, there were 950,000 people living in Britain who had been born in Ireland compared to only 250,000 in the United States. More Irish-born people live in London than in any other city except Dublin and Belfast.[18]

Emigration has left an indelible mark on Irish society. Over the past two centuries, the Irish have become used to the steady flow of family, friends, neighbors and colleagues leaving and rarely or never coming back. In his study of 6,900 families in 1989, Mac Laughlin found that one in four had a family member living abroad, prompting him to classify them as transnational households.[19]

In his book *Transnational Connections*, the anthropologist Ulf Hannerz defines globalization as "increasing long-distance interconnectedness." As an example, he describes a visit to Carna in the Connemara *Gaeltacht* on the west coast. He and his wife were staying with an Irish-speaking family. The mother was going into Galway later that day for a family reunion. She hoped that her brother who lived in New York would be flying in for the event. She had spent most of her adult life working in London.[20] People from the Irish diaspora have become part of what it means to be Irish. They have become a badge of Irish identity as much as if not more so than other traditional cultural markers such as the language, the GAA, Irish Catholicism and faded dreams of cultural uniqueness and economic self-sufficiency.[21]

On 7 May 2003, Mary McAleesse, the President of Ireland,

was in the United States. She gave a speech at a conference on "Re-imagining Ireland" in Charlottesville, Virginia. As well as speaking to the audience that night she, like de Valera 60 years previously, was speaking to the people back in Ireland. She talked about its recent success. "The little impoverished island off the West coast of Europe which became an unremarkable member of the European Union thirty years ago, has become the symbol of the Union's potential, the place with the economic success story that everywhere else wants to imitate." She talked about the global connectedness of the Irish that had arisen through centuries of emigration, of how where they had gone and, no matter how long ago they had left, Irish people around the world were deeply rooted to the local.

> No other nation holds on to its children and its children's children like we do. Five generations away from Ireland living in Chicago, Kuala Lumpur or Canberra we meet them and we interrogate them until the parish is found and the *botherin* their emigrating ancestors set out from and the cousins of theirs we know back home in Ireland. We have ties of family so extraordinary that when fifteen thousand of our young people go off around Australia annually on their year-long working visa, they feel instantly at home in that land twelve thousand miles away with its population that is one-third Irish. We are a connecting people. It is our strength and our global Irish family is today one of our greatest resources, feeding our culture, expanding its imagination, opening doors, keeping faith with our intriguing homeland.[22]

The success of the Irish is, then, linked to the increased value of embodying an Irish habitus—an Irish way of being in the world and presenting oneself—and accumulating Irish cultural capital in the form of music, literature, art and so forth. Moreover, the value of this cultural capital has extended beyond the specific field of the Irish diaspora. It is increasingly sought after by cosmopolitans around the world. In the same way that embodying an American habitus and accumulating American cultural capital was important to Irish cosmopolitans, particularly in the latter half of the twentieth century, identifying with being Irish and accumulating Irish cultural capital has attained higher value.

MISSIONARIES

The flow of people in and out of Ireland is not new. The most significant inflow was the arrival of Christians. The influence of a Christian way of life and, specifically, of the Catholic Church and its teachings, has been enormous. St. Patrick is credited with having brought Christianity to the island from the European continent in the fifth century. But then over the next centuries Irish monks exported their brand of Christianity throughout Europe. This close religious connection with Europe has lasted through to today. From the seventeenth century, many Irish priests were trained in Irish colleges around Europe. In the nineteenth century, the flow changed direction. There was an influx of religious Orders of nuns and priests from Europe who established houses here and then the schools, hospitals, orphanages and homes that were to become the backbone of Catholic Ireland. In the latter half of the nineteenth century the religious flow changed direction again with thousands of Irish priests and nuns going on missions primarily to Africa, Asia and Australia. These Irish missionaries had a profound influence throughout the world, on the Irish diaspora and on the Catholic Church itself.

Going on the missions meant, for the most part, going into the British Empire to minister to Irish migrants and to convert the locals. There was a broad division in the missionary destinations and objectives. Those who went to Africa, Southeast Asia, Oceania and parts of South America concentrated primarily on bringing education and health care to indigenous people. In Africa alone it is estimated that one-tenth of all missionaries (Catholic and Protestant) were Irish.[23] The intention of the Irish missionaries was to help westernize indigenous people. Religion was taught within a classical curriculum based on language, mathematics, science and history. The Irish missionaries were often portrayed as ascetic, dour colonists who remained aloof from the indigenous people, who rarely learnt to speak the native language, eat the local food, or engage in local customs.[24] On the other hand, education was open to all children at primary levels, and selection was based on merit for higher levels. Moreover, provision was made for females "in societies where there were deeply-rooted prejudices against their education and where they were widely exploited as servants by the colonial classes."[25] In many instances, Irish missionaries to America, Australia, New Zealand and the other destinations of Irish emigrants were motivated, above all else, by a desire to sustain the faith of their compatriots which was at risk through lack of pastoral care.[26] Such was the missionary zeal of the Irish that from the 1860s onwards they gained control over the Catholic churches in Australia, New Zealand, South Africa, English-speaking Canada and the United States of America.[27] Hogan estimates that in 1965, Ireland had 7,085 priests, sisters, brothers and laity working in Africa, Asia and South and Central America.[28]

ST. PATRICK'S DAY

If the Irish are known throughout the world, it is probably because of St. Patrick's Day more than anything else. Each year, on 17 March, there are parades, dinners and festivities held in honor not so much of St. Patrick, not so much of the Irish, but of being Irish. There are parades held in almost every large city in almost every state of the United States. There are also parades in Japan, Taiwan, Korea and Turkey, countries which do not have any direct link to Ireland.

The origins of St. Patrick's Day lie in the celebration of the Irish "pattern"—the celebration of the local saint's day—and the custom of staging fairs and markets. It had become well established in Ireland in the seventeenth century and, while a religious occasion, was "followed by plenty of food and drink, Irish music and dance, and playful physical activities."[29] However, the actual celebration of St. Patrick's Day originated in the United States and was effectively imported into Ireland. The first record of a St. Patrick's Day celebration was in Boston in 1737, which, ironically, did not include Catholics as the idea of the celebration had been transplanted by Ulster Protestants. The first St. Patrick's Day parade took place in New York in 1762 when Irish soldiers serving in the English army marched through the city. As with most subsequent parades, the parade and the music helped to affirm their cultural difference, their Irish roots, and to create a bond with other Irishmen serving in the army.

The most remarkable aspect of St. Patrick's Day is that there is nothing that is remotely equivalent to it around the world. Why do so many people in so many countries, particularly America, celebrate St. Patrick's Day rather than the patron saint of some other country such as Poland, France, Italy? There are many reasons. First, it is a celebration of Irish successes and achievements within an emigrant host society or in Ireland itself. It is a display of Irish cultural capital. In the past it enabled those living as the poor Irish to rise above their usual station in life, and proudly proclaim their presence amidst "like" others. "In its entirety, the day offers an opportunity to understand how the Irish have been transformed from feckless beggars, brandished exiles, and a people oppressed in their own land, to a group eyed with envy by others for their achievements, culture and success worldwide."[30]

Second, the Irish have no colonial baggage. They are white, Anglo-Saxon, English-speaking, and mostly middle-class. They have become one of the most successful ethnic groups in the world, the global "other" with whom it is easy to identify. Third, in many countries, but particularly the United States, the Irish became a cohesive political group who not only developed a "green machine," especially in cities like New York, Boston and Chicago, but also were key swing voters whose representatives often held the balance of power. Fourth, Catholic Irish have a reputation for letting go and partying, self-emptying and surrender to the group. St. Patrick's Day offers an opportunity to bring a relief to the everyday demands of being rational, predictable, strategic and calculating. Fifth, and perhaps most significant of all, it has much to do with the time of year. The middle of March is a change in the season. In the northern hemisphere it is often the first occasion to celebrate the end of winter and the beginning of spring.

When Aileen and I lived in Carbondale, Illinois we sent our son Arron to a state-subsidized crèche in the more deprived side of town. As we traveled down to collect him on St. Patrick's Day we could see black people gathered together on door-steps with their brown paper bags covering bottles of alcohol, enjoying the early evening spring sunshine. One St. Patrick's night I went to one of the bars in the town and when I asked people why they were celebrating so much, they said it was because they were Irish. When I told them that I was actually Irish, they laughed and told me that on St. Patrick's Day everyone was Irish.

But it would be wrong to think that the celebration of

St. Patrick's Day and the parades that are held around the world are occasions of ethnic solidarity. They have become subject to debate and contestation in much the same way as the more general debate of what it means to be Irish. Consequently, as Wilson and Donnan point out, there are Protestants in Northern Ireland who feel that St. Patrick's Day has become a republican festival and there are Irish gays and lesbians who have felt excluded from the annual parade in New York. Indeed it would seem that complexities around the celebration of St. Patrick's Day and what it means to be Irish may be best studied on the Caribbean island of Montserrat where the local people, some of whom are descended from marriages between Irish landowners and slaves, have had an annual festival since 1970.[31]

THE DRINKING IRISH

In a scene from an episode of *Young Indiana Jones*, the young lad gets transported back to Ireland during the time of the 1916 rising. Like many a modern tourist, he goes into a pub in search of contacts. It is very busy. The *craic* (fun) is good. People are laughing, drinking and talking. Suddenly a row breaks out. Two men start fighting. Then, as if some Pavlovian bell had been rung, everyone in the pub jumps up and starts to beat the hell out of each other.

The image is simple. The Irish love to drink and have a good fight. The myth of the fighting Irish, reenforced through films like *Gangs of New York*, is as strong as the myth of the drinking Irish. It is as if we have no choice. It is in our genes. We are natural-born drinkers and fighters.

In the lead-up to the St. Patrick's Day celebrations in Ireland in 2005, there was considerable debate in the media and the public sphere generally about binge drinking, particularly among young people. There was a fear that there would be major outbreaks of public disorder and drink-related offences. In effect, 714 people were arrested. Given that hundreds of thousands were out celebrating at different festivals and parades around the country, this may seem very small. But an editorial in the *Irish Independent* claimed that those arrested were "just a small proportion of the overall number of drunken youths who were looning [*sic*] around, many fighting, vomiting and urinating in public, frightening children and shocking ordinary people." The editorial went on to ask: "What is it about our youth that compels them to do this? Why is there such a vacuum in their psyche? Why is drinking themselves into a stupor, anti-social behavior, mindless aggression and vandalism, the only way they can celebrate?"[32]

When President McAleesse was addressing the conference in Charlottesville, she too drew attention to this dark side of being Irish.

> More money in pockets has visibly lifted standards of living but it is being badly spent too, on bad old habits that have never gone away. The Irish love of conviviality has its dark side in the stupid wasteful abuse of alcohol and its first cousin—abuse of drugs. They chart a course of misery and malaise so utterly unnecessary that we need to re-imagine an Ireland grown intolerant of behavior which it has too benignly overlooked for too long.

There is a stereotypical image of the Irish liking nothing better than to go down to the local pub for a few pints. Indeed the statistics would seem to verify this. The Irish like their beer (including stout and lager). It accounts for just over half of the total amount of alcohol consumed. And three-quarters of the beer sold is in draught form, mostly in pubs.[33] The statistics reveal some other related trends. Ireland has one of the highest levels of non-drinkers—23 percent. This is twice as many as, for example, Italy (11 percent). This means that those who do drink alcohol have to drink more to keep Ireland third in the European table. Second, Ireland has the lowest number who drink every day—less than 2 percent of the population compared, for example, with 42 percent of Italians. Third, when the Irish do drink, they are likely to drink more than their European counterparts. Ireland has the highest level of binge drinkers—people who drink the equivalent of four pints of beer or more in one session. In Ireland, 48 percent of adults admitted to binge drinking once a week compared to 11 percent of Italians. Fourth, compared to other Europeans, Irish people are more likely to die from alcohol-related diseases (e.g. liver cirrhosis), accidents and homicides.[34] Drinking alcohol is deeply embedded in Irish culture and the Irish psyche. It is seen as part and parcel of being Irish. The results of a national survey showed that over 40 percent of respondents listed drink-related issues as major elements of their "Irishness."[35]

THE IRISH PUB

It is difficult to estimate the number of Irish pubs around the world. Slater noted that Guinness had claimed to have opened 1,700 Irish pubs between 1992 and 1998. Most major global cities now have an Irish pub; Shanghai has three. There are four companies approved by Guinness to design and build "authentic" Irish pubs around the world.[36] The official Guinness website claims that over 1.8 billion pints of Guinness are sold around the world each year. The biggest sales per annum in numerical order are Great Britain, Ireland, Nigeria, United States and Cameroon.[37]

The success of the Irish pub can be seen, generally, as a form of ethnic commodification and, specifically, of making identification with an Irish habitus and "being Irish" as glamorous for cosmopolitans in global cities.[38] The same is true for the way in which, for example, Indian music, food, religion and philosophy became glamorous and a form of cultural capital for Irish cosmopolitans back in the 1970s. The question, however, is what makes going to an Irish pub attractive to cosmopolitans around the world. Why not English pubs, American bars, or French cafés? The simple answer is that going to an Irish pub is great *craic*. The more complicated answer may be, as it was in analyzing the success of St. Patrick's Day, that the Irish are neutral, white and successful. They also have developed a global reputation for partying and drinking.

In the years after the Famine, many men in Ireland were backed into a corner of permanent celibacy and learnt to sublimate their sexual frustration through drink. They may not have had any status as a landowner, farmer, husband, or father but in the sanctuary of the pub they were able to gain the status of a hard drinker and with it a strong masculine identity.[39] Those who emigrated to America brought the culture of the bachelor drinking group with them where hard drinking in saloon bars became not just a signifier of masculine identity but a spiritual value symbolizing one's Irishness or one's Catholicism.[40]

It may well be, then, that what attracts cosmopolitans to Irish pubs is partly the attraction of letting go, of becoming detached from over-involvement in the world, through a ritualistic form of self-elimination achieved through hard drinking. However, to ensure that there is no loss of status through drinking on one's own, this involves a party of colleagues or friends engaging in hard drinking together. The system of drinking in rounds forces members of the drinking circle not just to buy drinks for everyone else, but to accept and drink those that are bought for them. Ultimately it can be seen as a form of ritual self-surrender to the group and, in this respect, as a religious ritual.

The basis of Irish *craic* is a cultural practice that may take more time to develop. It revolves around group banter and teasing in which people take it in turns to make fun of each other, cutting down to size those who stand above the group—who are deemed "too big for their boots."[41] The *craic* in Irish pubs is, then, based on ritualistic self-surrender to the group which, in turn, means that any overt display of individuality that threatens the solidarity of the group is liable to be censured. Irish pubs are neither stylish nor sexy. They are not about the self. They have become an occasional haven in a relentless, heartless world of production, consumption and individualism. They are now a ritualized form of self-elimination, late modern forms of spiritual retreats developed in Ireland and, through global flows, deposited around the world.

RIVERDANCE

Global flows are serendipitous. There is no certainty to the way the deposits from global culture become adapted to local conditions. Sometimes the way global cultural flows become deposited in a society and, through cultural entrepreneurs, are mixed with local cultural forms can create a new hybrid which re-enters the global flow to be deposited elsewhere around the world. The ongoing hybridization of global culture takes place through individuals deliberately mixing elements of the traditional with the new This is what happened with the show *Riverdance*. Beyond the pub, *Riverdance* has probably become the next biggest global icon of Irishness. It has become a classic example of how, through commodification, Irish dancing was made attractive to a global audience which then, through achieving worldwide commercial success, had the effect of reinvigorating Irish dancing both at home and abroad.[42]

The show began life as a seven-minute interval event for a Eurovision Song Contest in Dublin in 1995. By 2006 it had more than 8,000 performances in over 250 venues in over 30 countries. It has been seen live by more than 18 million people and on television by over 1.5 billion. The video/dvd of the show has sold over 9 million copies.[43]

Riverdance brought together elements of contemporary dance forms with traditional Irish dance. Irish dancing became an icon of holy Catholic Ireland. It was blessed by the Church because it was different from modern dancing. It was a different form producing different forms of bodily contact. Irish dances could not, as Cardinal Logue, declared "be danced for long hours." More importantly, he said, "they do not make degenerates."[44] O'Toole argues that in most cultures dancing is where what is private—sexual desire, courtship and family relationships—is played out as a public display. However, Irish dancing became "an act of piety, a homage to the holy trinity of Catholicism, Irish nationalism and sexual continence."[45] As a cultural entrepreneur, Michael Flatley brought to *Riverdance* his enormous self-confidence combined with his experience of Irish-American music. *Riverdance* became a mixture of "Ireland and America, folk art and Tin Pan Alley, tangos and reels, the pure and the hybrid."[46]

Riverdance made Irish dancing exotic and spectacular. It transformed it from something that in the past took place in domestic kitchens and small halls onto the biggest stages of the world. Instead of traditional Celtic costumes, the dancers wore exotic, sexy ones that emphasized rather than hid the body. *Riverdance* symbolizes the "leap from a repressed and pur-itanical culture . . . where dancing was regimented and boring . . . into a neo-liberal one in which dance was transformed into something which was exciting, sexy and exuberant."[47] The skill, precision, power and virtuosity of the dancing help undermine the image of the Irish as being shy, physically awkward, lazy, inefficient and ill-disciplined.[48] *Riverdance* emerged from the flow of emigrants to America who brought their folk dances with them. They became enmeshed in the popular cultural shows where they were re-presented and reformed. This reformation was then brought back into Ireland primarily by Flatley and his colleague Jean Butler. Once constructed, *Riverdance* was exported around the world not just as a form of hybridized culture, but as a symbol of the new Ireland and the triumph of the modern over the traditional.

TOURISM

Tourism is the biggest and fastest-growing industry in the world. It is the biggest employer and is estimated to generate the largest export earnings of any industry.[49] Tourism revolves around the search for difference. It is the desire to look at and be in an environment that is different from the everyday.[50] The stereotypical image of Ireland—produced primarily for tourists but cherished by many Irish themselves—is of a rural retreat where people work to live rather than live to work, have time to meet, swap information, gossip and laugh at themselves and life. It is epitomized by postcards of village pubs and roads empty except for the odd donkey and cart loaded with turf. Tourism is one of the biggest global flows to affect Ireland. In 2005, almost 7 million people visited Ireland. Approximately half of these were traditional tourists, just over 2 million came to visit relatives and friends and just under 1 million came on business. These visitors spent €4.3 billion.[51] Even during the peak of the Celtic Tiger, tourism remained a major component of the Irish economy. If it were not for the transnational companies, the main industry in Ireland would be tourism. In the 10 years between 1988 and 1998, one in three new jobs in Ireland was in tourism. Half of these jobs are seasonal, part-time and low-paid and, increasingly, are being taken up by migrants from eastern countries of the European Union.[52] When visitors are asked what it is that attracts them to Ireland the most common answer is the scenery and the friendliness and hospitality of the people.[53] The next most frequently mentioned reason for coming was to be with friends/loved ones followed closely by a desire to relax and get away from things. As the report noted, "Ireland is rarely perceived as a destination for a luxury holiday or a scintillating nightlife." When asked what makes Ireland separate from other destinations, 40 percent said the people, 31 percent the scenery and 19 percent its culture and history; 85 percent said that the friendliness and hospitality of the people was a very important factor in their choosing Ireland, 69 percent mentioned the easy, relaxed pace of life and 59 percent said the different way of life.[54]

The arrival of millions of tourists each year in search of an authentic Irish experience has led to a greater commodification of Irish difference. Local and national culture become staged, consumers are given a formulaic packet of common icons. In this perspective, tourism becomes a parasite that grows on the Irish tree of difference. This "stage-Irish" approach is often decried by critics, intellectuals and high-minded protectors of Irish culture as a form of artificial difference. This perspective assumes that there is something essential and authentic that is being colonized through commodification. Many cultural nationalists in the nineteenth century propagated the notion that the Irish belong to a Celtic culture. This has been taken up by the tourist industry even though the evidence that there was ever a distinct Celtic culture and people is flimsy.

The problem, as has already been seen above, is that national difference, tradition, character and personality have always been intertwined with economic, political and social interests. There is a similarity in the way a nation or a people present themselves and self-presentation by individuals. The notion of there being an authentic, essential dimension to being Irish is as problematic as there being an authentic, essential dimension to one's self. In the same way as we have as many selves as people who recognize us, so too are there as many Irelands as tourists and Irish people themselves recognize.[55] On the other hand, it would be foolish to argue that there is nothing different about the Irish, about their language, sport, music and dance, about their culture, humor, character and sense of self. The question is how significant are these differences. It may also be that the tourist industry is colonizing and destroying these differences. But it may also be that the continual influx of tourists forces not just those in the tourist industry, but all Irish people, to reflect critically about what is the difference between "them" and "us," and to then embody the discourse and engage in the rituals and practices that distinguish "us" as being Irish. Tourists are a constant reminder of our difference, of what we are and what we are not.

Tourism is not a one-way global flow. There has been a dramatic increase in the number of Irish people traveling abroad for their holidays and, more recently, buying holiday homes, especially in Europe. In 2005, the Irish made 6.1 million visits abroad at a cost of €4.8 billion.[56] The global image of the Irish is, therefore, increasingly related to how people in other countries experience them as tourists. In 2002, the BBC conducted a survey of tourist boards in 17 different countries to discover who were the world's worst tourists. Categories included behavior, politeness, willingness to learn the language, trying local delicacies and spending on the local economy. Germans, Americans and Japanese topped the poll as the best tourists. The British finished bottom of the table of 24 nations. They were designated as the rudest, meanest, worst-behaved, most linguistically incompetent, and least adventurous holidaymakers. The Irish finished 22nd.[57]

DIVERSITY

Another way that the Irish are known and understood globally is through the number of people who come to live and work in Ireland. There has been a dramatic change of direction in the flow of people. The 1980s was a period of economic depression in Ireland. It led to heavy emigration. In 1989, it is estimated that 70,000 people left Ireland while 29,000 entered.[58] In 2002, the level of emigration had declined to 26,000 but the level of immigration had increased to 67,000.[59] In the 10 years between 1996 and 2006, Ireland, particularly urban Ireland, became a multi-ethnic, culturally diversified society. In the 1990s, thousands of refugees and asylum seekers came to Ireland to seek a new life.[60] The state introduced restrictions to stem the flow. However, with the expansion of the European Union in 2004 to include many Eastern European countries, tens of thousands of Poles, Lithuanians, Slovakians, Latvians and Czechs have come to Ireland to live and work. On a daily basis, the second language spoken in Ireland is no longer Irish but Polish. There are regular radio advertisements and notices in shops in Polish and other Eastern European languages. There are specialized shops selling produce for Eastern Europeans. There is also increasing religious diversity. For example, the number of Muslims increased from 3,900 in 1991 to 19,100 in 2002.[61] The arrival of so many new people has given rise to a wide range of new religious and ethnic groups with their own newspapers and newsletters, churches, choirs, sports, restaurants, pre-school and primary schools.[62] This is how Mary Corcoran captures this diversity in Dublin:

> The former Jewish quarter centred around the South Circular Road has, since the early 1990s, become home to many members of the Irish Muslim community. A former church on the South Circular Road serves as a mosque, and there are several halal stores on Clanbrassil. Harold's Cross in the south of the city now boasts a Russian Orthodox Church, while Mass is celebrated in Polish in St. Michan's Church in Smithfield. During the Polish presidential campaign in October 2005, election posters made a brief appearance on hoardings in South Great Georges Street. The Pentacostal Church on Pearse Street boasts a vibrant African congregation. So many Africans have set up grocery stores on historic Moore Street that it is known as "Little Africa."[63]

The rapid increase in racial and ethnic diversity is probably the main cultural transformation in contemporary Ireland. The island on which I grew up was small, mostly Catholic and very white. In the kindergarten I attended there was a little collection box for the Black Babies. When you put a coin in the box, the head of a little Black girl nodded in thanks. I did not encounter a Black person until I was about 10 years old—a foreign student playing rugby for Dublin University. My first job as a social science graduate in 1972 was as an interviewer on a survey about prejudice and discrimination in Dublin. There was a high level of latent discrimination. Almost 3 in 10 (28 percent) said they would refuse digs to Black people if they had a boarding house. A quarter believed that Black people were more highly sexed. Four in 10 believed there should be stricter controls on Black people entering Ireland. All of this was latent discrimination as, even as late as the early

1970s, there was hardly a Black person to be seen on the streets of Dublin. In a repeat of his 1972 study in 1988 Mac-Gréil found that while there had been a significant decline in latent racial discrimination, there was still a high level of racial prejudice. For example, while 79 percent of his respondents would welcome white Americans into their family, only 26 percent would similarly welcome Black Americans.[64]

It is estimated that there are people from more than 160 countries now living in the Republic. There are thousands of Chinese, Nigerians, Filipinos, Pakistanis, Romanians, Algerians, and many more nationalities. These are the new Irish. We are used to the term Irish-American. Irish people may soon have to get used to the term Polish-Irish, Chinese-Irish and so forth. By 2002, there were 9,400 African-born residents in Dublin city and county and 20,000 nationwide.[65] By 2005, the estimated total number of foreign nationals in Ireland had risen to over 350,000 which was close to 10 percent of the overall population.[66] Many of these have come to stay.

The most dramatic change in Irish diversity has come through the inflow of people from Eastern Europe that took place following the enlargement of the European Union in 2004. Over the following two years, just over a quarter of a million migrants from Eastern Europe registered to work in Ireland. The number from Poland (147,659) was higher than from the next four countries combined (Lithuania 40,237), Slovakia (20,312), Latvia (20,301) and the Czech Republic (10,302).[67]

The Irish may have a reputation among tourists for being very friendly and welcoming, but this may not be directed towards immigrants. Numerous studies have reported on difficulties immigrants have experienced in integrating into the workplace, schools, communities, and local voluntary organizations.[68] The most commonly cited problem for Black migrant workers is securing accommodation. Other problems include racist slogans shouted at them by children and drunks and their being ignored by shop assistants when paying for goods in shops and other public buildings.[69]

A survey in 2006 found that 70 percent of respondents did not want any more migrant workers to come to Ireland; a large minority of these would like to see at least some of them go home again. Over half (53 percent) said that migrant labor was making it harder for Irish people to get jobs.[70] Another survey found that 35 percent of respondents disagreed that ethnic groups make Ireland a more interesting place to live in, and almost half (48 percent) agreed that someone can only be Irish if he or she was born in Ireland of Irish parents.[71]

In 2004, a new panic began to spread through the island. It was the fear of the state maternity services being overrun by women coming in from abroad to give birth to children, thereby guaranteeing the children Irish citizenship. Those who propagated the "Black baby peril" conjured up images of women in late pregnancy coming over as tourists and ending up staying to give birth. It was claimed that this type of citizenship tourism was placing an inexorable burden on the maternity services. The state decided that it was necessary to hold a referendum to change the Irish constitution and remove the automatic right to citizenship for all children born on the island of Ireland. Eight in 10 voted in favor.[72]

Irish immigration strategies seem to be working. In 2002, even though the strength of the Celtic Tiger economy had weakened, there were 11,634 applications for asylum. In 2004, this had dropped dramatically to 4,265.[73] But there are still up to 30,000 people who are living in Ireland in a legal limbo (mainly composed of those applying for asylum). Between 2000 and 2005 there were over 43,000 asylum applications. Of these, 5,800 were granted refugee status and 2,200 were deported.[74] One of the key factors in the growth of the Celtic Tiger was that Ireland had a well-educated population of young people. This was important in attracting transnational corporations. One of the arguments made about allowing foreigners to come in to work in Ireland was that they were willing to do the more menial, low-paid jobs. It then began to emerge that these immigrant workers were significantly better educated. In 2004, the Irish population increased by 65,000. Over 60 percent of this increase was accounted for by immigrants. However, whereas only 27 percent of the Irish workforce had third-level education, the proportion of immigrants with such education is twice that figure.[75]

There are seeming contradictions at the heart of the Irish attitude to foreign nationals. Many see them as a threat and believe that they can never become truly Irish. And yet, on many occasions, there was a national outpouring of sympathy and concern for particular individuals.[76] It may well be that such concern emerges when people relate to the "other" as an individual rather than as a member of a group. In other words, the individual does not take on the stigma of the group. The concern may also be higher when the foreign nationals come from educated, middle-class backgrounds. There are thousands of Travellers in Ireland, a native ethnic group of semi-nomadic people, who suffer as much, if not more, prejudice and discrimination as do foreign nationals. And even though the established settled community has met and knows Travellers, because they are from a different class background the chances of their being accepted as different are probably far fewer than for most foreign nationals. When it comes to embracing diversity in Ireland, class makes a big difference.[77]

For three of the first five years of the new century, Ireland was ranked as the most globalized society in the world. There were very specific criteria used—openness of the economy, technological development, level of travel and so forth—to develop the rankings. However, if one was to develop criteria for ranking for the most globalized *culture* in the world, it would be interesting to see where Ireland would come. Certainly if one was to measure cultural globalization in terms of the flow of people, then on the basis of the number of Irish people around the world who claim Irish ancestry per head of indigenous population, Ireland would score very high. In 2004, the US Census Bureau reported that 34 million Americans claimed Irish ancestry.[78] Similarly if one measures the annual number of visitors per head of 100 population, Ireland with 176 ranks joint second with Croatia behind Austria (232) but ahead of Spain (133) and France (124).[79] Finally, in terms of the amount of Irish music listened to, books read, films watched, pubs visited, then it could be argued, again per head of population, that the Irish have contributed more than might be expected to the global flow of ideas and knowledge. This would suggest that as well as being one of the most globalized societies in the world Ireland was also the most globalized culturally, that is, in terms of contributing to the flow of people and ideas.

The final question that needs to be addressed in this chapter is whether the Irish with all these global connections have overcome their insularity and have developed a more heightened global consciousness or habitus, whether they tend more than others to see, understand and relate to the world as one place. In other words, instead of seeing the world as made up of numerous different international relations between societies, organizations and individuals, do the Irish have a greater sense of living in a global community and of everyone as belonging to humankind? This would mean that the Irish would be more aware of the world as a complex place made up of differences—civilizations, societies, ethnicities, regions and individuals who operate in different times and spaces. It would also mean that they would care more and have a greater sense of responsibility for other human beings around the world. When it comes to overseas development aid, Ireland ranks in the middle of its European neighbors. In 2005, it gave 0.41 percent of its Gross National Income, much below Sweden at 0.92, but higher than Portugal at 0.21.[80] Although it is estimated that private voluntary donations account for 21 percent of overseas aid in general, there are no accurate international comparisons available. However, Trócaire, one of Ireland's largest charitable overseas development agencies, reported that in 2004, the year of the tsunami in southeast Asia, its income from public donations increased dramatically to €60 million from €22 million the previous year.[81]

CONCLUSION

In the scheme of things, Ireland should be insignificant when it comes to the study of globalization. It is a small island. Its population is smaller than that of many world cities. And yet, the Irish have developed a global presence and reputation, particularly in the West. The reason, of course, is that during the nineteenth and twentieth centuries the Irish made a major contribution to the global flow of people. The cause of this contribution lay in the peculiar way in which Irish society modernized. The explosion in population that took place during the first half of the nineteenth century was brought to an abrupt end by the Famine. But this did not deter the Irish from having babies. For generation after generation through to the end of the twentieth century, the Irish had one of the highest levels of marital fertility. For a predominantly rural society with an underdeveloped system of agricultural production, the safety valve was emigration. So as well as being prolific at giving birth, the Irish became prolific at emigrating. For over 150 years they scattered throughout the Western world. Although the first Irish emigrants may have started at the bottom of the social ladder many have, over the intervening years, climbed to the top. They established roots and connections. This is particularly true of Irish missionaries who, through the schools they established, began to educate the social elites of the countries in which they worked. The global presence of the Irish has also been enhanced by their becoming an acceptable icon of ethno-national difference. The "black" Irish have become whiter than white. They speak English. They have assimilated. Their national difference is acceptable. In most of their host countries, members of the Irish diaspora have become part of the established middle class.

The permeation of the Irish throughout the West has also brought a cultural cachet to being Irish. There are rewards and benefits to being socially connected to the Irish and to engaging in and embodying Irish culture. Being Irish attracts social, cultural and symbolic capital. The Irish have become successful. They have no colonial or oppressive cultural baggage. They do not pose a threat. They are hard-working. They are good fun. People positively identify with being Irish. This helps explain why St. Patrick's Day is celebrated around the world. It helps explain why people like to go to Irish pubs to celebrate. It helps explain the global success of Irish film, music, theater and literature and shows like *Riverdance*.

But is there something else that makes the Irish attractive, that makes their cultural difference globally acceptable? Has it got to do with their maintaining their cultural uniqueness, their own language, music and sport? Or is it something more fundamental that is related to the way they see and understand themselves, their sense of self and how they relate to the world and other people? This is what I will now explore.

Four

The struggle between being the same and being different is at the heart of social life. As individuals we struggle to be accepted and liked by those with whom we identify, with whom we have a sense of bonding and belonging. At the same time, as individuals, we struggle to be seen and accepted as different if not unique. In our everyday lives we play a crucial game in which we balance this drive towards saying and doing things that mark us out as being the same and, often at the same time and in the same place, we say and do things that mark us out as being different. Social life is an ongoing process of balancing being the same—and accordingly practicing self-surrender and self-denial—with being different through developing, expressing and emphasizing one's uniqueness.

A sense of sameness, bonding and belonging, emerges primarily in families and small groups. It is often associated with a commitment to a shared habitus, a similar way of reading, understanding and being in the world. It generates beliefs and ritual practices which become central to creating and maintaining a collective consciousness and sense of bonding and belonging. This sense of sameness can extend beyond families and small groups to churches, neighborhoods, voluntary associations, organizations, churches, workplaces, sports clubs and so forth. At its furthest, it reaches to religion, race, social class, ethnic groups and nationality. At these extremes, collective identities are more likely to be contested. The sense of sameness that binds people together and generates a social bond is subject to more debate: The boundaries of membership become blurred. There is little debate or contestation about my identity as an Inglis, my profession, the university to which I belong and so forth. In the Ireland in which I grew up there was little debate about what it was to be Catholic or indeed Irish. This has changed.

It would, however, be wrong to think that there was no difference in the Catholic Ireland of 50 years ago. But the range, opportunity and acceptance of radical difference were limited. Difference was accepted as long as it was not seen as a threat to the group. There was a sense of sameness and belonging that came from speaking Irish, even if one spoke with a different dialect or accent. There was a similar sense of belonging that came from playing *gaelic* sports, regardless of whether it was football, hurling or handball. There were many different varieties of jigs and reels, as long as one played or listened to traditional Irish music. What has changed, however, in the last 50 years is that there has been a shift with increased globalization. The more that Irish culture has become open to global cultural flows, the more Irish people have become cosmopolitan, and the more being Irish has become commercialized and commodified, so the more that speaking Irish, playing *gaelic* sports, playing and listening to traditional Irish music and, in some respects, the more being a good Catholic have become less a form of sameness and more a form of individual difference.

IRISH DIFFERENCE

There are many cultural characteristics that mark the Irish as a distinct people with a different way of being in the world. One might refer to Irish literature, poetry, theater, film and art. Certainly people like Yeats, Joyce, Heaney, Beckett and others have added enormously to the cultural reputation of the Irish. I am interested more in popular culture, the way Irish people see and understand themselves rather than the way in which their difference has been captured by others. The most obvious differences are religion, language, music and sport. But how are these differences manifested in everyday life and how do they relate to the character of Irish people, their humor and sense of self? How important are these differences? In an age of globalization in which everyday life is becoming increasingly similar, does national culture really make much difference? Indeed, why, like so many other nationalities, do the Irish insist that they are different? Is this insistence on national difference linked in some way to the new relentless drive by individuals to be different? In many respects there is a similarity between the way a nation constitutes its difference and the way individuals assiduously work at creating and maintaining a unique self-image. What is crucial for national difference is the extent to which national cultural representations are incorporated into the struggle for individual difference and status.

Towards the end of the nineteenth century, people in Ireland—who had up until then differentiated themselves in terms of families, clans, townlands, villages and counties—began to see and understand themselves as a distinct people with their own culture and traditions. This drive towards cultural distinction was closely linked to economic and political interests. The Irish wanted to be different from the English, but they also wanted political freedom and ownership of the land. So in the late nineteenth century, as in many other parts of the world, the Irish began earnestly to imagine themselves as being different, as belonging to one unique national community. Like any young adult, the Irish wanted to break away from the limitations and restraints of their colonial masters and create a new image of themselves.

Much of this sense of national identity was achieved, as Anderson has argued, through the print media.[1] As elsewhere in the West, there was a dramatic growth in the readership of national newspapers in the nineteenth century. There was also a dramatic growth in social movements promoting national culture, particularly language, sport, literature and the arts. There was a determined effort to reinvent Ireland, to reimagine its past. The creation of Ireland as a nation-state was the result of "social and environmental engineering" which invented tradition, ethnicized historical records, claimed territories and systematically dismissed the claims of minorities and rivals.[2] There was a material, technological dimension to the creation of a national habitus. As well as print media, there were also the beginnings of post and telegraph communications and the development of an elaborate network of roads and railways.[3] Mac Laughlin argues that while the national press and universities were the main champions of nationalism and nation-building in nineteenth-century Europe, the process was a bit different in Ireland. He stresses the importance of a whole range of people working at local level "including map-makers working with the Ordnance Survey, priests and clergymen living in close proximity to their people, reporters and newspapermen writing in the provincial and national press, and schoolteachers teaching in national and secondary schools."[4] The detailed mapping of Ireland allowed people to see and read the island as one place in much the same way that, first of all, globes and then pictures taken from outer space, helped people to see and read the world as one place.

Irish culture was very unsettled throughout the nineteenth century. There were ongoing struggles about religion, education and language. Irish people wanted to be the same as their European counterparts: They wanted to be self-disciplined, moral, civil and polite. But they also wanted to be different. They most certainly did not want to be Protestants, to have an English Protestant education, and to behave like their colonial masters.

Much of what is written and said about Ireland creates an image of a unique people with their own culture and way of life. This has been reaffirmed by the anthropologists, ethnologists and travel writers who have come to study the Irish over the past 200 years. The histories of Ireland have tended to be national histories, re-creating the conception of the island as having always been on some trajectory to realize itself as a unique nation-state among other nation-states. It is as if there is a desperate need to believe in the uniqueness of Ireland, that we are people unlike any other.

This mirrors what happens at the level of the individual. The more people come in contact with those from other societies and the more daily life within the world capitalist system becomes similar, the greater the increase in the imperative to create and develop personal identities. In other words, there is a link between the psychogenesis of the individual and the sociogenesis of national society: the more global cultural flows reach into remote regions and increasingly permeate the lives of more people, the more there is an imperative to diversify. Increasing sameness produces within itself the need for increasing difference.[5] But whereas Irish national difference was created through a reinvention of the past, contemporary individual difference is mainly created in and through the media and the marketplace.

EARLY INFLUENCES

The global flow of knowledge and ideas is as old as the world itself and it was the particular way these ideas reached Ireland in the fifth century and the way they combined with existing local culture, that was to be the precursor of Irish difference. As a schoolboy, I was constantly reminded that AD 432 was the most important date in our national history. This was the year St. Patrick arrived. Until then Ireland was populated by pagans and snakes. He drove out the snakes—probably a metaphor for pagans and female goddesses—and turned them not just into Christians but into saints and scholars. St. Patrick can be seen as part of a global flow of Christian beliefs and practices that reached Rome from the Middle East and spread from there out across Europe. His ideas—particularly the simple device of using the shamrock to persuade the pagans that there could be many gods in the one God—changed the way the people saw and understood themselves and the world in which they lived. The rest is Irish history. St. Patrick and the shamrock have become universal icons of what it is to be Irish.

Christianity flourished in Ireland and the particular form of Christian life developed by Irish monks over the next couple of hundred years was exported throughout Europe. It became part of a global flow that had a profound impact on Western civilization. This is a reminder of the importance of the global flow of ideas and knowledge. What makes any society and culture different is the way global flows become embedded locally.

St. Patrick was not the first visitor to Ireland. The early history of Ireland revolves around the flow of people who arrived from time to time with new ideas, languages, equipment.[6] As part of this process, hunter-gatherers gave way to neolithic farmers, megalithic builders and so forth. The growth in sameness was linked to a growth in difference. By 1500 BC, as in other parts of Europe Ireland was made up of a number of tiny political units, settlements and tribes, which "jealously guarded their autonomy" but, at the same time, "were linked to an 'international commercial system.'"[7]

In the 500 years before Christ, Ireland, like the rest of Europe, became Celtic. But the extent to which this represented a distinct culture and way of life is questionable. While there was a Celtic language, there was no Celtic race. The Celtic age revolved more around war-bands or migrating tribes moving into settled areas. The Romans brought an end to the Celtic era in Europe. Although the Romans never physically came to Ireland, this did not prevent "their world"—in terms of ideas, knowledge, technology, ornaments and fashion—flooding the country.[8]

THE IRISH SOUL

The growth of globalization is intrinsically tied into the growth of individualism. The penetration of the market into everyday life has created a new individualism revolving around personal identities and lifestyles.[9] But what were the early foundations of this modern sense of self? When, where and how did people begin to think of themselves more as individuals? Part of the answer lies in transformations that took place in Ireland after the arrival of St. Patrick.

As Foucault reminded us, the modern notion of self and individualism emerged within a series of developments within Christianity, particularly the concept of sin, of individuals committing sinful acts, of their critically reflecting about their sins, confessing them, and then seeking atonement through forms of physical penance. This gave rise to unique forms of bodily discipline and, through them, of individuals saving their souls through strict control of their bodies. Many of these techniques of classifying and assessing sins and of devising appropriate penance were developed by Irish monks.[10] This ascetic form of self-discipline became combined, through confession, with a critical reflection of the self. Bodily discipline and critical self-reflection became the foundations of the notions of soul and salvation. They also became central to the creation of the heightened sense of self which lies at the heart of modernity and individualism.

When I was growing up, I was taught that it was up to each of us to save our own soul. In other words, just because you were born a Catholic did not mean that you would gain automatic entry into heaven. The struggle for salvation was an individual journey. Getting into heaven and avoiding eternal damnation depended on avoiding mortal sin. The greatest sins of all had to do with the body and sex. The body was a source of temptation and evil. Now while the notion of sex being the greatest sin is as old as the Christian religion itself, and while the Irish obsession with sex was not unique, what made us different was that this notion was inculcated deeper and lasted longer in the bodies and souls of the Irish than among the rest of the West. It is a key ingredient in what makes the Irish different. It was something that permeated beyond class, education, rural/urban boundaries. There was, therefore, nothing unique in my parents being unable to be openly sexual or even to demonstrate their love and affection, either physically or verbally, for each other or their children.

The lifestyle developed by Christian monks in Ireland during the fourth and fifth centuries had a profound impact on global culture and the world capitalist system. The monks set themselves the task of living a good life which for them meant an ethical life that followed the teachings of Christ and promised eternal salvation. As a means towards that end, they did four things which were to have a profound impact on Western civilization.

First, they introduced a taxonomy of sins and a scaled system of penance.[11] This represented a different ethical system to the one developed by the Greeks for whom ethics involved an overall arts of existence. The task of the individual was to develop a lifestyle in which, for example, there was a balance between pleasures and responsibilities.[12] The Irish monks helped develop a different system in which acts were deemed sinful in themselves. Although this cataloguing system was being developed elsewhere within Christianity, the Irish monks added an important extra dimension. They devised a system of penances or mortifications through which monks had to atone for their sins. They devised, so to speak, a suitable punishment to fit the crime.

Second, the monks rationalized the idea of confession and moved it from a public to a private practice. Not only did this increase the power of the priest, it also enabled the development of individualism through a greater sense of private guilt and shame. In other words, the Irish monks devised a moral life that was based on an accounting system of sins, in which there was a rational evaluation of individual acts. It may well have been that this way of thinking, of seeing life as a series of discrete acts which were critically reflected upon, played a key role in the rise of modern individualism. The other key ingredient was confession. In confession, Christians were expected to reflect about themselves in terms of discrete acts or particular sins for which they were given suitable penances and absolution. It may well be that this kind of critical reflection was responsible for generating the notion that there is no essential self, but rather a number of selves that act differently in different circumstances.

Third, they developed an emphasis on celibacy and virginity. The effect of this was to introduce a class division between Christians: the higher order who renounced sex and the lesser mortals who married. But in renouncing sex, the monks became obsessed with it. They were anxious to discover how temptation and desire operated so that they could develop disciplinary techniques to counteract them.

Fourth, the monks developed the practice of mortifying the flesh. As a means of discovering themselves, of discovering the soul of their being, the monks devised a system of living that was other-worldly and ascetic. They devised a moral way of being in the world, a way that was oriented to God and heaven. It encouraged a detachment from the material world which they considered to be full of evil temptations, particularly in terms of the body. They devised a series of penitential practices which they believed, if followed dedicatedly, would help monks to become detached from bodily desires.

Penitential practices are a defining characteristic of contemporary Irish Catholicism. They are what make Irish Catholics different from other Catholics. Again it is not that other Catholics, or indeed members of other religions, do not engage in ascetic practices such as fasting, walking barefoot on craggy rocks and, in general, mortifying themselves. It is just that the tradition is deeper and has lasted longer in Ireland. Every year, on the last Sunday in July, up to 25,000 people of all ages take part in the traditional penitential pilgrimage to the top of Croagh Patrick in County Mayo. Hundreds do it in their bare feet.

It is also important to remember that while disciplining and controlling the body has become a major feature of contemporary consumer capitalism, it is very different from religious mortification. Rigorous dieting and exercising may have become central to having a good body, being seen as a good person, and being seen to live a good life. The difference is that the end is self-fulfillment and self-glorification, the body becomes an end in itself as opposed to a means of attaining salvation.[13] It is the emergence of this form of consumer bodily practice in contemporary Ireland that makes the Irish less like the monks from whom their habitus or sense of being in the world emerged over generations and more like the rest of the West for many of whom salvation revolves around the development and maintenance of a beautiful, fit, healthy body.

CATHOLIC—PROTESTANT DIFFERENCES

For many people around the world, what makes Ireland different is the conflict between Catholics and Protestants in Northern Ireland. Probably more than anything else this conflict raised global consciousness about Ireland. There is an extensive literature on the conflict.[14] It is one of those small localities which has generated an enormous amount of research and debate. A key question has always been whether the conflict is more about political and economic divisions than it is about religion. I do not want to get involved in this debate here; however, it must be remembered that, for the most part, Protestants and Catholics not only have different beliefs and practices, they live in different communities, attend different schools and, to a certain extent, have developed a different habitus and lifestyle. I say to a certain extent because the question as to whether there is a difference between the habitus and lifestyle of Catholics and Protestants is similar to the question as to whether the Irish are really that different from their Western counterparts. Many features of the everyday lives of Catholics and Protestants, their cares and concerns are similar. However, the reality is that Protestants and Catholics continue to perceive and believe themselves as different and this perception and belief have real consequences.

The division between Catholics and Protestants in Ireland has a long history. It was not until the late fifteenth century when Irish lords became embroiled in ongoing battles to obtain control of the monarchy that England became more actively involved in the affairs of its neighboring island. As the English state started exerting greater control internally, it began to realize the strategic importance of Ireland in terms of an external threat. When, under Henry VIII, this military interest became enmeshed with the Protestant Reformation, the determination of the English state to conquer, subdue and control Ireland became persistent and brutal. The English state sent over soldiers, adventurers and bureaucrats to tame the Irish. In contrast with other conquerors, particularly the Normans, these colonizers did not intermarry with the Irish. Instead they created a new social elite, the Anglo-Irish. The divisions caused between the people of Ireland around this time, essentially between Protestant—English and Catholic—Irish, were to last through to the present day. Protestants wished to dominate the old Catholic elite and so, during the seventeenth century, there was an attempt to Protestantize and Anglicize Ireland. The gap between the new and old elites was widened by the attempt, through the Penal Laws during the eighteenth century, to exclude Catholics from property and civil society. Centuries of Protestant ascendancy and deprivation meant that religion became central to Irish Catholic culture. The Irish, de Paor argues, became like the Jews, a pariah people. But a pariah people in their own land.[15]

There was always a possibility that when the Reformation came the Irish gentry would follow in the steps of its British counterparts and switch its allegiance to Protestantism. But for a mixture of reasons, partly economic, partly social and cultural, many remained loyal to Rome. It was then, as Carroll argues, that something took place that was to have a profound impact on the nature of Irish Catholicism, which shifted it down a track quite different from the rest of Catholic Europe.[16] Those who remained Catholic, partly to assert their difference and partly their moral superiority over those who became Protestant, developed a culture based on embracing earlier penitential practices. These practices became the base of a religious sense of self that revolved around self-mortification and denial. Elsewhere in Catholic Europe, this penitential sense was balanced by a religious culture of celebration and festivity, of self-expression and fulfillment. The balance among Irish Catholics was tilted towards a culture of mortification and death rather than life.

During the nineteenth century, Irish Catholics began to emerge from under the yoke of Protestant oppression and with this emergence came the building of churches, schools, hospitals and a wide variety of social welfare homes for the poor and disabled. They flocked to their new churches. There was a devotional revolution. The Catholic Church developed a monopoly over morality and spirituality. The new Irish state founded in 1922 was by no means theocratic—it was not run by priests and bishops—but it was based on a very Catholic society. In the same way the new state in Northern Ireland was not formally Protestant, but it was effectively run by Protestants to benefit Protestants. In the Southern state, Protestants prospered but through a combination of push and pull factors developed separate social networks from Catholics. In the Northern state, Catholics survived as second-class citizens who were regularly discriminated against.

Anti-English sentiment was rooted in colonial oppression. It is hard for a people to embrace the disposition, manners, habitus and practices of those who dominated them not just economically and politically, but symbolically. For hundreds of years, thousands of Irish people lived in the shadow of big houses and huge estates most of which were owned by English landlords, many of whom rarely or never came to Ireland. Such places were often owned by a Protestant Anglo-Irish elite who willingly dipped their feet in the cultural pond of England. They liked and admired all things English. They read English newspapers. They liked English literature and art, listened to English radio, and followed English sport. The Irish cultural nationalist response was an equal and opposite reaction to this symbolic domination. There was, as Kiberd points out, a deep-seated antimony to the West Briton who "asserted his authority by imitating English manners." Irish Ireland countered this "with its own form of invented Gaelic snobbery." He goes on, "[a]nything English was *ipso facto* not for the Irish, as it might appear to weaken the claim to separate nationhood, but any valued cultural possessions of the English were shown to have their Gaelic equivalents."[17]

In the latter part of the nineteenth century, along with a struggle for religious equality and parity of esteem, ownership and control of the land, and political independence, there was a symbolic struggle to claim that Ireland was and always had been a unique people, a separate nation. There was a deliberate, concerted attempt to create and develop a distinctive Irish culture. Central to this was keeping the Irish language alive. Besides color and ethnicity, if there is anything that marks out a people as different, it is language.

IRISH LANGUAGE

Irish was the main language of the people up until the sixteenth century—although the authorities in the main towns demanded that people use English for legal and administrative purposes. In the nineteenth century, the Famine (1845–1849), and the massive emigration that followed, dramatically reduced the number of Irish speakers. In 1891, there were 680,000 Irish speakers out of a total population of 3.5 million—just under 20 percent. Of these only 66,000 spoke Irish alone; the number under the age of 10 represented no more than 3.5 percent of their age group. The language appeared to be on the point of extinction.[18] The decline of the Irish language is an example of the incursion and dominance of cosmopolitan cultural capital. English was not just the language of political and social administration, it was also the language of commerce and, predominantly, of the organizational life of the Catholic Church. But this suggests that the decline in the use of Irish came about through institutional structures: it was something imposed on people. This does not take into account that many Irish saw greater value in speaking English. Parents recognized the importance of speaking English to give those children who emigrated, particularly to America, and those who wanted to work in the civil service and various apparatuses of the state, the advantage of having good English.[19] The revival of the Irish language by the Gaelic League at the end of the nineteenth century was part of a protest against cultural homogenization. However, although cultural nationalists made arguments for reviving the language, to have an impact on public opinion and policymakers, most of these arguments had to be made in English. In the nineteenth century, the Irish language was mainly part of an oral culture. But the language within which the national culture of Ireland was imagined and invented was primarily print language which was almost completely English.[20]

From 1922, the revitalization of the language became a major cultural priority for the new Irish state. From 1925, Irish-language proficiency was necessary for entry into the civil service.[21] Article 8.1 of the Irish Constitution in 1937 designated Irish as the first national language. It was compulsory to teach Irish at primary- and secondary-level education. It was necessary to obtain a pass mark in the Irish exam to obtain an overall pass in state examinations. For most entrants, it is still necessary to have Irish to enter the National University of Ireland. There were numerous state "carrots" as well as "sticks" to help promote the language. Throughout the twentieth century the state provided generous funding to a wide variety of groups and organizations who sought to develop the language. Those areas of the country which were designated as *Gaeltachts*, or regions where Irish was the first language, were given special grants to enable them to survive economically. In 1972, the state broadcasting company RTÉ established *Raidió na Gaeltachta*, a national all-Irish radio station. Since 2000, the station has been broadcasting on the internet. In 1996, an Irish-language television service, *Teilifís na Gaeilge* (now TG4), was established. Despite the competition from transnational digital television stations it has grown in popularity and won a number of national and international awards. The station claimed in 2007 that 800,000 tuned into its channel each day.[22] Its popular soap opera *Ros na Rún* has an average weekly audience of 300,000.[23] There is also a national daily newspaper, *Lá* (published in Belfast), and a weekly, *Foinse*, both of which have sales of around 5,000 copies.

The success of state-sponsored developments of the language, together with numerous Irish-language interest groups, is that it is increasingly becoming not just accepted but a badge of distinction and a source of national cultural capital to be actively involved in supporting the language. This can be seen, for example, in the rapid growth of all-Irish schools that use Irish as the primary language in the classroom. In 2004, there were 159 such primary schools and 33 post-primary schools outside of *Gaeltacht* areas. Many of these are in the larger towns and cities and have arisen from parents wishing to preserve the Irish language and identity by having their children taught all subjects through Irish. Moreover, every year thousands of Irish secondary school students engage in what has become almost a rite of passage and go, at least once during their schooldays, to one of the 40 language schools in the *Gaeltacht* areas for three weeks in the summer. The approach in many *Gaeltacht* summer schools is one of isolation and purity. The children are put into a purely Irish-speaking environment and many of the schools operate a policy of expelling any student caught speaking English.

The success of the strategies of the state and other interest groups, as well as the desire by the middle classes to maintain and develop their national identity and cultural capital, is linked to a positive attitude to the language. The Census of Population (2002) showed that the number of people aged 3 years and over able to speak Irish was about 1.5 million—42 percent of the population. Nearly a quarter of those who indicated they could speak Irish said they did so on a daily basis—but three-quarters of these were in the school-going ages. However, two-thirds of those who said that they were able to speak Irish either never spoke it or did so less than weekly.[24] In other words, when Irish people say they are able to speak Irish it may just mean that they have a few words and phrases which, in reality, they rarely or never use—except perhaps when they are abroad to convince people that they are Irish and that they can speak the language. Despite the low level of practice, the positive attitude towards the language seems to have been maintained, if not to have grown. In 1975, a government report showed that three-quarters of the people believed the language was essential to Irish identity.[25] A survey in 2004 found that 89 percent of the respondents agreed that "promoting the Irish language is important to the country as a whole."[26]

The Irish language is, then, something that Irish people value very strongly. It operates as a powerful symbol that reaffirms national identity.[27] However, while people may like to hear the language, few are willing to speak it. It is one of those values that does not translate into practice. In some respects, the Irish language is following a similar path to Catholicism. Many Irish Catholics have a high level of religious values and beliefs, but these do not necessarily get translated into religious practice which has been declining steadily in recent decades.

The decline in speaking the Irish language is related to a general fragmentation in what it means to be Irish, and to the decline in the significance of using Irish as a form of cultural capital. While it is still necessary for teachers, civil servants and politicians to speak Irish, in general the cultural capital value of speaking Irish has declined. It is no longer a definitive statement about one's character and personality, about one's commitment to the Irish nation, to being Irish. Irish identity, a feeling of belonging, and a sense of being different, are generated more through music, dance, sport, humor and self-presentation. Speaking Irish has moved from being an ascribed social identity—an indication of who we are—to becoming an achieved personal identity—an indication of who I am.

One of the main reasons the Irish language has survived is because the state became its guardian. It put enormous resources into promoting and developing the language particularly through educational and media policies and funding Irish-language interest groups. The problem is that this state agency has not been matched by individual agency. People support but do not practice the language. The language has survived rather than thrived. Ireland does not come close to being a bilingual society like some of its European counterparts. Despite all the state investment and despite most schoolchildren learning Irish up until they leave secondary-level education, there is a reluctance to use Irish. Another reason it has survived is that there has been a change in policy regarding the language. Many of the programs on TG4, particularly films, are in English as well as Irish. Many programs have subtitles. In other words, the language seems to have survived when, rather than pursuing a strategy of purity and isolation, a policy of hybridism has been adopted. It also has survived because many cosmopolitan city-dwellers have recognized the personal kudos and cultural benefit to themselves of promoting and developing the language by sending their children to all-Irish schools. However, unless the parents speak the language themselves at home, the success of these schools may be minimal.

The Irish language will continue to be a potent symbol of Irish national identity and to be used on official state occasions, but there is a danger that the state investment will dwindle. It will not survive without language activists lobbying for minority language rights. The problem is whether these guardians of local culture can carry on without the state aid that they have been receiving.[28] It is also unlikely to survive if *Gaeltacht* areas are swamped by the incoming tide of consumerism and cosmopolitanism.

Many in the *Gaeltacht* feel English to be the better language. . . . There is a shyness about using the language unless we are sure the other person converses in it comfortably. Among the younger generation English is considered cool, Irish not.[29]

GAELIC SPORT

The development of sport was one of the lasting legacies of British colonial rule. Athletics, rugby, soccer and cricket grew in popularity throughout nineteenth-century Ireland; mainly organized by the gentry. Sport fulfilled a social interest in creating and maintaining healthy, fit, vigorous and efficient bodies as well as providing a form of passion and excitement, a controlled way of letting go emotionally.[30] One of the main institutional strategies used to create and maintain a sense of Ireland, of Irish people being different (particularly from the

English), was to re-establish the importance of *gaelic* sport. The *Gaelic* Athletic Association (GAA) was established in 1884. It represented a celebration of simple rural life. It eulogized a form of manliness and "muscular" Christianity.[31] It embodied the importance of strength and agility, fair play, morals and manhood. In this respect the GAA was no different from sporting and educational organizations in other Western societies. Michael Cusack, the founder of the GAA—who was also very involved in promoting and developing the Irish language—was part of a social movement to open sport to all social classes. He saw English games as a form of cultural imperialism, of humiliating and symbolically dominating the Irish. The main impetus behind the association—the first major guardians of Irish culture—was from teachers, minor civil servants, neo-traditionalist clerics and farmers' sons.[32]

As with all other social movements at the time, the Catholic Church was a major player not just in shaping the policies of the GAA but, on a daily basis, fostering its development in Catholic schools. The organization of the GAA is based on Catholic parishes. While the GAA was not a sectarian organization, and there are Protestants who are members, few Protestant schools in Ireland play Gaelic Football or hurling. The lack of involvement of Protestants is probably linked to the GAA's being, particularly in its early days, strongly associated with radical political nationalism. Again there was a very strong emphasis on isolation and purity. In 1902, the GAA passed a rule that any member who played rugby, soccer, hockey or any imported game was to be suspended from the association. As late as the 1950s, Michael Ó Donnchada, president of the GAA, could speak openly about the GAA standing as "a solid front of unyielding hostility to all forms of foreign aggression and infiltration."[33] The ban on members of the GAA playing foreign games was lifted in 1971. More recently, the ban on members of the British police or armed forces becoming members was also lifted—this mainly had relevance in Northern Ireland. However, rule 42 which prohibited foreign games, particularly soccer and rugby, being played on GAA pitches—which had most relevance to Croke Park which is one of the biggest and best sports stadiums in Europe—remained in force up to 2005. At that time, there was a public debate, nationally as well as within the GAA, about lifting the ban. What is remarkable is that while it was forbidden to play soccer and rugby in Croke Park, it was permissible to hold a Michael Jackson concert and an American football game between the Navy and Notre Dame. It was equally permissible biannually for the GAA to allow an International Rules Football game—sponsored by Coca-Cola—to be played in the stadium.

Similar to Irish-language guardians, the GAA used a strategy of non-contamination and isolationism to protect Irish sport, but, in comparison to Irish language organizations' attempts, it has been far more successful in maintaining *gaelic* sports as major symbols of Irish identity. In 2004, there were 2,595 GAA clubs in Ireland. There were 300,000 Irish adult members of GAA clubs—10 percent of the adult population. GAA sports account for almost 60 percent of all sports attendances in Ireland and for 42 percent of all those who spend time volunteering in sport.[34]

The GAA is not just local and national. It has followed the Irish diaspora around the world. There are 88 clubs in Britain, 120 in the United States (50 in New York), 70 in Australasia, 21 in Europe and 13 in Canada. As well as football and hurling the GAA is also responsible for women's football, camogie (women's hurling), handball and rounders. In 2004, almost 2 million people went to grounds throughout the country to watch games. Millions more watched on television and listened on the radio.[35]

There were fears, particularly in the 1970s when television began to broadcast foreign sports into most Irish homes, that support for the GAA and *gaelic* sports would wither away. The opposite has happened.[36] The GAA and *gaelic* sports have thrived. The primary reason lies in the development of difference as a response to increasing sameness. The GAA responded not just to a need for national identity difference but, as it had always done, to county and parish difference. To understand the success of the GAA it is necessary to appreciate the intense but mostly friendly rivalry between counties and within counties between parishes. The second reason for the recent success of the GAA has been television. The more Irish television gave greater time and resources to broadcasting *gaelic* sport, the greater the interest, which, in turn, led to more participants, players and supporters. Third, in contrast to the Irish language whose main guardian has been the state, the guardians of Irish sport are almost entirely voluntary. The success of the GAA is based on volunteers working at local level. Through them, it has been able to develop modern club-houses and sporting facilities. Fourth, what makes the GAA successful is the advertising, merchandising and marketing of GAA products. People who travel around the island during summer will see towns, villages and homes bedecked with the county flag and bunting, and children and adults wearing their county jerseys. Fifth, participation in the GAA has not only become a major source of local identity and pride, it has also become a source of local cultural capital. There is enormous value in being involved with and playing for the local parish or, better still, the county. It can be a significant source of economic, political and social capital. As well as honor and respect, it can lead to better jobs, higher incomes, better business, better social networks, better chances of political success.

But as well as a source of cultural capital, participation in the GAA is about identity and belonging. Most people in Ireland see and understand themselves as being from a particular county, and this sense of identity and belonging is often sustained and developed more through the GAA than anything else. Throughout the year, but particularly during the summer when the All Ireland football and hurling championships are played, matches between parishes and counties are a major source of public debate and discussion. What perhaps characterizes participation in the GAA is the nature of the rivalry. Supporters of opposing teams are rarely segregated and will generally mingle together. While there are occasional hostilities on and off the pitch, the rivalry is generally good-humored. The debate and discussion about players, teams and matches are generally based on a sophisticated practice of people teasing and ribbing each other.

This is how Humphries has described the social significance of the All Ireland GAA finals:

> The All Ireland finals in football and hurling are events which define autumn in our culture, great gatherings of the clans, afternoons when a farmer in Mayo will sit down to watch the same game as a labourer in the Bronx or a displaced school-teacher in Sydney. Once upon a time, winning an Ireland medal in September virtually guaranteed you a seat if you ran for Parliament the next time there was an election. That era has passed maybe, but the social phenomenon of the All Ireland series continues to grow.[37]

The GAA, then, brings together the confused mixture of Ireland incorporating local, national and global culture. It shows that despite an incoming tide of American culture, consumerism, liberal-individualism and hedonism, there is still a very strong sense of identification with and belonging to the local and, from this, to the national. The more Ireland becomes globalized the more the GAA fosters greater social bonds at local level which, in turn, feeds greater national identification. As Cronin remarks, "the strength of Gaelic games, the very peculiarity of its parochial nationalism, is that it allows Ireland to say to the rest of the world, 'this is us, this is our game.'"[38]

IRISH MUSIC

Irish language and sport are important identifiers of Irish difference, but their significance is greater at home than it is abroad. Most people around the world do not hear Irish being spoken or see Irish sport being played. However, they are likely to hear Irish music. It is important to make a distinction between Irish music and the popular music played by Irish bands such as U2 which is generally a variety of Western popular music.

Even within Irish music there is a distinction between Irish folk and ballad music, popularized by groups ranging from the Clancy Brothers and Tommy Maken and artists such as Enya, and traditional Irish music which is mostly either dance music (jigs, reels, hornpipes, polkas and so forth) played with fiddles, pipes, accordions and the like, or *sean nos* or unaccompanied singing. Like many other national forms of music, traditional Irish music has become globalized. It is played and listened to in Irish "theme" pubs, both by members of the Irish diaspora and by cosmopolitans who have developed a taste for something different and authentic. Traditional musicians have a relationship to their repertoire that is different from classically trained musicians. Though the repertoire is formally a very simple one derived from accompaniment to Irish dancing, traditional musicians know vast numbers of tunes but with a wild variety of versions, names and histories. The result is that a particular tune played by the same musician on different occasions will not be the exact same tune. It may even have a different name. The tune is relative, it all depends on context. In this sense traditional Irish music is postmodern. It is learnt through listening and playing. There are very definite rules about tunes and how they are played, but they cannot be learnt from a book.[39]

Irish music is a classic example of the links between global and local culture and how elements of local culture can become part of global flows only to be deposited back in the culture at a later date, sometimes in a different form. The way Irish music has thrived in the midst of global culture follows a similar path to Irish sport. In the 1960s, cheap portable transistor radios—mostly manufactured in Japan—flooded the Irish market. Linked to this was the sudden increase in radio stations, many of them based in Britain and Europe, which began to broadcast popular music. Suddenly young people were no longer dependent on the musical offerings of the state's public broadcaster Radio Eireann. Irish music began to decline not just as a major and often necessary ingredient in Irish broadcasting. The cultural and moral expectation that people should play Irish music, sing Irish songs and dance to Irish music began to wane.

There were fears that the dramatic increase in the flow of popular music would swamp Irish music. But what happened was that through technology more people were able to listen to more music more often. Again the increase in the sameness of Western popular music brought with it a demand for difference. Irish music may have declined as the dominant form, but that did not mean that it did not thrive as a minority form. The global flow of technology, which enabled more people to listen to more music more readily and cheaply, helped Irish music survive. New forms of technology also helped players experiment, mixing and matching "native" and "foreign" elements to produce a new sound. Technology allowed them to amplify instruments. Editing machines enabled them to remix sounds and produce new ones. These technologies were important for a small minority of professionals, but the most influential technological effect was the cheap portable recording device used by all musicians to capture music when and where it is played, in sessions, live concerts, off the radio or TV, and now streaming through on the internet. This has vastly increased the volume and velocity of the global flow of tunes. Today cell phones are used to record performances, and cheap digital recorders have replaced expensive recording studios in the production of commercial recordings. There was a hybridization of form and content. This led to traditional dance tunes being made from the theme to *Dallas* and the Beatles' song "Hey Jude." On the other hand, there was increasing interest within the subculture in authenticity and regional purity.

As I have said, Irish music is full of examples of how, through the global flow of people, local culture is taken up and becomes deposited in another part of the world where it takes new forms. Later through the flow of technology these new forms are changed from their originals and deposited back in the local form. The first major book on traditional Irish music was published by Francis O'Neill in 1903. He was general superintendent of the Chicago Police. The *Music of Ireland* contained the 1,850 tunes, most of them noted down from "the playing musicians in the Chicago area, many of whom O'Neill had recruited to the force."[40] The American influence continued throughout the twentieth century.

Michael Coleman was a fiddle player who attained cult status both in America and Ireland by being one of the first traditional musicians to have been recorded. When Coleman's recordings were issued in the 1920s and 1930s, they had a "devastating effect on traditional music, particularly in Ireland." Coleman's recordings displayed a level of virtuosity that was unheard of in Ireland. This virtuosity, combined with the fact that the music was delivered on newfangled machines on 78 rpm discs with the imprimatur of prestigious American recording companies, led to his achieving a cult status.

> It is not too fanciful to suggest that Coleman's adoption by an Irish audience (so much so that the gramophone sometimes replaced the local fiddle-player at house dances) represented something more than musical taste. . . . Ownership of a gramophone was itself a mark of economic status—representing a link with the New World, it was often quite literally "money from America."[41]

Another example of the way traditional Irish music became hybridized through global flows was the concert organized in March 1969 by the famous traditional music composer Séan O'Riada. This was a seminal event which was to push traditional music down very different tracks. In the first instance, instead of the musicians playing in small pubs, houses or halls, they played in the Gaiety Theater, the most fashionable venue in Dublin. This was an attempt to lift traditional music from its peasant roots; to bring it closer in line with classical music, to make it accessible and appealing to a new successful urban bourgeois. There were ten players on stage all wearing tuxedos. But it was not just the setting. O'Riada reinterpreted the rules of playing. As well as having the top musicians of the day playing, O'Riada introduced a wide range of instruments. Although the musicians did not play formally composed pieces—which might have been too unorthodox—they played "in unprecedented and formalised settings, interspersing ensemble playing with highly rehearsed solo pieces."[42] The concert was an attempt to give air time to each musician and instrument and, at the same time, to knit them together into an overall composition. It resembled a jazz concert. While Coleman's recordings had great influence on individual style and performance (and not just on fiddle players but also, for example, on the way the accordion was played), O'Riada revolutionized ensemble performance. In Coleman's lifetime the dominant ensemble was the *ceilí* band, a format that had become somewhat moribund by the late 1950s. O'Riada crucially opened up ensemble performance by presenting it in a form that was autonomous, different from dance or other social functions and rituals.

But what made this revolution possible was that as well as being a cosmopolitan, a man of the world, O'Riada also had enormous national and local credibility. When he was young he learnt to play the piano and violin. In 1952, he attained a classics degree from University College Cork. While at university he used to play for local jazz and dance bands. A year after graduating, he went to Paris and worked in French television. He came back to Ireland and in 1959 composed the music for *Mise Éire*—the first feature film on the history of the Irish revolutionary movement during the first two decades of the twentieth century. The score was traditional Irish music, but it was played with a full symphony orchestra. Some of the players at the Gaiety that March night in 1969 went on to form The Chieftains who over the next two decades became the global sound of traditional Irish music, who played in some of the most prestigious concert halls around the world and who, as Coleman had done years previously, brought a new respectability to Irish music among the record-buying population of Ireland.

Like Irish sport, traditional music is not just surviving, but thriving. A traditional Irish database developed in 1990s listed the following elements in the field of traditional music: 1,441 informal sessions, 250 *feiseanna* or *fleadhs* (festivals of Irish music), 178 pay-in-performances, 77 concerts or series of concerts, 42 competitions, 20 awards, 382 people who make, repair or supply instruments, 299 people or places that provide tuition, 47 formal schools and 196 agencies, bodies and organizers.[43] In 2004, the annual *Fleadh Cheoil* was held in Clonmel. This is the biggest traditional music festival of the year. It attracted more than 200,000 people with up to 10,000 Irish and international musicians. At the *fleadh*, *Comhaltas Ceoltóirí Eireann* announced a proposed €27 million grant in Irish traditional arts and music. *Comhaltas* is the largest of the national organizations. It claims to have 400 branches on four continents, with over 1,000 classes being run weekly by almost 600 teachers. Finally, according to the organization's figures, 25,000 performers have their standards validated in the *Fleadh Cheoil* network on an annual basis.[44]

Vallely points out that the reason for the success of Irish music is because, like traditional rural life generally, it has become an important source of cultural capital for the "comparatively wealthy middle class." Irish music has, he argues, become an emblem and icon of cultural distinction for the urban bourgeoisie in the same way that it has become a badge of Irishness for the Irish diaspora. The problem with this success is that "the majority of such people don't know the difference between one tune-type and another, let alone different tunes." However, and again this reflects the symbiosis between the cosmopolitan and the local, he points out that the local and regional differences in the styles of playing Irish music—for example, there is a difference in style between East Clare and East Galway—have been maintained in an age where Irish music has become part of world music.[45] Entry into the global flow of culture has not diminished the impetus to remain authentic and different. These differences are then hoovered up by consumer cosmopolitans as emblems of their cultural distinction even though they may be ignorant of what makes them authentic or different. Instead of remaining isolated and retreating into the local, Irish music became part of world music and has thrived through people at home and abroad searching for authentic traditional as well as hybridized forms.

IRISH CATHOLICISM

More than anything else, and certainly more than language, music and sport, what makes the Irish different is that for over 150 years the majority of Irish people gave their hearts, minds and bodies to the Catholic Church. The Church helped create and maintain a Catholic habitus, a collective consciousness and a collective conscience that became central to Irish identity, people's sense of belonging, and the way they behaved. It became entwined with their everyday lives. Being Catholic became synonymous with being Irish. It became the sameness which made the Irish different.

Catholic prayers and rituals were at the heart of family life. Homes were festooned with crucifixes, holy pictures, statues, holy water fonts and other religious iconography. God, Christ Jesus, Mary and Joseph were woven into interpersonal communication. Most people began and ended their days with morning and night prayers. The family rosary was a regular event in most Catholic homes. People knew the time of year as much by religious events as by the seasons and months. There was Advent, Christmas, Lent, Easter, Trinity, May Devotions, pattern days, October devotions as well as annual novenas, missions, retreats, pilgrimages and so forth. Priests, nuns and brothers were at the heart of social life. They were more than just religious leaders, they were paragons of virtue. They dominated social and cultural life not just in rural areas, but in towns and cities. They controlled crucial services such as education, health and social welfare. They had enormous influence over the state, the media, public debate and discussion and civil society generally.

There has been considerable debate as to whether Ireland became a theocratic state during the heyday of the Church's monopoly over morality. Whyte, who conducted the most extensive study of Church–state relations, concluded that there was little evidence of the Church interfering in the running of the state.[46] On the other hand, he said that the Church was so powerful that it operated like no other interest group. But what Whyte failed to grasp was how this took place. It was because the Church dominated family life (particularly wives and mothers) as well as education, health and social welfare, that everyone that grew up in Catholic Ireland was saturated with a Catholic habitus, a Catholic way of reading, understanding and being in the world. Politicians, civil servants, teachers, doctors, nurses and so forth embodied the discourse and practice of the Church, fulfilled its teachings, rules and regulations and, although they may sometimes have disagreed with the Church and its bishops and priests, they rarely did so in public. For the first half of the twentieth century, the Catholic Church's vision of what it was to be Irish held sway.

The task of the Church was to create and maintain Ireland as different, as a place where there was a commitment to living a deeply spiritual, pious, humble life, to develop a Catholic culture and society which would be an example to the rest of the world. At the center of this difference was the creation of a disdain for and detachment from materialism, that is, for seeking satisfaction through involvement in the world, particularly through material comforts, consumer products and sensuous pleasures. Irish Catholics had to be protected from anything that distracted them from their monkish way of life.

The idea of maintaining a sense of difference, of not becoming the same as the rest of the West, was fostered not just by the state but by numerous Catholic interest groups such as Muintir na Tire. This is how its handbook of 1953 described the task.

> When we all dance the one way, wear the same costume, eat the same meals, enjoy the same standard of living, speak the same language, share the same entertainment, what is there to mark us from one another except shades of colour, marks of our being weather-beaten? This is part of the equalising tendency in modern society. Visions of levelling up and of levelling down divide men into two camps and even these use slogans of "under-privileged" and "over-privileged", for a flat world is an uninteresting thing, with no surprises over yonder hill. All the local loveliness may pass away.[47]

The vision of Ireland expounded by Muintir na Tire was not significantly different from that expounded for many years by politicians and the state. In 1927, Eamon de Valera who was Ireland's longest-serving Taoiseach (Prime Minister) during the twentieth century announced the policies of his Fianna Fáil party: "I have said repeatedly that our guiding principle will be to make Ireland as self-contained and as self-supporting as possible. That is the only basis on which we can prosper materially. It is the only basis on which we can build a spirited, self-reliant people."[48] His view of Ireland was epitomized by a radio broadcast he gave on St. Patrick's Day 1943 in which he developed what has come to be recognized as the classical vision of Ireland.

> That Ireland which we dreamed of would be the home of a people who valued material wealth only as the basis of right living, of a people who were satisfied with frugal comfort and devoted their leisure to the things of the spirit—a land whose countryside would be bright with cosy homesteads, whose fields and villages would be joyous with the sounds of industry, with the romping of sturdy children, the contests of athletic youth and the laughter of comely maidens, whose firesides would be forums for the wisdom of serene old age. It would, in a word, be the home of people living the life that God desires that man should live.[49]

What is most significant about the broadcast is that it was part of an ongoing annual series of addresses produced primarily for an Irish-American audience: it was taken up by numerous radio stations across the States. Most of the broadcasts were reviews of the past year in Ireland, similar perhaps to a State of the Union address in America. However, it is another example of the interplay of the global and the local and, in particular, of how an image of Ireland produced for a global audience was reflected back in Ireland. De Valera and his party Fianna Fáil were locked in a close election race at the time, so this speech can be seen as a mixture of a political manifesto and a party-political broadcast. What is extraordinary about the speech is that it advocates a rural, non-industrial, self-sustaining, low-economic growth vision of Ireland. In many ways it is the exact opposite of the suburban, post-industrial, transnational-dependent, high-economic society that Ireland has become. His ideal "was built on the basis of a fundamentally dignified and ancient peasant way of life."[50] His suggestion of a non-material, spiritual way of life was deeply redolent of the type of social order advocated by the Catholic Church at the time. The speech could have easily come from a bishop. But, as Lee points out, there were already signs that Irish people were not happy with their lot. They wanted more. Urban workers wanted higher wages. Farmers wanted higher prices, and the only way homesteads would be cosy would be through rural electrification.[51] The pressure to become the same as the rest of the West was already mounting.

The Church's monopoly over morality has declined significantly over the last 30 years. The Church teaches that the use of contraceptives, sex outside marriage, divorce and homosexual behavior are immoral but not only has the state made them legal, they have become acceptable among many if not most Catholics. However, although Catholics may have become detached from the teachings and regulations of the Church as a guide as to how to live a moral life, being Catholic is still an endemic part of most people's lives. The Church is still at the heart of Irish cultural life. Irish Catholics have one of the highest levels of religious practice in the West. The Church presides over education and the major events in people's lives, particularly birth, marriage and death. Being Catholic is part of most people's cultural heritage. It is a way of being in the world, of understanding themselves, that they are happy to accept.

While Irish Catholics may no longer be deeply immersed in the Church, the teachings of the Church are still deeply immersed in the sense they have of themselves, the way they present themselves in everyday life, the way they relate and communicate with others, and their sense of humor. The Catholic Church reigned so long over Irish souls, its teachings and dispositions penetrated so deeply into their bodies, that being Catholic and adopting a Catholic way of being remain second nature to most Irish people.

Of all the virtues that the Church instilled in the Irish Catholics, none was more important than a deep sense of humility. The strength of the Church revolves around its members surrendering themselves, their interests and desires, to the Church's greater good. This notion of self-surrender became central to the modernization of Irish society in the nineteenth century, particularly after the Famine. The success of family farms depended on children learning to surrender their interests and desires, particularly in relation to sex, to the greater good of the family. Family members were encouraged to sacrifice themselves for the good of the family as Christ had sacrificed himself for the good of humanity.

As mentioned above, the art of self-deprecation became central to symbolic capital. People are honored and respected by putting themselves down. They willingly tell stories against themselves, about how they made idiots of themselves. And they love to hear stories about how the great and mighty humbled themselves before others.

For many years, Sir Anthony O'Reilly was director and chairman of Heinz, one of the biggest food companies in the world. He likes to tell stories about Jack Lynch, a former *Taoiseach* of Ireland. When Lynch was Minister for Finance he was being briefed one day by a civil servant. When the civil servant left the room, Lynch was heard to say that the man knew "shag-all" about what he was talking and remarked "why he knows as much about finance as I do." Another story that O'Reilly tells is about the day Lynch, who was a great GAA player, was playing in the final of the All-Ireland championships. When he went to get a public bus to the grounds, there was a long queue. Everyone was going to the match. Several buses went by full and when one did stop, it took only a few from the queue. But Lynch never pushed forward out of the queue. He eventually got a bus but only arrived at the ground minutes before the start of the game.[52]

What we have here is one of the richest, most successful corporate businessmen in the world telling a story about one of the most successful sportsmen and politicians in Ireland and the story revolves around humility and self-deprecation. In telling the story, O'Reilly indicates how much he values self-deprecation and perhaps how despite all the pomp and glory that surrounds his wealth, power and fame, he is, at heart, just a modest, humble man like Jack Lynch.

Again, it is important to remember that although humility and self-deprecation are part and parcel of other cultures, what makes Ireland different is how important and endemic it is in social and cultural life, and how skilled the Irish have become at playing the game. One key strategy learnt at home and at school is to how to belittle yourself before you are belittled by others. Laugh at yourself and the Irish will laugh with you. In Catholic culture, self-denial and making do were so central to being a good person that they became an almost automatic, second-nature way not just of presenting oneself, but of being in the world. One of the main legacies of the culture of self-denial was the way in which taking pleasure and being seen to be enjoying oneself became problematic. Self-indulgence was a mortal sin. It was the sin of Eve: turning one's back on God in order to taste forbidden fruit. The practice of self-denial has become so embedded in the minds and hearts of Catholics over generations that, regardless how materialistic Irish society has become, it will take a long time to become disembodied.

The dominance of the Catholic Church in Irish society raises fundamental questions about sameness and difference. The story of modern Ireland is deeply embedded in the struggle by Irish Catholics to create and maintain a sense of difference from Protestant English. This struggle for national difference is linked into the process of globalization. However, the bonds of identity and belonging became so strong that they tended to strangle the type of individual difference that is promoted and developed today through the media and the market. This is not to say that there were no individual differences in Catholic Ireland 50 years ago. There were, but they were housed in very strong social bonds.[53] Most Irish people were immersed in Catholic culture and realized themselves as individuals and struggled for status, distinction, honor and respect within this culture. For example, one of the main forms of status and prestige for mothers was to create vocations for the Church, to have a son become a priest or brother or a daughter a nun. My mother failed in this respect. However, she achieved enormous dignity and respect by going to Mass every day and receiving Holy Communion. Like many Catholic women of her era, she carved out a sense of difference through her choice of religious icons and artifacts, through her devotion to particular saints or causes—for many years she was part of a campaign to have Blessed Martin de Porres canonized (made a saint). She regularly made the pilgrimage to Lough Derg. She was sometimes fortunate when someone who had made a pilgrimage to Lourdes brought her back some holy water.[54]

Globalization has influenced the way Irish Catholics seek to attain honor and status. This has occurred in two ways. In the first instance, there was an opening up of different ways of being Catholic. The development of the charismatic renewal movement in the 1970s was an example of this. This was part of the global flow of new Catholic ideas and practices. Charismatic prayer groups sprang up across the country which were not always under the control or auspices of the institutional Church. Second, cheaper travel meant the development of Catholic tourism. An increasing number of Irish Catholics are choosing to be married in Italy and other European Catholic countries. And while thousands still flock to climb Croagh Patrick, thousands of others go on organized holiday packages to Rome, Lourdes and Medjagorie. Like many other aspects of Irish culture, the survival of Catholic culture may depend on the way it accommodates to commercialization.

An examination of the transformations in the Irish religious field helps us understand the mix between locals and cosmopolitans. For a long time, religious cosmopolitans were priests. They were the ones who were most likely to have traveled, to have been on the missions, to have been educated or served abroad, to have been to Rome. They were also the most likely to be among the best educated people in the parish. They exuded a knowledge and an understanding of the world. Many locals, on the other hand, might not have ever traveled far beyond the parish. Now the situation is often reversed. It is the locals who can now afford to travel abroad on pilgrimages, to see relatives and friends, visit and shop in big cities and stay in exotic holiday resorts.

But globalization has also brought other changes. The Catholic Church no longer has the same influence on people's lives, their sense of self, the realization of themselves as individuals. It has been replaced by the media and the market. The bonds that tied people to family and Church have been loosened. Irish people are not immersed in Catholic culture as they used to be. Over the last 50 years, being Catholic has become a cultural question, a lifestyle option, another choice that people make. Being Catholic has become more like being Irish, speaking the Irish language, following Irish sport, listening to Irish music; something that is no longer inherited as an ascribed part of one's identity. Today's cultural representations, like building blocks, are put together by people in the construction of their identities as individuals. The problem, of course, is that in a globalized consumer culture these cultural representations may lose their depth. They become identity accessories rather than cultural givens. Because people are no longer immersed in the culture, because they critically reflect about cultural representations and pick and choose between them, they no longer generate the same social bonds.

IRISH IMAGINATION

I have concentrated on the more generic or popular dimensions to Irish culture, and have eschewed references to Irish high culture and, in particular the way Irish novelists, writers, artists, film-makers and musicians have made significant contributions to the global flow of culture. However, it is tempting to make a connection between the dominant Catholic habitus that emerged in Ireland, with its repression of the body, sex, self and desire, and the emergence of a vibrant Irish imagination. Was this imagination generated from a peculiar mix of a visually rich religion, a climate that lent itself to an indoor life and story-telling, and a moral regime that demanded the repression of self? Andrew Greeley is a well-known American priest, sociologist, journalist and novelist. He loves Ireland and all things Irish. Following an argument developed by the theologian David Tracy, he argues that because of the rich sacramental form of Catholicism that developed in Ireland, God came to be seen and understood as an immanent force in life rather than as an external transcendental figure. Irish Catholics, Greeley claims, developed a rich analogical imagination that saw God "lurking in the ordinary object and events of life—the blackbird singing, a great pool of ale, a cat, a river, trees, the rising sun or moon, fish rushing upstream, the close bonds of family and community."[55] He argues that in describing these experiences and events, the Irish have a propensity to use elaborate and playful descriptors that bring together, recklessly and outrageously, elements which seem in contradiction to one another. Greeley claims it is this religiously inspired imagination that is evident in a wide variety of works of art such as the plays of Brian Friel, the poetry of Seamus Heaney, the films of Neil Jordan, and the novels of Roddy Doyle. However, there is plenty of evidence of God being an external authoritarian who demanded obedience and whose image instilled fear as much as awe. It may also be that the Irish imagination is founded on a rigorous ethical program of sexual repression and self-elimination which, compensated by drink, talk and humor, gave rise to tall stories whose validity and reward depended on how much entertainment they gave.

SMALLNESS

It is sometimes difficult for outsiders to understand how small Ireland is not just in terms of its geographical size but also its population. In terms of population (4 million) it is about the same size as the metropolitan areas of cities such as Boston, Atlanta, Milan and Hamburg. It is about the same size as the state of Indiana. It is slightly smaller than the Netherlands but it has only a quarter of its population. But what makes Ireland different is that it is an island nation. Most people who live in cities have rural backgrounds: 90 percent are white, Catholic and English-speaking. When this is combined with the fact that most people have been reared in Catholic families and have attended Catholic schools and that they have developed a similar habitus, there is a strong sense of common identity and belonging. As we shall see, when established villagers meet in Ballivor they immediately place each other in terms of families and surrounding townlands. But this practice extends to a national grid. When strangers meet they will often place each other by county, village and family. This practice, combined with a shared outlook on life, facilitates access, communication and social networking. The degree of separation between people in Ireland is small. People may mix in different circles but there is a dense social network: it does not take Irish people long to make connections with each other. Strangers quickly discover that they mutually know other people. But, perhaps what is most important is that when strangers meet in Ireland there is a desire for, an interest in, the cognitive mapping of each other in terms of mutual friends and acquaintances. In this way, when it comes to favors being done people can be easily put in contact with each other. Most can get to meet any politician, media personality, church leader, or business person. Moreover, because these people mix regularly in open society, there is a feeling that they can be approached without any formal introduction. This links back to the culture of self-denial and self-deprecation and the felt need that political and economic leaders have to be close to people.

There is, then, an intimacy between Irish people that is almost parochial. Young and old still meet, greet and begin to relate to each other in terms of the county, parish and family to which they belong. People from small villages like Ballivor have a conceptual grid of people, the families to which they belong and the townland in which they live. When people meet, they are placed into this grid. The national grid operates in a similar fashion. When someone introduces himself as a man from Mayo and then says he is from the village of Shrule, there is social and cultural capital in knowing where Shrule is, being able to cite some of the family names and, most important of all, to refer to Conor Mortimer, one of the stars of the Mayo football team.

When I was in Ballivor interviewing people from the GAA club, they mentioned that the previous weekend Ballivor had hosted a visit from two teams from Shrule. I was able to ask if Conor Mortimer had come. He was one of the stars on the Mayo team that got to the All Ireland final that year. I do not have any background in GAA. My family is steeped in middle-class Dublin. I went to a rugby-playing school. I follow GAA, but only through the media, and only superficially. However, my brother-in-law comes from Shrule. So when Shrule was mentioned, I was able to nonchalantly mention Conor Mortimer as if I knew him personally. They said no, he hadn't come, but they were surprised. By making the connection between Shrule and Mortimer I had obviously increased my status.

This parochial sense of Ireland is not just maintained through social relationships, it is evident in the media, particularly in traffic reports. For example, on 16 June 2004 on national radio (RTE 1) the traffic report announced that there were no major problems to report from around the country. The only item of significance was that the *gardaí* had cleared the cattle that had been on the Spiddal to Moycullen road. This is a minor road in County Galway in the West of Ireland. Something as global as a road traffic report has the effect of producing a sense of place, intimacy and belonging.

CONCLUSION

My argument is, then, slightly different from Greeley's. I agree that what makes the Irish different is that for generations they were devoted to the Catholic Church. This devotion revolved around practices of self-denial and self-sacrifice particularly in relation to pleasures and desires, especially in relation to sex.

Since the middle of the nineteenth century, the Irish have had the lowest levels of marriage. Those who did marry, married late. There is little evidence about sexual activity, but the level of births to married women was very high while the number of births outside marriage was low. The standard of living was fairly low—most people lived a life of frugal comfort—and the level of emigration was very high. The Church was central to this social system. When families were large and incomes were low, it was crucial that individuals were disciplined and controlled, particularly when it came to desire, pleasure and sex. The Church promoted a culture of large families and, at the same time, was the source of the discipline and control necessary to regulate pleasure, desire and self-indulgence. It was also a source of comfort and consolation. There was a willingness, as well as an expectation, for individuals to deny and sacrifice themselves. It was this culture of self-mortification, of the control of pleasure and desire, combined with a rich tapestry of religious stories, symbols and iconography, which was a major source for the Irish imagination.

There was another long-term historical practice that became central to the Irish being different. The low level of marriage, combined with the lateness of those who did marry, meant that from the nineteenth century many Irish men found sanctuary, comfort and solace in the pub, not just in hard drinking, but drinking in rounds whereby everyone in the drinking group takes turns to buy everyone else a drink. As mentioned earlier, this is associated with a surrender of the self to the group and, at the same time, an elimination of the self. Over the last 150 years the Irish became masters at the art of self-denial, self-deprecation and self-elimination. Language, music and sport are important factors, but this was this system of self that made us different.

The balance between difference and sameness is central to

social life. If individuals, groups or societies become too different they are in danger of becoming isolated from or ostracized by the wider social whole to which they belong. On the other hand, if the social whole becomes too strong, if it inhibits difference and individuality, the self cannot grow and develop. And yet, if the social bond that binds the whole together is not strong enough, the differences that emerge will be weak and shallow and will not allow for the genuine difference on which sustainable growth and development depend. If individuals grow up in families in which there is a strong social bond, the difference can be tolerated and sustained. If the social bond is weak, there is a danger that the difference will be shallow and will not contribute to the family's strength in diversity. The same goes for groups and societies. From the micro-world of the individual to the macro-world of organizations and societies, there is a continual struggle to achieve a balance between sameness and difference.

This raises a number of questions and issues in relation to Ireland. Did the homogeneity of *gaelic*, Catholic Ireland create a social bond that strangled difference and individuality and did this contribute to Ireland's isolation and backwardness during the twentieth century? Or was the social bond strong enough to allow for the type of ingenuity, imagination and strength of character which became a key component of Ireland's recent economic and social development? Are some of the differences that I have described in this chapter what statisticians would call "significant", or are they just minor variations? Has Ireland lost much of whatever difference it ever had and is it being drowned in the sea of sameness that characterizes global capitalist culture? In moving from a more Catholic form of capitalism to a more fully fledged consumer capitalism, have we lost our authentic difference?

Although we are rapidly moving towards a conflation of global time and space through which the world is increasingly becoming one place, there are very few analysts of globalization who would argue that there is a global culture. There are so many languages, religious beliefs and practices, inherited traditions, forms of family and community life, types of music, dance and sport and, generally, ways of being in the world, that it is ludicrous to suggest that there could ever be a common disposition or orientation to life that produces similar practices and forms of everyday life. And yet there seems to be an increasing similarity to the pattern of life for most people living in the world capitalist system. The swiftness, intensity and penetration of global flows seem to lead to more people working the same way, consuming the same products, obeying comparable laws, rules and regulations, living in similar spaces, engaging in the same forms of entertainment and so forth. The question then is whether the similarity in everyday life has become so strong that there is effectively little difference not just between cosmopolitans living in global cities but between locals living in rural Idaho and rural Ireland. Would someone living in rural Ireland today have more in common with someone living thousands of miles away in rural America than they would, for example, have with someone who lived in Ireland 100 years ago? Does this suggest that what is happening around the world is that the material base of everyday life is becoming similar and that while there are cultural differences in language, habits and customs, these are increasingly becoming superstructural and insignificant? Despite all the differences described in the previous chapter, has social and cultural life in Ireland become the same as in the rest of Western society? More importantly, because of the similarity in outlook and lifestyle practices, have Irish people developed the same sense of self?

For many of us there is something revolting about sameness. The idea of having to live in the same house, sleep in the same bedroom, dress in the same clothes, eat the same food, drive the same car, do the same work, watch the same television programs, and read the same newspapers, seems to be abhorrent. It would be no different from living in a prison or the worst form of state socialist society. And so there seems to be increasing universal agreement that, whatever else happens, individuals have to be free to choose who they are, what they do, how they live their lives. The cry of the liberal is that the more opportunity individuals have to make their own rational choices within open markets, the better for them, the better for their society, and the better for the common global good. It does not matter if the free choice is more illusory than real, if people are trampled on in the marketplace, or if the long-term consequences of unrestricted short-term freedom of choice are environmentally disastrous: the individual is god. And yet in this age of narcissism and individualism there is an increasing sense of sameness about everyday life in the West.

America was the equivalent of Mecca for many aspiring Irish cosmopolitans during the 1950s. It was where they made those wonderful movies, cartoons and television programs that brought excitement and glamor into our rather dull and drab lives. There were cowboys and gangsters as well as smooth sophisticates who "dressed to the nines" and drank swanky cocktails. Like many other kids in the 1950s, I knew exactly the meaning of Christmas; it may have been Jesus's birthday but my world would fall apart if I did not get the latest cowboy outfit. There was nothing incongruous in seeing hundreds of kids out early on the streets of Dublin on Christmas Day dressed in their new costumes, playing Cowboys and Indians. There was enormous kudos to having the latest cultural artifacts from America. In the 1960s this was to grow into wearing jeans, eating hamburgers, drinking Coke, going bowling, and, complete salvation, getting to Disneyland. The global flow of culture coming from the States was overwhelming. There was a feeling that it would not be long before most people in Ireland would be sitting down in their living rooms to watch American football on television with a packet of popcorn in one hand and a Bud in the other.

I remember when I first went to Southern Illinois University in Carbondale in 1979, having managed to extract myself from the apron strings of Catholic Ireland. I had arrived in the land of freedom where individuals had the right to pursue life, liberty and happiness. Yet I was amazed by the lack of difference. It seemed as if I had arrived in some sort of boot camp in which the students were required to dress in T-shirts and jeans, eat the same food (mostly meat and potatoes), drink the same drinks (mostly soda and beer) and watch the same sport. They lived in the same dorms, drove the same cars, listened to the same music and went to the same shopping malls to buy the same clothes and groceries, many of which they didn't really need. People seemed to live and work to consume. At the weekend, taking a break from work, they would drive to the mall and walk around huge stores filling enormous trolleys with great bargains. If they hadn't consumed enough, there were always the numerous yard sales where you could buy some of the great, hardly-ever-used bargains for knockdown prices. It was not just the way of the market, it was the way of the world in the land of the free.

The notion that not just Ireland but the rest of the West would be swamped by American culture was in line with what many sociologists and global analysts thought was happening in the latter half of the twentieth century. We would be swamped by low-cost goods produced by American trans-national corporations, we would not only eat more fast food but our social, work and private lives would become McDonaldized. Everything would become more rational, pre-dictable, calculable and efficient. Our concept of leisure and entertainment would become Disneyfied.[1] It was "cool" to be American. There was cultural capital as well as profit to be made in Ireland from aping all things American. Being American became so common, it was obvious. O'Toole gave a description of a hamburger restaurant in County Mayo nearly 30 years ago:

> Inside the Nevada Burger fast food restaurant on Westport's Mill Street, established, as the sign above the door proudly proclaims, in 1979, one wall is boldly emblazoned with the stars and stripes. Underneath the sea-blue Nevada state flag on the opposite wall is the motto: All For Our Country.[2]

ALL-CONSUMING SAMENESS

American icons and cultural motifs are still big business in Ireland. Unlike Britain, making associations with America can sell products. Even today, as the peace continues in Northern Ireland, it would be rare to go into any restaurant, pub or store and find it festooned with Union Jacks and pictures of the royal family. However, it is common to find public displays of cultural insignia not just from other European countries, particularly France, Italy and Spain, but also from India and

China. What makes the world the same is that culture is less tied to place. National cultural icons have become swept up in global flows. Culture increasingly becomes context-less, a mélange of disparate components drawn from around the world and borne upon the modern chariots of global communication systems.[3] As far back as 1983, Theodore Levitt argued that different cultural preferences and national tastes were vestiges of the past. The only ones that would survive would be those that entered the global mainstream. He cited ethnic markets such as Chinese food, country and western music, pita bread, as examples that confirmed global homogenization.[4] The world is shrinking in terms of diminishing time and space differences. But it is also shrinking in terms of the content of what people consume. There is a growing convergence of consumer tastes and preferences. A study of consumption patterns across 22 countries (including Ireland) from 1985 to 1999 examined expenditure on food, beverages, tobacco, clothing, rent, fuel, household equipment, health care, transport, communications, education, recreation and other miscellaneous goods and services and found that there was robust evidence of strong convergence in cross-country consumption patterns.[5] The rapid flow of goods and communications has turned the world into one marketplace which, in turn, means that those companies that can operate in the global marketplace can produce huge economies of scale by selling the same product all over the world at once. As Friedman predicted, everyone everywhere is increasingly looking like everyone everywhere else.[6] And yet, in the midst of the growing desert of sameness, there is a desperate search for difference. Cultural entrepreneurs search for authentic local difference that can then be marketed globally. In this process, "standardized, commercialized mass commodities draw for their contents upon revivals of traditional, folk or national motifs and styles in fashions, furnishings, music and the arts, lifted out of their original contexts and anaesthetized."[7]

The sameness in people's lives around the world is more at the level of the material practices of everyday life, literally the patterns of sleeping, eating, working, commuting and consuming. In recent years there has been a renewed interest in sociology in describing and analyzing the specific practices of everyday life and the logic and meaning people bring to the ordinary happenings in their lives.[8] However, the origins of the interest in the everyday go back to the middle of the last century and, particularly, to the writings of Henri Lefebvre. He argued that the penetration of capitalist forms of production and consumption has eliminated the organic connection in pre-modern societies between time, space, work, leisure, sense of belonging and identity.[9] In his view, modern capitalist relations have eliminated genuine forms of social relations, have eradicated the centrality and importance of local festivals, and have led to an obsession with self, work, consumption and career. He emphasized how, in this system, the time of nature and seasons is replaced by the time of technology, work and consumption. Work and leisure become rationally differentiated in time and space; people work harder to fulfill the desires and fantasies that have been created for them by the advertising industry.[10]

What makes everyday life in the West the same is not just that people are involved in the same practices of getting and spending, but that there is an increasing standardization of how people earn their living, in the way corporations, businesses and companies are run, in the way work is evaluated and pay is linked to performance. Much of global sameness is, then, based on the rationalization of production and consumption that is embedded in the workings of the modern world system. The world capitalist system thrives on difference, providing an enormous range of different products and services, stimulating people to purchase these to fulfill their needs, have new experiences, explore new tastes and, in doing so, develop a portfolio of choices that constitute not just a unique lifestyle but an ongoing unique sense of self. And yet despite this frenetic, desperate search for difference, the demand for constant transformation, there is a sense that everything is becoming the same. People may drive different cars, listening to different sounds, along different roads to get to work in different buildings to do different jobs, eat different food, go home to watch different television programs and go to their different beds and, yet, it is all very much the same. It is the same difference.

The more identity, sense of self and individual difference are realized through consumption, the more the economy grows and the world capitalist system penetrates deeper into people's bodies and souls. The more the world becomes the same, and the more the relations people have stretch across time and space, the more social bonds become stretched. The more individuals spend more time being with and communicating through technology and less time creating social bonds through spending time in the same place with the same people, the more fragile their sense of self becomes. It is one of the emotional costs of globalization.[11]

This is not to deny that Irish people live different lives. They do and, equally important, insist that they do. Like most other people, the Irish talk to each other about the different things that have happened to them, their experiences, feelings, responsibilities, cares and concerns. This is the stuff on which social bonds are built. We are anxious to hear about people we know, love and care for. People may be globally connected, they may travel the world, but there is generally a home, a place of strong social bonds to which their hearts and minds are connected. People increasingly act globally but they still think locally. The question is to what extent what is going on in their minds makes any significant difference to their practices.

ECONOMIC TRANSFORMATION

The way in which Ireland has slowly become like the rest of the West dates back to the second wave of modernization that began in the late 1950s and early 1960s.[12] For a long time there had been a struggle within the government and apparatuses of the Irish state between the traditionalists and modernists, those who wanted to keep Ireland different and those who wanted it to become the same. The traditionalists wanted to keep building up around Ireland the walls that protected our native industries and our Catholic innocence. We had to be shielded against foreign competition and filth. Slowly but surely the modernists began to infiltrate the habitus of the traditionalists and, through reasoned debate and rational argument, persuade them that the pursuit of economic growth was not necessarily wrong in itself, that dismantling existing trade barriers would strengthen rather than disable Irish industry, and that reducing the level of censorship on books and films would not destroy our Catholic souls.

There was also a realization that economically Ireland had become too dependent on Britain. There was a need to diversify our markets and, in particular, to reach out into Europe. During the 1960s, the state campaigned actively to become a member of what was then called the Common Market, which has become the European Union. During the 1970s, the boom in the Irish economy continued. It got even better when we eventually joined the European Union in 1973. Irish farmers, in particular, did really well from the grants they received under Europe's Common Agricultural Policy. However, Ireland was never going to become rich from agriculture and tourism, then the mainstays of the economy. The state recognized that any long-term economic development depended on enticing transnational companies to come to Ireland. It put a huge effort into selling Ireland to these companies some of which had a greater annual turnover than the state itself. The government gave incentive grants. It changed the education curriculum away from a classical Catholic one to greater emphasis on science and technology. It lowered the level of corporation tax. It got together with the social partners, mainly representatives of employers and trade unions, to reach national agreement on pay and conditions and thereby reduce the number of industrial disputes and strikes that had previously undermined the economy.

The reality is that the transnational companies who came to Ireland did not need much inviting. There were rich opportunities in Ireland. The Irish were a relatively young, socially stable, culturally homogeneous, well-educated, self-disciplined people who were eager to earn some good money and have a slice of the good life. The state and the transnational corporations have had a successful partnership for the past 40 years. It takes two to tango, but the transnational corporations have done most of the leading. If they decide they no longer want to dance with the Irish, there is nobody else for the Irish to dance with. It is the transnational corporations that helped Ireland go from being an isolated, economically backward, almost peasant society to becoming one of the wealthiest, most globalized societies in the world. More than anything else it has been the transnational companies that have led the move from a Catholic to a consumer capitalist society. In this chapter, I want to explore in more detail the nature of this sameness.

The main reason why the Irish have become the same as others in the West is that they produce as much as them. Between 1961 and 2002 there was an average of 2.75 percent growth in Irish labor productivity (measured by Gross National Product by worker). This mirrored the growths in productivity in the EU and the USA. However, much of the Irish growth took place during the 1990s. Between 1996 and 2002, Ireland had the highest level of labor productivity in Europe.[13] This increase in productivity is related to a number of different factors including state management of the economy, access to risk capital, the level of education of workers and, finally, research and development activity. However, it also relates to allowing for greater competition and reducing restrictions on the operation of free markets, particularly labor markets, and reducing state expenditure. Cassidy points out that OECD reports show that when there is strong employment protection legislation this can have the effect of reducing labor productivity and discouraging the entry and expansion of firms. In other words, one of the main reasons why Ireland has become the same as the rest is because we have more transnational companies, who pay good wages, but who are not restricted in the way they employ people. Cassidy also argues that when state taxes are too high this can restrict household choices thereby reducing productivity. In other words, the primary way Ireland has become rich is that it has allowed the market and transnational companies free rein. With less interference from trade unions, we have learned to work harder, produce more and earn more. With less interference from the state, we have been able to spend more on what we like. This is the way of world capitalist system, the way of the world; there is much greater freedom and wealth, but less security, much less trust and, generally, much more risk.[14]

There is a myth that with the arrival of the Celtic Tiger, Irish people are working longer hours. The reality is that between 1983 and 2000 the average hours worked fell from 44 to 38 hours.[15] Moreover, the average number of hours worked in Ireland is quite similar to those across Europe.[16] However, what is increasingly at issue in Ireland is not so much the number of hours worked as the type of work and the levels of productivity. We are constantly told by the state, its agencies and transnational companies that to maintain our global competitiveness and standard of living it is necessary to create more high-value jobs producing high-value outputs. We are also told that we have to work harder. Irish state agencies such as FÁS, the National Training and Employment Agency, insist that economic growth can only be maintained by increasing labor productivity. Forfás, the national policy advisory board for enterprise, trade, science, technology and innovation, has put it quite clearly: "Ireland's ability to catch up with the living standards of the world's richest regions now depends on increasing the productivity levels of those already in work."[17]

The struggle to extract more productivity from workers is probably the second oldest profession in the world. It became a science and technology with the concept of the division of labor advocated by Adam Smith in his *Wealth of Nations* (1776). This was developed further with Taylor's *Principles of Scientific Management* (1911) and reached a peak with the Gilbreths' motion and time studies.[18] Management is crucial in extracting productivity because it dictates the precise manner in which work is to be performed and then monitors and evaluates the performance. There have, of course, been new developments in management strategies—collective decision-making, democratic and humanistic management, empowerment of workers and so forth—but the more the productivity of workers can be scientifically calculated, the more management is able to improve performance and get "the best out of people."

NEC, the Japanese corporation that was based in Ballivor for 30 years, was the same as most other transnational companies. It wanted to get the most out of its workers. A global company, it operates in the highly competitive electronics market. One of the ways it maintains its competitiveness is by getting subsidiaries and branches within the company to compete not just against other companies but against each other. NEC Ireland was semi-autonomous. It manufactured logic microchips, primarily for European motorcar industry. What it manufactured was negotiated with headquarters in Japan. Often it would make proposals for new capacity and equipment on the basis of promised returns. Once its budget and production were decided, the task of the Irish plant was to increase productivity, efficiency, turnaround and performance. It had discretion when it came to whom it employed, what it paid people, how it treated them and how it monitored, evaluated and rewarded efficiency and productivity. As Tom Malone, the human resources manager, put it to me:

> The key factor is to remain competitive. How you measure that is very debatable. There are four key performance indicators for any manufacturing plant: cost, on-time delivery, quality and customer service. We are not strong on all four. We are best at on-time delivery and customer service. [On] quality we would be okay. We are not the most cost-competitive in comparison with Singapore. We are okay in comparison to Japanese plants.
>
> The quality of the people that we hire is quite good, because the tests are quite strict. We have never measured the effectiveness of the tests. But I know that some of the people we have excluded have gone on to other jobs and done very well.

> What we are looking for is people who can apply themselves. Who are self-motivated, who have good skills, are punctual (a basic thing) and are looking to get on. We are looking for "Theory Y People" in McGregor's theory.

In his book *The Human Side of Enterprise* (1960) McGregor identified two models of individuals at work.[19] Theory X managers saw people as basically disliking work and consequently they had to be controlled and threatened before they worked hard enough. This gave rise to tough management with punishments and tight controls. Theory Y managers saw people as wanting to work in the same way as they wanted to rest or play. They would direct themselves as long as they were committed to the organization and their job was satisfying. In Theory Y, workers, under proper conditions, not only take on but seek responsibility. Using their own creativity, imagination and ingenuity, employees are seen as wanting to work together to solve most of their work problems.

During the 1990s productivity among Irish workers increased dramatically. However, studies showed that this increase came mainly in high-tech, foreign-owned sectors like pharmaceuticals, chemicals and information technology. The rise in productivity in the domestic sector, particularly in utilities and construction, was shown to be more modest. The general rise in productivity was attributed to better management techniques, improving technology and foreign know-how about labor utilization.[20]

In his study of a team of Irish software developers, O'Riain gives a description of how global corporations are constituted, how they operate across time and space, and how they extract performance from workers.[21] The company Womble Software is an example of a new "global web" corporate structure. It was formed as a spin-off from a large hierarchical corporation. The company has no more than 15 employees. It is partly owned by the four founders, partly by the major transnational company USTech, partly by a major customer, and the rest by a venture capital fund in Silicon Valley. The development team of six people was based in Ireland and was officially contracted to provide software development services to Womble. O'Riain gives a detailed description of the daily communications between the team and Ramesh, the managing director of Womble based in California. Through being only a phone call, email message or plane trip away, Ramesh was able to mentally preside over the Irish team in its physical absence. The Irish team had to use their own creativity, imagination and ingenuity to get the work done and the way in which Womble and all other companies exert control in the global workplace is through controlling time, specifically the imposition of project deadlines. O'Riain sums up this approach by quoting a "thank-you" email message that Ramesh sent to a contract graphic-design firm:

> Our project team was truly an international virtual-team, with up to 8 hours of time-zone difference among the different team members. We expected you to work at such a hectic pace, yet, we also demanded flexibility from you in all aspects. It is very rare that anybody of your caliber would be able to excel on both these fronts.[22]

Towards the end of the project deadline, the team in Ireland was working up to 60 hours a week which, O'Riain maintains, is not long compared to other software development firms in Ireland.[23] He claims that the trend in the software industry in Ireland, especially in small firms, and particularly among managerial and professional workers, is towards the Japanese and North American pattern of executives and managers working particularly long hours.

The result of this corporate work structure is seen most obviously in the work-family nexus, "where work demands come to dominate family life, leaving very little space for workers to negotiate alternative work and family time arrangements." He argues that although there is increasing evidence of a move away from highly centralized bureaucratic organizations, the intensification of time control, through the imposition of project deadlines, results in the same level of control.[24] The greatest form of discipline and control in the workplace, in Ireland as elsewhere, is the eye of the clock.

What is at issue here is that not just in NEC but throughout Ireland, workers are increasingly becoming more subjected to the same science of management, the same technologies of productivity that are being created, maintained and developed all over the world. There are two important points. First, there has been a gradual transition from harsh regimes of management to softer forms—from Theory X to Theory Y. This corresponds to Foucault's argument that governance generally and regimes of discipline and punishment have over the centuries moved from brutal forms of body control to more subtle penetrative forms: children, for example, are governed more by psychological techniques rather than being beaten.[25] It also corresponds to Elias's argument that over the centuries, people have moved from external forms of self-constraint to more internalized forms.[26] What is crucial, however, is that not only do more people discipline and control themselves, but that they want to. They have internalized and embodied the discourse of the scientific management of work. There is an expectation and perhaps a perceived demand that it is not enough just to work, but to be good at it, to be successful. Obviously this has been an imperative throughout history.

What makes globalized modernity different is that not only has it become far more rational and scientific, the notion of efficiency and productivity has trickled down to many other forms of everyday life. In resting, playing, and even in making love, there is a desire to be more productive and efficient, to get the most out of life, out of people, out of every situation and event.

Years ago, Jacques Ellul described contemporary life as being driven by an imperative to find the one best way of doing everything.[27] And what is best has to be fast. We live in a world where the unquestioned orthodoxy has become that money is time, that everything has to get faster and better. This is the rhetoric that is embodied by those at the top and it does not need an idiot to figure out that those at the top expect it of those at the bottom. Doing things faster and better is what keeps companies on top, the economy growing and world capitalism thriving.

The theory is that ever-increasing, better performances at every level of everyday life are necessary if we are to survive economically, to continue to have high levels of economic growth and to improve standards of living. We are led to believe that it is necessary that at every level of society, whatever people are doing, they strive to achieve the best. This means that all aspects of life have to be monitored and evaluated for performance. Who is producing more? Where is this happening, how, why? This reaches into the center of family and community life, into the hearts, minds and souls of nearly every Irish person. It begins with education.

Throughout their education, children get used to being tested, to the demand to produce good results. This feeds back into their family and personal life. Who they are is increasingly associated with educational performance. The system of examination becomes increasingly pervasive and persistent.

The monitoring of schoolchildren is almost as relentless and rigorous as of patients in intensive care. Pupils are seen and understood, and see and understand themselves, in terms of their educational performance. Schools and colleges are places where young people learn to become orthodox capitalists. They learn to survive in a world of examinations, tests, time-tables, deadlines, evaluations, levels, points and so forth. As in the Catholic Church, there is little or no room for unorthodoxy let alone heterodoxy.

To produce more, people have to behave in a more rational, predictable, standardized and calculable manner. High levels of production are not amenable to people being emotional and spiritual. If people wish to show some emotion, it is impera-tive that they do so at appropriate times in an appropriate manner. The fluid and efficient interdependency that is central to increasing production depends on people dealing with their emotions. Because it is too dangerous to bottle them up, there is an expectation, if not a demand, that people deal with their emotions in a way that does not impinge on others, that does not interfere with the production process. Letting go of one's emotions is important, but it has to be done in a controlled manner; a controlled, decontrolling of emotion.[28] Similarly, there is a need for people to be spiritual. But whatever way people get in touch with the meaning of life, human connectedness, the supernatural and the transcen-dental, has to be done in their own time and private space. What is most important is that it is compartmentalized from, or at least does not interfere with, production.

It is easy to slip deeper into the habitus of the world capitalist system. It moves from being an accepted to an unquestioned orthodoxy or *doxa*. It becomes part of the air we breathe. We are like fish in water. The rhetoric and practice of consumer capitalism have seeped into everyday life in Ireland, into the body and soul of most people, particularly workers. The obsession with time is part and parcel of the obsession with productivity and performance.

CONSUMPTION

Not only have the Irish jumped on board the treadmill of increased productivity, they have also taken to consuming like a duck to water. It is this combination between production and consumption, between working hard and spending hard, which has been central to the success of the Celtic Tiger and to the Irish behaving more like their Western counterparts. Consumer spending has been an essential part of Irish economic growth. In 2000, when economic growth was peaking, the National Income and Expenditure Accounts showed that the value of personal consumption accounted for 49 percent of Irish Gross Domestic Product (GDP). Another reason the Irish are becoming the same is that they have become accustomed to borrowing more to spend more. In 1993, the Irish level of private sector credit was close to 6 percent, the same as the rest of Europe. By 2006, the Irish level had risen to almost 30 percent—three times higher than the European average. Most of this, however, was by companies borrowing to make investments to make profits and, where it was household borrowing, the bulk of it went into obtaining mortgages to buy houses.[29] Nevertheless, there is plenty of evidence of the Irish wanting to indulge themselves. In 2001 a survey showed that the top five spending or financial priorities were to buy a good holiday, a new car, new clothes or shoes, to increase short-term saving, and to have a good time (meals, drinks, cinema).[30]

The Irish obsession with house ownership fueled the construction industry which also grew dramatically during the Celtic Tiger years. The annual number of new dwellings completed rose from 22,464 in 1992 to 86,188 in 2005, an increase of 283 percent. In the ten years between 1995 and 2005, there were 584,073 new houses built, an enormous increase in a population of just over 4 million.[31] And, as McDonald and Nix point out, it is not just the number of houses that is growing exponentially but their size: "the Irish vernacular tradition of housing, particularly thatched cottages, has been ... comprehensively rejected in favour of the imported idioms derived from Spanish haciendas or the antebellum pastiche of Southfork, the Ewing home in *Dallas*."[32]

The explosion of house building is linked to two other phenomena that bring the Irish into line with the rest of the West, suburban sprawl and commuting. Between 1996 and 2006, the population of Ireland increased by 9 percent from 3.6 million to 4.2 million Dublin city and the Greater Dublin area grew substantially during the second half of the twentieth century. But there is now little room left for suburban housing estates. Thus between 1996 and 2006, the population of County Dublin increased by only 12 percent from 1.1 million to 1.2 million, but the population of the surrounding counties increased dramatically: Meath (48 percent), Kildare (39 percent), Wicklow (23 percent) and Louth (20 percent).[33]

The obsession with purchasing cars is almost as strong as purchasing houses. In the 10 years between 1995 and 2005, the number of cars in Ireland almost doubled from 1.26 to 2.14 million.[34] One might think that because Ireland is relatively small and such a large proportion of the population live in the mid-east region, the Irish would not have much use for cars. However, a report in 2000 showed that Ireland had become one of the most car-dependent societies in the world. It stated that the average car in Ireland traveled 15,250 miles. This was 70 percent higher than France or Germany, 50 percent higher than Britain and 30 percent higher than the USA.[35]

Not only are there more cars on the Irish roads, but as in America, they are getting bigger. It was estimated that in 2005, about 14,000 SUVs (Sports Utility Vehicles) were sold in Ireland, or 8 percent of total new private car sales. This represented a 41 percent increase on 2004.[36]

Keohane and Kuhling have pointed out that many car accidents in Ireland occur where minor rural roads interconnect with highways—where the slow local meets the fast global.[37] The roads in the West of Ireland are a maze of endless twists and turns. Traveling on these roads is more about traveling slowly back in time than fast forward through space.[38] When people travel fast on these slow roads, the results are often deadly. A study in 2000 by the National Roads Authority found that the preponderance of road deaths involved young, inexperienced males driving at excessive speed on rural roads late at night at weekends.[39] It is estimated that young men between the ages of 17 and 24 are seven times more likely to be killed in a car crash compared to the general population.[40] There are, then, emotional costs and benefits to globalization. Fast cars bring a quick sense of freedom and excitement. They can also bring death, long-lasting trauma and tragedy.

The new Irish obsession with houses and cars represents the descent into the material world which the Catholic Church warned about for over a 100 years. Property prices in Ireland have risen rapidly. Between 1996 and 2005, the consumer price index rose by 30 percent but the price of houses in Ireland rose 270 percent. What survey results do not reveal is the extent to which this rapid rise in property values has come to dominate Irish conversations. For those who were lucky enough to be in the property market, it has developed a sense of economic well-being and an interest in the comparative value of their own property. Between 1995 and 2005, the average price of a new house in Ireland increased from €77,994 to €275,810.[41]

The way, then, that the Irish are becoming the same revolves around having a home, and a car to drive to and from home. The home and the family have been central to most human societies. A home fulfills traditional functions of a place of retreat and recovery from work, of rearing children, and of self-realization. It may still be a haven in a heartless world, but instead of being a quiet, private, spiritual place, it has become more of a center for consumption. What makes life at home in Ireland more the same is the emphasis given to watching television, listening to the radio, using computers, keeping in contact with family and friends through the phone, email and text messages, maintaining and revamping the home and garden, buying clothes and, then, arranging to go out (mostly to the pub) and away on holidays. A survey in 2001 found that seven of the top nine most popular soap operas, drama series and comedies in Ireland were made in the UK or USA.[42] We can agree that UK soaps such as *Coronation Street* and *EastEnders* and US situation comedies such as *Friends* are received, interpreted and assimilated differently by Irish audiences: They use different interpretive repertoires.[43] But while these programs may be interpreted differently what links audiences is the practice of watching television and the exposure to the lifestyle that is depicted.[44]

Consuming has become serious work. It requires a great deal of skill and effort to read through advertisements, to find the best rate, to create and maintain credit balances, to decipher bargains.[45] The major social practice in consumer capitalism is shopping. Shopping has become a common global experience.[46] Shopping malls are now contemporary temples of consumerism and hedonism.[47] It is through shopping that people are stimulated and excited. It creates a sense of freedom and agency. What has happened in Ireland is that as it has switched from Catholic capitalism to consumer capitalism, the number of people who realize themselves as individuals through a Catholic discourse, habitus and practice has declined and the number who realize their difference through consumer choice and lifestyle has increased. Instead of rituals, prayers, penances and sacraments, they increasingly realize themselves through fashion and food, lifestyles and diets, sports and entertainment. Like the rest of the West, the Irish have become global cultural bricoleurs, they pick and choose their cultural icons from around the world. The way they decorate themselves and their homes becomes a signature statement. Instead of being called to pray, they are called to consume. The Catholic Church was never able to compete with the sophistication of the advertising and marketing industries. Ireland is no different. Everywhere people go they are reminded of the need to buy. Advertisements are no longer notices about the availability of goods and services, they have become ethical, spiritual and aesthetic messages. In Ireland, there has been an ongoing debate about the broadcasting of the Angelus—a Catholic call to prayer—twice a day on radio and television. Nobody complains about the amount of calls to consumption. The more money the Irish have, the more intent they become on achieving distinction, honor and respect by the pleasures they have had, their great excitements, the beautiful places they have visited, the people they have rubbed shoulders with, their latest purchases, the exotic food they have eaten, the fine whiskeys, wines and beers they have drunk. They travel through the world and daily life hoovering up differences as a means of developing their personal identity.[48] Salvation is gradually moving away from the supernatural other-world of God and saints to an inner world of self-realization and fulfillment.

For centuries in Ireland as elsewhere, time was gauged by the sun and the seasons. This has changed now that the Irish are on the global treadmill of production and consumption. Like the rest of the West the Irish are becoming timed to perfection. The development of modernity is closely linked to the development of the mechanical clock and the precise measurement of time.[49] By the end of the nineteenth century clocks and watches existed among all classes and life in factories, offices, schools and homes had become disciplined by time.[50] A strict sense of time is central to a strict sense of self. We impose time on each other and ourselves. It has become an internalized mechanism of self-control.

What makes Irish people similar to other people in the West is the acute sense of time and the different time zones in which people are operating. Behaving in a timely fashion, or keeping good time, is part of good order and discipline. It allows people to organize their lives more predictably and, therefore, more effectively. It is part of the instrumental, rational organization of life.

The operatives in NEC in Ballivor developed an acute sense of time. Except for Christmas week, the factory operated 24 hours a day, 7 days a week which, for them, meant working 12-hour shifts from 7.00 to 7.00. The management devised a monthly cycle so that operatives would work two weekends a month—one on nights, one on days. The average number of hours an operative worked in a week was just over 40. For example, a typical pattern could be to start on Thursday and Friday on days, be off for the weekend, back in Tuesday and Wednesday nights, off Thursday and Friday, and back in Saturday, Sunday and Monday during the day. During each 12-hour shift, the operatives got two 20-minute and one 40-minute break. There were, however, many small, unofficial breaks, to go to the toilet, smoke a cigarette, and so forth. The problem for management was to maintain efficiency and productivity, particularly when the work was often boring and repetitive. The main instrument for achieving this—resisted to the end by the operatives—was pay-related performance.

Rigorous time-keeping demands disciplined bodies. Operatives had difficulty with eating patterns and lack of sleep. One operative described how at 1.00 or 2.00 a.m. her body would be crying out for sleep, not food. She said that while she needed food for energy, digesting it took more time and made her sleepy which resulted in her not eating enough. There was an over-reliance on sugared water, tea and coffee—one operative admitted to drinking four cans of soda a night.

The measurement of time may have been introduced within the realm of production but it has penetrated into the world of free time, time supposedly outside of the constraints of work-time. And yet, like the rest of the West, Irish people are probably as much stressed and harried trying to get away from their time at work as they try to get to and from their holiday destinations, squeezing in as much time as possible doing all the expected activities, seeing all the necessary sights.[51]

Time has moved from an external to an internal form of self-constraint. It is something that people voluntarily impose on themselves. It has become a badge of status and prestige to be punctual and, at the same time, to complain about the lack of time in a day. There is also the increasing realization that time is money: wasting time is a waste of money. It seems that more Irish people are becoming the same as other busy people, they get frustrated—if not angry—when they are delayed and, generally, when they encounter people who are not the same sophisticated movers through time and space as they are.

BEING IN THE WORLD

As well as a keen sense of time, the Irish have developed a similar way of being in the world. As with the rest of the West, they have become increasingly rational and predictable. We used to be the opposite but that was often because, as with time, we wanted to resist the controlled way of being in the world that was being imposed on us by the English. Now we willingly embrace rational predictable behavior as part of the global habitus. It is central to the trust that makes the world go round.

The increase in the volume and rapidity of global flows of capital, goods, services and people has led to an increase in the number of people around the world who have become dependent on each other, even though they have never met face-to-face. Increased interdependency can only succeed if people become more rational and civilized. Irish people have become self-restrained. They do not spit, belch, fart, puke, pee and shit as openly as they used to or with the same sense of freedom. They are more careful with their bodies. They have become more reflective and sensitive about how bodily functions can cause offence. They have learnt to control their instincts, passions and emotions.[52]

Much of this way of being in the world trickled down from the higher to the lower social orders, from the aristocracy to the bourgeoisie to the working class. Being civilized has become part of the global habitus and is central to attaining all the different forms of capital and social position. What has changed is that instead of different national elites who produced different manners and ways of being in the world, we now have a new global elite who, as Berger suggests, "dress alike and act alike, both at work and at play and, up to a point, think alike ..."[53] How many Irish people already ape the manners and way of being in the world of this global elite?

It used to be that it was only an international class of corporate and governmental people who traveled on airlines, stayed in hotels and ate in restaurants. The explosion of global travel has meant that many people from all levels of social life have experienced being in foreign countries and, through the agency of people who guide tourists, have been externally constrained to conform to these manners. Over time this habitus becomes second nature to them. The self-constraints become more internalized. It is through travel and exposure to strangers and the dependence on interdependency that the codes of behavior of global elites begin to be adapted.[54]

HEAVENLY BODIES

In the last chapter I argued that what made the Irish different was not so much that they had a different language, music and sport, but that the dominance of Catholic practices and beliefs in Irish culture, had given rise to a different sense of self. I emphasized in particular practices of self-denial and self-mortification, of people emptying rather than asserting or fulfilling themselves. These practices, I suggested, dated back to the penitential practices of the early Irish monks. The monks became experts at realizing themselves as individuals—discovering and saving their souls—through their bodies.

Take, for example, Cosrcah Thruaghan. He came from a long line of anchorites who avoided the temptations of the world by retiring from society and living a life of rigid self-mortification. As a means towards this end he lived in a tiny cell or confessional in a monastic community on an island in the middle of Lough Derg on the River Shannon. The cell still exists: it measures approximately 12 feet by 8 feet.[55]

The Irish are still into their bodies but in a different way. Instead of retreating to penitential cells, they go to the gym, sports club, health center, spa and so forth. As Baudrillard declared 40 years ago, "the body has today become an *object of salvation.*"[56] Instead of the body being a means towards salvation—that is, through a renunciation of bodily pleasure— the body has become an end in itself. It is something to be pampered and adored. Brooklodge is a spa hotel and resort in the heart of the Wicklow Mountains. It is one of many that have opened in Ireland in the past 10 years. The Spa Wells in Brooklodge is very different from Thruaghan's cell. The emphasis is on self-indulgence. The Wells has a number of "daily essentials" including massage, waxing treatments, eye care, hand and foot treatments, tanning and cosmetics. It has 8 types of different facials and 14 different body treatments including Aroma Perfect Bust, Aroma Perfect Legs and Aroma Vital Eyes. The facilities include a large ornate swimming pool, mud chambers, aroma baths, a flotation room, Finnish baths, an outdoor hot tub, heated loungers and various Jacuzzis.

Irish people have become the same as the rest of the West in that their struggle for self-realization revolves around an obsession with their bodies and how they are looking and feeling. They have increasingly left aside their shy, awkward, demure, chaste bodies and embraced strong, confident, sexualized, disciplined bodies. They have a new sense of self. They have moved from a Catholic culture based on the principle "Lord, I am not worthy" to a consumer culture based on the self-justification principle "I am worth it". The rigorous discipline and control of the body practiced by Irish monks as a means of eternal salvation has been replaced by a habitus of discipline and control that is oriented towards an inner-worldly salvation of attaining perfect health, beauty and sexuality.

The yoke of shame and guilt about sex and the body has been slowly removed. The fear of being too sexual has been replaced with a fear of not being sexual enough. Religious icons have been replaced with sexual gods and goddesses. As elsewhere in the West, public life is plastered with sex. It is everywhere we look, on our television screens, in our newspapers and magazines, on billboards and advertising hoardings. Like many others in the West, the Irish have accepted the need to be sexual. It has become part of who they are. People see being sexualized as a form of freedom whereas, as Foucault reminded us, it is the most subtle, most penetrative form of discipline and control. If the Irish have become over-productive, over-stimulated consumer capitalists, if they have become efficient and disciplined, it is, more than anything else, related to having become sexualized.

When it comes to sex, what was once hidden, silenced, and discouraged is now openly portrayed, discussed and promoted.[57] There is greater public acceptance of the notion that indulgence in private sexual pleasures is part of the overall right to the pursuit of life, liberty and happiness. What people watch on their televisions, download from the internet, read in books and wear in bed are increasingly seen as being within the realm of permissible personal preferences and private pleasures. The rules on sexual morality are being rewritten. What used to be regarded as major transgressions—premarital sex and pregnancy outside of marriage—are now common-place.[58] In 1980, one in 20 births was outside of marriage, by 2000 this had risen to one in 3.[59]

Results of the first comprehensive survey of Irish sexuality in 2004/5 suggest that when it comes to sexual attitudes and practices, the Irish are rapidly becoming like the rest of the West.[60] The survey by the Economic and Social Research Institute (ESRI) found that among those aged 18–24 years, the average age of first intercourse had dropped to less than 17 years, which is the same as in Britain.[61] Not only are the Irish having sex earlier, younger people are having sex with more partners. Six in 10 men aged 25–34 years had sex with five or more partners. An analysis of partnership patterns over more recent periods and by age group showed that young Irish people have converged with their peers in other countries in terms of numbers of partners.[62] Attitudes have also changed dramatically. In a national survey in 1975, 7 in 10 Catholics (who formed over 90 percent of the population) said that sex outside of marriage was wrong. Thirty years later, the ESRI study found that this had fallen to 6 percent. When asked about one-night stands, only 40 percent said that they were always wrong.[63]

Although the ESRI study tells us a good deal about sexual attitudes and practices, it does not tell us the extent to which sex has become written into the Irish body. It reveals little about the degree to which everyday life and the sense of self have been colonized by an obsession with the body and being sexually attractive. It used to be that Our Lady was a role model for young Irish girls, of how to be pure, chaste and virginal and how to realize oneself through a life of prayer, devotion and self-sacrifice. It used to be that young girls in Ireland were given replicas of young baby infants to play with as children. The dolls helped socialize the young girls into a life of loving and caring for others and of becoming the next generation of Irish mothers. But Our Lady and baby dolls have given way to Barbie.

Barbie exemplifies a very different life to Our Lady and to traditional Irish mothers. She is not pure, chaste, modest and pious. She is a sexed doll. She has to be continually dressed and undressed, brushed and groomed. She is an example of what a sexually successful woman should look like. She has a completely different sense of self.

> Barbie represents the sort of contemporary selfhood some see as embattled and others see as liberated. Hers is a mutable, protean, impression-managing, context-bound self whose demeanour shifts from situation to situation and role to role . . . Her personality is inchoate, even ethereal; her morals and values are more implicit than expressed or affirmed; her intimate life— her dreams, her passions, her abiding attachments—remains a mystery.[64]

Barbie is more than a commodity. She has become an icon, a sign of the value of a highly sexed body.[65] She helps socialize children into the importance of a sexed body as a major form of cultural capital that has global value and that can be traded for other forms of capital across the world. And Barbie is a global phenomenon. By 2002, over 1 billion Barbie dolls had been sold. In 1997, global sales of Barbies peaked at $1.8 billion.

There were few signs of sex in the Ireland in which I grew up. Films should have been a great source, but any instance of semi-nudity—a woman's midriff or bare legs—was a target for the censor.[66] Even to see the word sex was unusual and exciting. Whatever global flow of sex there was in the 1950s, there were few deposits in Ireland. Now, like the rest of the West, the signs of sex are everywhere. Pornography has become one of the facts of Irish life. Accessing pornography on the internet is child's play. Go into the world's best-known web-browser, and confining oneself to pages from Ireland, type in "porn" and immediately there are detailed explicit pictures of everything from group to anal sex with the offer of free full-length videos which do not require either a credit card or email address. It is ironic that in an age where everything can be measured, there is no accurate measurement of how many Irish people visit pornography sites every day.

A study of 302 Dublin students in 2001 found that 94 percent of the male students had accessed pornography, of whom three out of four had used the internet.[67] An international study of pornography claimed that in the five years between 1998 and 2003, there was 1,800 percent increase in the number of pornography-related web pages, from 14 million in 1998 to 260 million in 2003. It claimed that internet pornography accounts for $2.5 billion of the $57 billion worldwide market, that one-quarter of daily search engine requests are for pornographic material and that 20 percent of men access porn at work.[68] However, it must be remembered that obtaining reliable information about internet use is very difficult. Another study of computer domains in 2004 found that there were over 46 million pages of pornography among the top individual country suffixes. The study found that there were some 300 registered sites with porn within the .ie Irish domain giving it a rank of 22nd place out of 41 countries. Germany, the UK and the Netherlands topped the list.[69]

HAPPINESS

The Irish seem to be riding two happy horses, a spiritual religious one and a secular materialist one. The majority believe in God and life after death: to add to the "feel good" factor, the level of belief in heaven is significantly higher than the level of belief in hell. Moreover, unlike many of their European counterparts the Irish put their religious belief into practice. They have one of the highest levels of religious practice in Europe. Sixty percent of Catholics go to Mass at least once a week.[70] Most Irish people would, then, seem to believe in the promise of eternal happiness.

On the other hand, the Irish, as we have seen, have become the same as their Western counterparts in their immersion in the material world, their pursuit of pleasure, quest for excitement, fulfillment of desire, obsession with consuming, and obsession with self. They have moved from being quiet, poor Catholic Church mice embodying a discourse and practice of piety and humility, to becoming busy, productive, self-indulgent rats searching for the next stimulation. They seem to have learnt the trick of rendering unto God the things that belong to God and to Mammon the things that belong to Mammon. The Irish are now evidently much better off, live in lovely houses, have nicer cars, fridges and televisions, faster computers and more holidays for which they work harder, commute more, and suffer more stress. But are they happier?

The pursuit of happiness is obviously a global concern, even though there has always been disagreement over the means to the end.[71] Within the world capitalist system, happiness has become conflated with well-being, particularly health and economic well-being. If people are not healthy and wealthy then they may not be able to consume. Worse still for the system, if people become happy consuming less, there is the threat of economic depression. If people stop believing in the need to earn more to spend more, there is a danger the golden egg of world trade and globalization might become just a thin shell with no yolk to sustain it.

But there is little evidence of any crack in the Irish egg. The majority of Irish people seem satisfied not just with their health and wealth, but life in general. A national survey in 2004 found that 84 percent of respondents said their health was good. A similar proportion (86 percent) felt satisfied with their family/personal life. Seven in 10 were satisfied with their financial situation and 8 in 10 reported being satisfied with life in general.[72] This is not to say that people do not suffer from stress, but the level of stress does not appear to be very high. Less than 1 in 10 of the survey respondents reported feeling stressed "always" or "very often" and less than 1 in 3 mentioned their job as their main source of stress. Eight in 10 (82 percent) were satisfied with their work/life balance—three-quarters actually reported combining their work and family and personal life as easy. A similar proportion (73 percent) said that their commute to work was not stressful.[73]

It may well be, of course, that the Irish have always had strong social bonds which have been associated with a strong sense of identity and which have been the base of a strong sense of well-being. When this mature sense of belonging and emotional well-being became combined with the pleasures and comforts of consumer capitalism, the Irish began to experience the best of both worlds. As we saw in Chapter One, in a worldwide quality of life index in 2005, Ireland easily came out on top.[74]

CONCLUSION

No matter what part of the world one is in, there is a similarity about airports, hotels, banks, shops, restaurants and so forth, a similarity in the design of houses and buildings and, within these, of rooms and offices.[75] There are phones and computers which operate on similar systems. There is a similarity in the way social life is regulated and controlled by states which pass laws that are enforced by police. But perhaps what is most similar about life in different parts of the world is the increased rationalization and homogenization of the practices of everyday life. All over the world, there is a familiar pattern to getting up in the morning, washing, dressing, eating breakfast, preparing for work or education, commuting, operating in an organization, using information technology, traveling home, shopping, cooking, eating, reading, watching television and going to bed. Work and educational life are rounded by weekends and holidays. At a more fundamental level, there is increasing similarity in the meeting and greeting of people, in the way people communicate and talk.

Look into any Irish store, supermarket, shopping mall or town center. Look into any Irish house, bathroom and bedroom. Look at the places where Irish people work, the type of work they do and the way it is done. Look at their general lifestyle and practices of everyday life. Look at their anxieties and concerns about life, the way they read and understand the world and, most important of all, the way in which they see and understand themselves. Irish life has become the same as the rest of the West.

The question then is to what extent does Irish culture produce real significant differences in the way people see and understand themselves and the world in which they live? Ireland used to be the jewel in the crown of the Roman Catholic Church: an island of saints and scholars who valued the beauty of the mind, spirit and soul rather than the self, the body and things of the material world. The Irish still go to church, but have they sold their souls to the shopping malls and cathedrals of consumerism that dominate the urban landscape? Are they lured more by the prospect of excitement and gratification than by the prospect of eternal salvation?

There are no simple answers to these questions. Of course the Irish are the same, but they are also different. However, it would be wrong to think that Irish people and life in Ireland will ever become the same as, for example, life in China or Japan. The state, Irish law, the institutional and organizational structure of Irish civic society, and the type of interest groups will always reflect long-term, inherited, cultural differences. There is a significant difference between going to work in a bog, as many of the people in Ballivor used to do, and going to work in a factory run by a transnational corporation like NEC. However, to coin an old phrase, "you can take the Irish out of the bog, but you cannot take the bog out of the Irish." In other words, inherited customs, habits, dispositions and, generally, ways of being in the world do not die away with structural transformation. There is, as Ogburn identified many years ago, a cultural lag between economic change and the transformation of people's attitudes and values.[76] However, there is mixed evidence as to whether this has caused what Bourdieu refers to as an "hysterisis" effect, a failure of the Irish to adapt their traditional Catholic habitus to the new demands of globalized forms of production and consumption.[77] There has been a homogenization in the modes of production, consumption, urbanization, housing and commuting. The question is how do these coexist with a more traditional, Catholic way of being in the world. To help answer this question, I will now focus on Ballivor and see to what extent this small village has managed to combine economic growth and rapid social change with what *The Economist* referred to as "the preservation of certain cosy elements of the old, such as stable family and community life."[78]

Six

Ballivor is a small village in County Meath. It lies at the edge of the bog that occupies much of the middle of Ireland. However, the village is surrounded on all other sides by good farming land. For most of its life, the village provided a center for the local farming community. It consists of one wide main street about half a mile long which includes three pubs, a couple of churches (one Catholic, one Protestant), a post office, a Credit Union, a mini-supermarket, a petrol station, a butcher, a greengrocer, two hairdressers, a pharmacy, a veterinary supply store, a bookmaker, a hardware shop and a home oil supplier. The local primary school is on the Mullingar Road on the outskirts of the village. The GAA club is on the Kinnegad Road. For most of its twentieth-century life, Ballivor had a population of about 300.

The established villagers talk about Ballivor in relation to other villages such as Raharney, Kildalkey, Killucan and Killyon and to towns such as Trim, Mullingar, Athboy and Kinnegad.[1] It is part of a cognitive mapping process, placing the village and its people in relation to other villages and towns. Villages are a bit like families. To the outsider they all look the same. People do the same things, live the same lives. Yet for the villagers they conjure up a world of fine difference.[2] When the established villagers of Ballivor speak of Kildalkey and Raharney, it is as if they were in another land with different families, histories and ways of being. Differences are often inherited dispositions into which people have been socialized.

M.J. McGearty was born in Ballivor at the beginning of the last century. He grew up on the main street. His father and uncle were both in the Royal Irish Constabulary—the police force that existed prior to the foundation of the Irish state in 1922. M.J. taught in the primary school in Kildalkey for most of his life. He is one of Ballivor's main cultural guardians. He suggested that the perceived differences between the surrounding villages go back to old practices. For example, he told me that when people from Coolronan came to Ballivor for Mass on Sunday they used to arrive in advance of the Mass time and line up on the opposite side of the road.

When established villagers meet each other they are immediately mapped in terms of where they live and of their extended family and its history. Among them, a person's social identity is still primarily his or her family identity. Villages and townlands are identified by the families living in them. Much of the relational difference between villages revolves around *gaelic* football and hurling. The GAA plays a big part in the social life of rural Ireland; this part of Meath is no exception. GAA clubs are based on parishes, and parish schools are the main breeding grounds for new team members. The rivalry between schools and parishes can be intense. And then there is the distinction between these villagers and those who live in the nearby towns and, in particular, those who live in Dublin. Like all small villages near big cities, Ballivor has always lived in the shadow of Dublin. The Greater Dublin Area absorbs one-third of the national population. Although Ballivor was outside that area for most of the twentieth century, the main flows of finance, goods, services, people, knowledge and ideas were to and from Dublin.

Ballivor was on one of the main link roads between Dublin, the Midlands and the West of Ireland.

One of the hubs of Ballivor is the petrol station at the end of the village. It stands at the beginning of the Dublin road. As with petrol stations all over the world, the station in Ballivor has a shop attached to it that sells the essentials for people on the go—newspapers and magazines, soft drinks, sweets, a limited range of grocery products but, most of all, a fast-food, take-out section serving primarily tea, coffee, hot food, sandwiches and rolls. It has become a place where people oriented to the outside world, often Dublin, meet and greet each other.

Dublin is central to understanding the logic of social identity in Ireland. The first great social division in Ireland is between the "Dubs" or "gurriers" (the colloquial terms for those from Dublin) and "culchies" (those from the country). People who have lived most of their life in Dublin will still hold on to their county identity. So they may say, for example, "I am a Meath man but I have been living in Dublin for twenty years." County identity is still very strong and, again, revolves around the GAA. The rivalry between Meath and Dublin in *gaelic* football is legendary.

In the last 10 years, Ballivor has been absorbed into the Greater Dublin Area. The majority of the people come from, commute to, work in, and are oriented to Dublin. In the late 1990s, rapid economic growth, combined with a shortage of housing stock, and a rise in population, resulted in a mushrooming of housing estates around Ballivor. It has become another satellite village with most of the outsiders coming from and being oriented towards Dublin 30 miles away. The established villagers distinguish three types of outsiders. Council people are those from other parts of Meath who, dating back to the 1970s, were placed by Meath County Council in two small housing estates at either end of the

Figure 6.1
Ballivor Village 1974
© Ordnance Survey Ireland/Government of Ireland: Copyright Permit No. MP003207.

Figure 6.2
Ballivor Village 2004
© Ordnance Survey Ireland/Government of Ireland Copyright Permit No. MP003207.

village. The "blow-ins", mainly Dubs, are those who have moved into the large private housing estates that have mushroomed up around the village. The "foreigners" are mainly migrants from Eastern European countries, particularly Poland. The transformation in the population of Ballivor has been dramatic. In 1971, the population of Ballivor was 287. Over the next 25 years, it increased to 383. Between 1996 and 2002 the population doubled to 793. The census results for 2006 are expected to show another doubling of the population in four years. It is this rapid growth in population which has been the main force of social and cultural change in Ballivor. When one looks down on Ballivor, the rapid growth in housing development is easily evident. Aerial photographs show that while Ballivor used to be encompassed by fields, it is now surrounded by housing estates.

Ballivor is, then, the same as many other villages within a 50-mile radius of Dublin. Every weekday morning there is a steady flow of people leaving the housing estates to work in the Greater Dublin Area. It is this colonization of local village life by global cities such as Dublin which effectively is the most substantive connection between the local and the global. When I originally chose to study Ballivor it was because NEC, the Japanese transnational corporation, had established a manufacturing plant there back in the 1970s. I thought it would be interesting to study globalization and, in particular the way the global and the local interacted, by looking at the impact of the arrival of a large transnational corporation on life in a small village.[3] I had an image of local villagers trundling up the main street each day and in through the factory gates, a modern version of a Lowry painting of industrial Manchester. The reality is that besides bringing prosperity to a number of villagers, NEC Ireland had little or no impact on the village. It sat out of on the Mullingar Road like an enormous spaceship. But the flow of people who went in and out of its gates came more from the surrounding 50-mile area than from Ballivor. It was not until the emergence of the Celtic Tiger in the mid-1990s that the structure and social life of Ballivor changed dramatically. Up until 1995, it was like any other village in Ireland. Within 10 years it had become like any other satellite town within commuting distance of a large city.

The story of Ballivor is inextricably linked to Dublin. The city has become an ivy whose tentacles have engulfed the village and, more than NEC Ireland or anything else, has altered its character for ever. As I mentioned previously, I grew up on the outskirts of Dublin surrounded by green fields. We used to walk to Dundrum village which was then 5 miles from the city center. Throughout the 1960s and 1970s, the city slowly encroached on Dundrum. For years the established villagers held out. But they died away and with them the collective memory of Dundrum as a village. Now it boasts of having the largest town center in Ireland.

Like the Irish riding the two horses of religion and materialism, the agents selling houses in the new housing estates try to sell Ballivor both as a traditional quiet village and a satellite town with all the necessary amenities. One agency referred to Ballivor village as providing a country-style atmosphere which it noted was quite hard to find these days. It went on to say that "while recently there have been a number of residential and retail developments constructed both on the Main Street and on the outskirts of the village, they have been completed in a tasteful manner and have added to the attractiveness and vibrancy of the village." Another agency referred to Ballivor as "a quaint country village within commuting distance of the city." It claimed that the village had plenty of facilities with supermarkets and shops but was also within commuting distance of Blanchardstown Shopping Center (on the outskirts of Dublin).

BALLIVOR AS DIFFERENT

From a geographical perspective, what makes the center of the village different is the streetscape and the type of housing. They are quite different from what one finds in villages in the West of Ireland and very different from English villages. It is far from being a picturesque village. Ballivor does not attract many tourists. Most visitors are emigrants returning home for holidays. It seems to have suffered from spasmodic and haphazard development. The original growth of the village is in stark contrast to the rapid, uneven and haphazard development of the housing estates that have grown up around it. What makes the outskirts of Ballivor the same as any other satellite towns around Dublin, is its housing estates.

Ballivor is not a haven of traditional Irish culture. You are far more likely to hear popular music in the pubs than traditional Irish music. There are no occasional, let alone regular, sessions of traditional Irish music. Nor does Ballivor have a thriving Irish-language community. You are more likely to hear an Eastern European language being spoken in Ballivor—often into a mobile phone—than Irish.

What makes Ballivor different from other villages in Western society is what makes it the same as many other villages in Ireland—the vibrancy of the Catholic Church. The majority of the people of Ballivor are practicing Catholics. As mentioned previously, the centrality of this difference is not in the architecture or religious artifacts, but in the habitus and practices and the sense of self that being religious brings to everyday life. Another aspect of Ballivor that makes it different from other villages in Western society is the strength of the GAA. Most of all, however, when one goes beneath the surface, what makes Ballivor different is the nature of the social bonds, the collective memories that have been developed, the accumulated history of interactions between individuals that have given rise to a particular sense of identification and belonging. What makes Ballivor different is the way this local habitus has been maintained and protected and how it manifests itself in everyday life.

Ballivor, then, like Ireland itself, rides two horses. It is a mixture of the old and the new, something between a traditional village and a new satellite town. The established villagers still invest time and effort in maintaining the local habitus. They engage in the gossip and conversations that are central to community survival. They have the knowledge necessary to be able to decipher new information about what has happened to whom, when, where, how and why. They are able to engage in the nuanced game of conversational give and take. They show the necessary deference and reverence, shock, dismay and despair when the latest news is discussed, names mentioned, and events recalled. It is a world to which outsiders do not belong. It is based on a language they do not know how to speak, a habitus into which they have not been socialized, and a form of self-presentation which they cannot easily embody. It is a world into which blow-ins have difficulty gaining access. Villagers who spend time engaging in conversation, who participate in parish life, who are members of the local GAA club, and who help out at community functions and events, accumulate local cultural capital which adds to their position and standing in the community.

For Ballivor village to survive as a community and for people to maintain a sense of identity and belonging, it is necessary that the accumulation of local cultural capital leads to the attainment of other forms of capital. It used to be that being connected locally led to the development of social networks which would enable individuals to accumulate social capital which, in turn, could be used to attain economic capital through hearing of job vacancies or work that needed to be done. For example, many local men and women who first went to work in NEC became important filters and gate-keepers for other local people who wanted to work in the factory. For local cultural capital to remain significant, it is also necessary that Ballivor has its cultural guardians, people who work assiduously at keeping the village, its culture and habitus, alive. Ballivor will remain different from the rest of the West as long as people go to the local Catholic church, participate in the GAA, meet in pubs, take an interest in local history, help organize and attend local events, and so forth. These are the practices central to maintaining a sense of identity, place and belonging.

CULTURAL GUARDIANS

M.J. McGearty is one of the village's principal historians. He has amassed a considerable archive on the history of Ballivor. He is actively involved in the local history society and hopes eventually to complete a history of the village. He is also involved in the parish church and the Community Council. He is treasurer of the local Credit Union. He is the keeper of general knowledge about Ballivor. He learned the history of Ballivor from his family—his mother and aunt taught in the local school. He also learned a good deal as a young man from Mrs. Conway who belonged to one of the best-known—and one of the few Irish-speaking—families in the village. He is at home with the established villagers, being able to place families within the geography and history of the area.

M.J. insists that nothing much changed in Ballivor for most of the twentieth century. The three pubs that were there in the 1950s, the Greyhound, Byrnes (formerly the Harvester) and

McLaughlins, are still there. The first major change in the village was when Bord na Mona (the state body responsible for Irish bogs and the peat industry) developed a scheme of eight houses at the end of the village back in the 1950s. Like the 1980s later, it was a time of large-scale emigration from Ireland.

M.J. talks of former parish priests with great reverence. He sees many of them as having been central to the maintenance and development of the village. The parish priest was the most important person in the locality. Many of them were responsible not only for getting resources for the local primary school but for representing Ballivor at county and national level and, in one instance in the early 1950s, getting a small scheme of houses built. As the main cultural guardian, the parish priest also became involved in the economic development of Ballivor. There was not the same differentiation between social fields as there is now.

Bríd Hiney is another cultural guardian. She was principal of the local primary school until she retired. Now she is an active member of the local historical society. M.J. and Bríd are able to list names of others in the area, many elderly, many dead, who are or were authorities on the local history, people such as M.J.'s sister Maureen, Jimmy Bagnall and Sam Lewis from Portlester, Tommy Kelly from Carnstown, Jimmy Murray from Cloneycavan, Norman Pratt from Scarrifbridge, Pat Clarke from Donore. Again what emerges is the detailed cognitive mapping of people and places. Ballivor is identified by its relations to other villages. The question is how long will it be before this cognitive mapping fades away.

Long before NEC came, the lives of most villagers revolved around cattle and turf. The main street of the village was dominated by cattle being herded to and from the surrounding fields. Jamsie McKeown was the last man to do this. He died about six years ago. He was a bachelor farmer with little

Figure 6.3
Main Street Ballivor 1994
Kind permission of Marie McClake.

Figure 6.4
Main Street Ballivor 2007
Kind permission of Arron Inglis.

income and yet he was well known—nicknamed "Buddy Bear"—and liked for his sharp tongue and wit. He was a man who survived and thrived on local cultural capital, one of the great characters of the village. Up until the 1990s, even when NEC was at its height, Ballivor remained a predominantly rural village. Everyday life was marked by local farmers walking their cows to and from their fields, up and down the main street. It was their space and was part and parcel of living in an Irish country village. By the 1990s, most had given up the practice, but not Jamsie. He was the last to do it on a daily basis, even in the middle of the day.

The established villagers talk about the bog with great reverence. There is an annual Mass held in the bog in August. Bríd Hiney remembers her first year teaching in the school. As soon as the weather got warm, the older children would be gone to work on the bog earning money cutting turf and making a vital contribution to the welfare of the family. The established villagers talk about the 1950s and the time when the state company Bord na Mona began cutting turf on a commercial basis. The company built a small housing complex for workers at the edge of the village, and became a major source of employment for many local people.

The backbone of Ballivor, what keeps it alive as a community, is the local school and the way people come together for sports, special events and meetings of the parents' association. The school is where established villagers meet blow-ins and foreigners on a regular basis. There are also events such as the annual horse show and the activities of small voluntary groups such as the Community Council—which produces a newsletter, "Revolve"—the Active Retirement Group, the Ladies Social Club, the Tidy Towns Committee, Father Murphy's Athletic Club, the local Scout group, and the crèche that NEC helped establish.

However, the most important voluntary association, and the biggest cultural guardian in Ballivor, is the local GAA club. The club has 150 members with about 100 players, 50 non-playing members and about 25 active volunteers. It fields up to 12 teams from Under-8-year-olds up to Juniors, Seniors and Under-21s but with some overlapping between the different teams. The club also has two girl teams. The GAA club is a repository not just of local history but of local difference. Its identity and existence are determined by its relation to other clubs. The main identity of Ballivor GAA club is that it does not have any hurling teams, even though many people in the village play hurling. Meath is mostly known as a football county, but South Meath is renowned as a strong enclave of hurling. But hurling is the traditional preserve of two other village clubs, Killyon and Kildalkey. I was told that as a result of this arrangement, there was a recent Meath senior hurling final in which there were 15 players from Ballivor, 8 on one team and 7 on the other. This is a major issue for the Ballivor club. The accepted tradition of not playing hurling in the club affects its strength. And yet there is a deep reluctance to break the tradition.

To understand Ballivor and its GAA club, it is again necessary to understand a world of fine difference. There is a logic to tradition which defies rational logic. It is difficult to articulate reasons when practice is embedded in unquestioned tradition. It is part of a logic of self-sacrifice, of the necessity for Ballivor to make the sacrifice for Killyon to survive. When I spoke to Andy Feeney, Connie Fitzsimons and Philomena de Lacy, all strongly connected to the club, they recognized that the hurling issue was moving from an unquestioned orthodoxy to one that is increasingly questioned. Similarly, the rivalry between local villages is traditional; it is part of a collective memory that is inherited within the club into which each new generation of players is socialized. And yet, when it comes to the county championship and particularly when Meath is playing its neighbor Dublin, the rivalry between the villages is transcended as they come together to support the county team.

The future of the GAA club looks good. It is confident that it will have extensive new playing fields and a new clubhouse when the Cow Plot (the village common) is developed. The future of the club is probably linked less to the hurling issue than it is to the growing dominance of women and blow-ins and, most controversial of all, the admittance of soccer to be played in the club. Finally, as a mirror of the expansion of the village, the raising of the funds necessary to build a new clubhouse is dependent on its being able to sell off its old grounds for housing development.

NEC IRELAND

Transnational companies are a bit like the cargo cults that developed in islands in the Pacific after the Second World War. The natives on these islands had been living alone in isolation from the rest of the world for centuries when suddenly American forces landed and, of course, brought with them goods and technologies which, for the natives, were out of this world. The Americans were seen as deities. When anthropologists visited these island years later, they discovered that the natives had developed shrines around the cargo that had been left behind. They seemed to be worshiping the machines in the hope perhaps that the American gods would return.

Although NEC Ireland had been established in the village for 25 years before I arrived, I did not really expect to find vibrant examples of creolization when I went there first. Certainly there were no sushi bars. In fact, there wasn't one sign in any part of the village of anything Japanese. I wondered how the villagers and the employees got on with the Japanese. It used to be said that the attempts to colonize Ireland in previous centuries had failed because the colonizers had intermarried with the locals and become more Irish than the Irish themselves. Was this the case with the Japanese in Ballivor? In fact, I never saw a Japanese person in the village— most of the Japanese who came to work in the factory lived outside the area. Even in the factory the small number of Japanese—who were mostly managers or engineers—tended to congregate together in the canteen.

Bertie Cunningham said that the arrival of NEC was "a huge change for a rural village from anything that went before . . . People went from working in *Bord na Mona* [the state-sponsored peat company], from working on farms and working in garages and all that sort of thing . . . to go into this state of the art [factory] . . . Every day it had to be specially cleaned for the microchip." The workers had to wear protective clothing and special slippers. Bertie said, "It was just like walking into the moon."[4] It was indeed another world: it was a different type of space, time and work. But other than some villagers selling their labor and coming out richer, the factory did not impinge on the everyday life of the village.

NEC is one of the biggest electronic companies in the world. It was founded in 1899. By 2006, it had 372 subsidiaries and 69 affiliated companies. It has over 150,000 employees worldwide. Its annual sales to the year ended March 2006 were €32 billion.[5] To put this in perspective, the total Gross National Product for Ireland in 2005 was €136 billion, just four times higher.

There are three segments to NEC's business. The IT Solutions segment provides hardware and software mainly to government agencies and enterprises (43 percent of sales). The Networks Solutions Business concentrates on broadband

and mobile communications (36 percent). The final segment, the Electron Devices Business, provides semiconductors and electronic components mainly to equipment manufacturers (19 percent of sales). NEC Ireland belonged to this final segment. It opened in 1976 and closed 30 years later.

The arrival of NEC in Ireland was part of a worldwide expansion that led it to establish manufacturing companies in America, Europe and Singapore. The NEC representatives who came scouting for sites in Europe were taken by Ballivor. In Japan, NEC had a history of establishing plants in villages rather than on the outskirts of cities. The philosophy was that if the plants became important to the people, you would get good workers who would stay and build an identity with the company and respect it. Moreover, as the former managing director was told, because it was not in an industrialized zone, there was less likelihood that the workers would be polluted by trade unions. When it opened in 1976, NEC manufactured both memory and logic chips. It started off employing 30 people. It peaked in 1998 with 570. By 2002 it was down to 350. It closed in 2006. During its 30-year reign, NEC Ireland was effectively competing against other NEC manufacturing plants.

There were two main ways in which the headquarter company controlled NEC Ireland. First, it controlled capital investment. Any major new investment in equipment had to be approved by the central engineering office in Tokyo. Second, headquarters decided the amount of product to be allocated to NEC Ireland—the product allocation map. That was done on a quarterly basis where all the forecasts were looked at and the amount of product was allocated. Most of NEC Ireland's allocations were for the European market, particularly the motorcar industry. It was up to NEC Ireland to make proposals to headquarters. For example, in 1999, they proposed to move out of memory chip manufacturing and concentrate solely on producing logic chips. The memory chip business was directed to a much larger NEC plant in Scotland. But in 2002 the memory chip market dived and NEC closed the Scottish plant. NEC Ireland breathed a sigh of relief. However, four years later it too was closed down. It was the last of NEC's manufacturing plants in Europe. The simple reason, announced to the workers and the world, was that by moving the manufacturing of the semiconductors to Singapore, Malaysia and China, NEC would reduce its labor costs by 75 percent.[6] The NEC factory stands empty at the end of the village. It is a now a bleak monument to the wealth and prosperity brought by the Japanese. It may not be worshiped, but it seems to be remembered fondly by most of the villagers. However, many of the workers to whom I spoke, had bitter-sweet feelings.

LOCAL CONTROL

As a transnational company, NEC conceded a considerable amount of control to NEC Ireland, the local plant in Ballivor. As Tom Malone, the human resource manager, pointed out to me, in comparison with American companies, there was much less central control in NEC. Indeed what was most unusual for NEC was that for almost half of its time in Ireland, the managing director was an Irishman, Larry Murtagh. NEC Ireland had discretion about who was employed, what they were paid, how performance and efficiency were rated. The key factor was to remain competitive. Tom Malone told me that half of their controllable costs were labor, 30 percent was depreciation and the remainder went on maintenance, consumable items and so forth. He said there were four key performance indicators: cost, on-time delivery, quality and performance.

NEC controlled what happened in Ireland by having Japanese employees in certain key positions. In 2002, there were four senior managers, of whom three were Japanese, eight middle managers, of whom two were Japanese, and eight technical experts, of whom one was Japanese. Malone felt that the loyalty of the Japanese managers was more to the overall corporation rather than to the Irish company. They generally came to Ireland for four years. When I interviewed him, before the factory closed, he saw the circulation of managers as a form of control.

> We had an Irish senior manager and my view is that if we did not have him there, we would not be still in business. . . . The Japanese in Ireland don't have to worry about their jobs, because when they go back [to Japan] they go back to senior management.

Larry Murtagh had worked for the American transnational company General Electric before joining NEC in 1986. He said that there was an enormous contrast in the management style of General Electric and NEC. In the American style there was much more direct control and a system of continually promoting, demoting and firing managers. They would be given two years in charge of a section, assessed, and then move up, down or out. The HQ of General Electric could be on the phone each day whereas NEC operated on the basis of intensive twice-yearly board meetings, but after that they would generally leave the Irish company alone on a day-to-day basis.

Murtagh likened the habitus among American managers to that of a football team. "You were kind of 'rah, rah' you know, make it great for '88 or something like that, that sort of culture you know, very robust culture." The managers seemed to want to develop a collective consciousness and effervescence that was not too dissimilar to the Catholic Church: salvation (or success) was through complete surrender to the corporation. He told me of how once when the directors of General Electric were on a European tour they had come to the Irish plant in Dundalk and had gone out for dinner to the local hotel. At the end of the meal, the cigars were passed round and everyone lit up. But then someone announced that they were Cuban cigars and, to a man, all the cigars were immediately extinguished.

The habitus among the Japanese managers in NEC Ireland was very different. Murtagh described it as much more philosophical, reflective and calmer. He learnt how to play GO, the Japanese board game similar to chess. He said that he and some of the Japanese managers used to go regularly on a Wednesday afternoon to a pub in Trim, the nearby town, and play GO for a few hours.

GLOBAL COMPETITION

As mentioned in the previous chapter, one of the trans-formations that transnational corporations brought with them to Ireland was a dramatic increase in productivity. But for manufacturing plants like Ballivor to survive they had to be able to compete globally which effectively meant having to produce more for less. The main problem for NEC Ireland was always cost. They were good at on-time delivery and customer service. They were okay on quality. But in comparison to other NEC plants, the level of productivity was low for the cost of labor. NEC Ireland was always under threat because in comparison to other factories they were not able to produce more for less. Back in 2002, Tom Malone specifically compared labor costs and productivity with Singapore. In 2006, NEC announced the closure of the Ballivor plant: it was transferring that part of its operation to Singapore, Malaysia and China where they would be able to reduce labor costs for general operatives by 75 percent. The company claimed that although the Ballivor plant had made a profit of €2 million for each of the previous two years, it had accumulated losses of €21 million.

For NEC Ireland to have survived, the workers would have needed to become the same as other NEC workers—to have been able to produce the same output of chips with the same quality in the same time and with the same customer service for the same wages. The name of the global game is continually increasing productivity. When Larry Murtagh was out in Japan, he learned about a new technique of managing workers, Total Production Management, which had been implemented successfully in Toyota, the car manufacturing company, and which was based on using management techniques to increase productivity by making continuous improvements in output through greater teamwork.

Over the intervening years, the Irish management team tried to get the workers to be more productive. Effectively, the workers refused to "become the same." This seems partly to have been a cultural response by the Irish workers: they reached a limit of productivity beyond which they could not go. Despite the job security, wealth and prosperity the company had to offer, the demands of higher productivity seems to have been a step too far. The workers I interviewed agreed that there were wonderful benefits to having a well-paid job. But, as Gerard, one of the operatives, said, the company kept on raising the demands for productivity. "They set a benchmark, a draconian benchmark I might add, that basically is going to be impossible . . . to achieve."

Another cultural dimension was that while many of the local operatives tended to work for and support each other, they did not work together as a team for the company. The operatives I talked to were adamant that people on a shift would look out for and help each other. But the level of genuine teamwork seemed to be confined to certain groups or cliques within shifts who knew each other from outside work through family, school or community connections. Frank was adamant about this: "If you are in my clique and if anything happens to you I take care of you. If you belong to no clique you're on your own and anything that happens to you, you face it on your own." Alec talked about how some operatives would deliberately try to exploit others by putting material through machines before finishing a shift. The incoming shift would have to process this material even though the productivity would be accredited to the previous shift. "You come in and the machine that you need to basically earn your money is working with somebody else's material that they are getting paid for . . . so they will dump on you big time, you have lost four or five hours of your production time carrying on their work."

Most of all there seems to have been a culture of distrust. Operatives admitted that it was a game between them and management: they were trying to get their weekly pay while giving as little as possible of themselves to the job. As Ellen described it:

> They all know by coming here pretty much what they need to do, just to kind of tread water, not to basically attract attention, not to be loping off, but they know that there is a median point and a kind of comfortable zone where they can come in, do their job, produce some material, go home and they just pretty much come in and do the numbers.

Brian insisted that the two biggest problems for people on the floor were lack of trust and lack of communication. He said they had had several meetings with management to discuss how things might be improved: workers would make suggestions, but nothing would be done. He said that at a meeting with a manager the previous week, the workers told him that they were not going to make any more suggestions because nothing ever happened. But it went deeper. "We don't trust them, so when they say something to us we don't know if it's actually true or not. They cried wolf so many times." He said that managers were "caught red-handed saying a non-truth and nothing happened; no heads rolled, nothing got changed."

On the other hand, management also claimed a lack of communication and trust. When I talked to Kenji Yamashiro, the Japanese managing director who took over from Larry Murtagh, he told me that the Irish workers were not the same as the Japanese. In a Japanese plant if a machine broke down—causing a major loss of productivity—the operative would only need to be asked once what happened to find the reason for the human failure. In Ireland, he said it would often take four or five whys. The worker might begin by saying he did not know why. When asked why again, he might say that he was tired. When asked why he was tired, he might say because he did not sleep well. When asked why, he might eventually admit that he had been out late and that he might have drunk too much.

The main reason why the NEC Ireland eventually closed was because workers in Singapore, Malaysia and China were able to produce more for less. Another important reason was lack of investment; without the advantage of latest technology it is difficult to produce more for less. But there is also a cultural explanation. From my interviews with the operatives, it seemed to me that despite the managers' efforts to increase performance and productivity, a habitus had emerged among the operatives as to what constituted a fair day's work for the pay that they were being given. Although productivity was continually monitored and evaluated by management, when it came to day-to-day production, much depended on the relation between the shift supervisor, the union shop stewards and the operatives. However, it would be wrong to think that the operatives were pawns in this process. While there was some movement between shifts, many of the operatives had a history of working on one of the four shifts. Since pay was not performance-related, there was no direct competition between the shifts. The result may have been that overall productivity tended to be defined by the lowest common denominator, by the shift with the lowest level of productivity.

The shift supervisor is the link between factory-floor productivity and management targets. I talked to a number of women operatives from the shift with a reputation for the lowest productivity. There was a very strong social bond between the shift supervisor and the operatives. She had been promoted from among the operatives. She had a good relationship and a strong social bond with many of the operatives, particularly with some of the older women who had been in the factory for nearly 20 years. Three of the women operatives declared that they were the "backbone" of their shift—there were four shifts. The operatives I interviewed said they would be most reluctant to move shifts. As one of them declared, "It would be like moving house." The routine extended to sitting in the same seat at the same table in the canteen. The camaraderie among these women extended to discussing personal problems and having party nights out together. There seemed to be a norm of balancing work and productivity with other interests: "Like the work was always done you still have your laugh and your chat and your cigarette." The central women in this clique had been originally hired through a local social network. The unintended consequence of being located in a small village and then employing local people to be in charge of hiring was that vacancies were often filled through word of mouth within the social network.

The woman at the center of hiring operatives for many years described how she would have known or heard of suitable new workers, and how others had called at her house, and she would get them an interview, and how she had often to go out on a limb to employ them.

> They would come in raw into an interview and you could see, oh my God every time they opened their mouth they were putting a nail in the coffin, and only that I would know the background, know the girls, know what they were made of and kind of overlook that, and 9 times out of 10 would get my way, you know what I'm saying, I'm taking her. I know where she lives. I know what she's made of. It's just the girl hasn't experience of interviews and I would take them on and some of those girls are still in the factory and brilliant operators and have got promotion within the factory.

The new girls were looked after and socialized into the existing work patterns. It seems that many of the more experienced women operatives took over from the women who hired the girls and acted as kind of surrogate mothers until they had integrated into the clique and the shift generally. This clique mixed socially outside of work and had become personally involved in each other's private lives. The management may have been experts at increasing productivity but the women operatives that I talked were equally skilled at using a variety of tactics to prevent their work from becoming too demanding or stressful. There seemed to be particular resentment for supervisors, technicians and engineers who tried to interfere with their work routines. The women knew how to handle such people: "We'd take them down a peg or two and after a while then they'd fit in." In their own words, their shift was known as "a tough crowd," "the rebel shift." They knew how to make life difficult for supervisors who did not fit in, with the result that many supervisors moved on. "We went through a lot of them, [our shift] was kind of a rocky shift for supervisors."

This, then, is another example of glocalization. The global flow of ideas and expert knowledge of techniques for increasing labor performance and efficiency is always operationalized in specific local conditions. The unintended consequence of handing over shopfloor hiring and supervision to local women—combined with an ethos in NEC of developing loyalty and not regularly firing workers—may have been that, over the years, it enabled the operatives to develop tactics that subverted management demands. The global flow of knowledge about worker management and productivity is constantly being adapted by agents to local conditions.

Outside of the particularities of the Ballivor plant, there may have been broader cultural factors at work. Japanese workers may have a sense of self, of being able to announce the truth about themselves, that is different from Irish workers'. The Irish, as we have seen, were for centuries colonized by English. They learnt to be disingenuous when giving responses to those in power, never to reveal themselves fully, never to say exactly what was on their minds. But it may also be that the operatives in NEC Ireland refused to be sucked any further into the grand illusion of the world capitalist system, that there is a balance between living and working and that when it came to the final judgment they decided that they could not increase their productivity by 50 percent: they would not be the same as the NEC operatives in Singapore. It may also be that with the success of the Celtic Tiger and the optimism about work opportunities they felt spoilt for choice and that they would find other jobs in which they did not have to work so hard for so little. They introduced their own informal life–work balance. In talking with the operatives, particularly the women operatives who had been with the company for more than ten years, the economic benefits no longer overcame the emotional and domestic costs of shift work. It may well be that despite the global conditions, the condition of the locals meant that NEC Ireland had come to the end of its line.

LOCAL BENEFITS

When I talked to the operatives we discussed the ordeal of working 12-hour shifts on a rotating basis. I asked them if it was worth it. They were almost unanimous in their agreement. This is how Brian, one of the Nigerians working in the factory, put it:

> I think it's worth it because here in Europe if you are working the sky is the limit. No matter what kind of job you are doing you will be able to go on holidays. You'll be able to arrange the lives of your children, what plans you have for them and what you want them to become in the future, so you'll be able to earmark how much you earn per annum and this gives you the idea of what you can do. If I like a very big car . . . I know sitting there at home I'll not be able to get that. . . . And you find that there are a lot of goodies for you if you are working rather than sitting down doing nothing.

The operatives talked about the benefits that came from having a job, the ability to buy houses and go on foreign holidays. There was agreement that not just Ballivor but the surrounding 20-mile region had all benefited from NEC. Kathleen Byrne worked in the factory from the very beginning. She told me:

> When it started people went into work on bicycles. There was an area for bicycles that had a cover on it but you could see after a year a few got cars, maybe old ones. But give it about seven or eight years there wasn't a bicycle to be seen. People became financially a lot more secure and you could see, the rate of cars becoming newer and newer.

Kathleen told me that at one time there was a local family that had seven members employed in NEC. She said she did very well herself. Without NEC she said she would not have been able to buy the house and car she had and, more importantly, to put two of her three sons through third-level education.

Bríd Hiney emphasized the importance NEC had for local women, particularly married women. She could think of families who were transformed by the mothers being able to go out and work in the factory. Not only did it give them income, it gave them independence, self-confidence and social standing. "They were able to go up, work in the canteen and they had their own money to spend, probably for the first time in their lives and as well as that then, they were pensionable, you know and I think it really improved their standard of living and their happiness."

During its 30 years in Ballivor, it is estimated that NEC contributed €600 million to the local economy.[7] As well as employment and income, the company provided sponsorship for local schemes, most notably the establishment of a créche, the annual horse show, the development of the old Protestant church as a center for the historical society and, back in the 1980s, a scheme which introduced computers into 20 primary schools in the area. Bríd thinks that the changes that have come about in Ballivor have made a positive difference. "I think it has given young people confidence in the way that they meet, they travel a lot now and they meet people from all over the world and you know they meet on equal terms, they have no reason to feel inferior." She talked about how her daughter had just returned from a peace camp in Italy where there were 17 nationalities represented and how she was better able to cope than most because of her ability to speak foreign languages. She thought the days of the Irish feeling inferior had gone and that they had also gone in the village.

> The young people you know, I know some of them err and drink too much and that sort of thing. But only recently I was just looking at a group of them we were out for a drink in McLaughlins. . . . [T]here was about twelve. I think they were going on to a party or something there. The fellows and girls say 17, 18 [years old] all locals and I was just looking at them and thinking how wonderful it was. I mean they were very smartly dressed and they were there, and they were chatting. I mean they could be from anywhere you know.

M.J. McGearty was more skeptical. He looked back to the 1950s with a sense of nostalgia and regret. He remembers a time before television when the church was full, the parish priest dominated village life, there was a *garda* sergeant and four *gardaí* stationed in the village (even though there was little or no crime), there were two postal services a day, two traveling banks and, most of all, when people relied on each other and made their own entertainment—at one stage there were three local drama societies active in the village.

Bríd Hiney, on the other hand, is much more positive and optimistic. She points to the success of the local GAA club, the many annual events organized locally, the success of the Community Council and, most important for her, the increasing integration of blow-ins into the community.

LOCAL COSTS

There is, then, an ambivalence among the established villagers. Many of them have done well from the development of Ballivor through selling land for housing, developing businesses and providing new services. However, for many the familiarity of the village, the sense of belonging and bonding, is disappearing. The influx of blow-ins has transformed the village. In 2006, a local survey of 324 households in the surrounding estates found that there were 534 adults commuting to work from the Ballivor area on a daily basis.[8]

The rapid increase in blow-ins has altered the nature of village life. There used to be a plaque to Bertie Cunningham in McLaughlins pub in the village. He was a member of the Meath team that won the All Ireland championship in 1967. He was voted GAA player of the year. He is a local, county and national hero. Bertie said that when he walks down the main street of Ballivor now, he may as well be walking down O'Connell Street in Dublin: "You'd know nobody, nobody talking. . . . I'm there 67 years, if I walked down it ten times I'd be lucky if out of the ten I'd know three people walking up or down." He felt that while people on the different housing estates knew and were friendly with each other, there was little or no integration. The rapid development of the village has put an excessive strain on the infrastructure. He blamed the county council and said that the village had been destroyed by bad planning that was evident way before the new wave of housing estates. He said that when the council itself developed social housing estates back in the 1970s and 1980s, it never gave any consideration to how the people who moved into these estates would be integrated into village life. The same mistake, he suggested, was now being made with the new private housing estates.

The established villagers maintain a collective memory of what Ballivor once had and what it has lost, through similar stories about the decline in village community life and the way that people don't know each other as intimately anymore. They also tell stories about the rise in theft, vandalism, violence and drugs. It is a classic example of what Elias and Scotson referred to as "blame gossip."[9] This is where stories are told about outsiders that have the consequence, often not intended, of casting them in a bad light. But there were real incidents on which these stories were founded. M.J. McGearty told me about how a ladder had been stolen from the back of the Credit Union one night and how it had been used to cut the telephones in a raid on the supermarket in Kildalkey, the nearby village. The raiders were caught on CCTV cameras. It may not have been a strange or startling event for many other people in many other parts of the world, but for M.J. it was revelatory and upsetting. It was another story that seemed, for him, to characterize the changes in the village.

I was told many stories about incidents concerning drugs. As in all village stories there is an element of myth and scapegoating as well as an element of truth. Nevertheless there is little doubt that many of the established villagers see that among the blow-ins that came from Dublin in the late 1990s, there were one or two individuals who introduced drugs and who, through drug dealing, brought a type of crime and violence that was unheard of previously. There were stories of houses being used for buying and selling drugs. For a couple of years the village was beset by regular outbreaks of violence, of fights in pubs and arrests.

There was a dramatic increase in fear and anxiety. Another story was that a bartender in one of the local pubs refused a young man drink and when she got home later that night she found her car had been burnt out in her driveway. The same night, an elderly woman who lived alone out on the Mullingar Road had the gates to her house rammed—which she already had padlocked out of fear—her car stolen and taken out to the bog where it too was burnt out. She had just had the tall trees surrounding her house cut down because a gang of youths were using them to gather under. I was told about "marauding gangs" of youths—wearing hooded sweatshirts to avoid recognition–parading around the town with dogs. "They used dogs as their protection and I mean I'm not talking about poodles, we are talking about vicious animals so that they became people that weren't easily approached." Ballivor developed a reputation throughout the county for being over-run with drugs. There was a front-page story in the *Meath Chronicle* claiming that drugs flooded the village. The local *gardaí* were having difficulty coping. A meeting of the Community Council was called to discuss the problem. The following Saturday night after Mass, one of the ringleaders of the gang was standing on the footpath on the opposite side of the road wearing a hooded sweatshirt, and with two large dogs on either side of him.

CREOLIZATION

Creolization involves the coming together of local, national and global cultural strands to form a new, ever-evolving, cultural fabric. One of the main centers of creolization in Ballivor is the local post office. This is where the local meets the global, and where established villagers meet blow-ins.

The post office has traditionally been at the center of village life in Ireland, its postmistress or postmaster the main conduit of local stories, gossip and information. It was the place where people came to make contact with the outside world, either sending or receiving letters and parcels. In the past, the post office was also the local telephone exchange.

Like many others around the country, the post office in Ballivor is at the back of a shop. But what is unusual is that as well as selling newspapers, magazines, greeting cards and stationery the shop also includes a continental café that sells expressos, cappuccinos, lattes as well as paninis, wraps and baps. The post office is owned and run by Brendan Bagnall. Brendan is a cultural entrepreneur. He grew up in the village—his mother was the local postmistress—went to America for 10 years during the depression in the 1980s and then came back home. As well as running the café, shop and post office, Brendan runs a small security company. He lives in Dublin and commutes to Ballivor.

I talked with Brendan one Monday morning at the beginning of September. The card rack was filled with back-to-school cards—in the world of consumer capitalism there is a card to mark every possible occasion. The bold headline on the front of the local *Weekender* read "Cocaine 'Epidemic' sweeps Meath."

Brendan may not live in the village but he knows the established villagers and is able to meet and greet, swap and receive information. He has a cognitive map of the established villagers and all the roads around the village and he is able to put them all in their proper place. That morning a woman came in with the news that one of the well-known local women had died. She told Brendan about the funeral arrangements. Immediately Brendan began to enquire about the rest of the family. He told me that being able to know who has died is crucial in case relatives or friends of the dead woman come into the post office later that day. But he said that the days of the post office being a local conduit for information are quickly dying off. He told me that there are over 600 houses in Ballivor and that with an average of 2.5 householders the population of the village would be nearly 1,500, but that of these the established villagers would only be 400. He pointed out that the established villagers only come to use the post office. They rarely buy anything in the shop and they never stop to have a tea or coffee. He is dependent on the blow-ins from Dublin for that part of his business. It is difficult to get the established villagers like his father to break old habits.

> I'd know from my own parents that, like my father, would come up you know to get the newspaper here every morning. And he lives three miles out of town, and he would leave the keys in his jeep parked in the middle of the road. You know what I mean? And come in and he'd buy the newspaper. That's all he would do. That's all he would have been used to doing. But he would not sit down and talk to me for five minutes over a cup of coffee because he's never done that.

The blow-ins have been central to Brendan's economic prosperity and to the prosperity of many other traders. He has done well from the increase in customers. But he recognized that the price of prosperity is an increase in risk and fear. He suggested that this sense of risk and fear may have been unwittingly brought in by the blow-ins. For example, it is they and not the established villagers who take their keys and lock their cars before coming into the post office. Bertie Cunningham felt that the village which he had grown to know and love so well, in which he was once a cultural king, was disappearing before his eyes. He is adamant that bad planning has been exacerbated by two factors. People do not go to the pub as much as they used to. He said the price of drink in pubs has led to what he called "six pack friends" who buy beer from the off-licence and go back to each other's houses. The other problem is that even when they do go out, the established villagers and the blow-ins tend to socialize in different pubs.

As we saw, the notion of Ballivor being a village is central to the way in which local estate agents try to sell their houses. Coming to live in a village conjures up images of a slow traditional unchanging form of life, where people know and have time for each other, where there are strong social bonds and a real sense of belonging. The reality can often be very different. This was what one young mother wrote when describing her life in Ballivor in an on-line discussion group.

> I wish i could be nearer to people i know as well . . . im in a small village called Ballivor its just outside of Trim . . . but have no transport yet so am very isolated out here and people seem to keep themselves to themselves around here, there is no mother and baby group here so its hard to meet others around . . . and to make matters worse we had a attempted breakin on monday night 3 local lads we think it was . . . its just a scary thing and finding it hard to sleep at the moment as you would guess . . .[10]

GLOBAL MEDIA, LOCAL GOSSIP

Another major site of creolization is the local pub. I was in McLaughlins one very wet August day. It was lunchtime. There was a handful of customers. They were being looked after by Tina, a confident young woman. Two of the customers seemed to be an English couple who had come back on holiday. There were five local men stretched out along the small bar. At the end of the bar, above the customers, the television was on and switched to the MTV channel. A woman who looked very like Madonna was offering her body to the viewer as she spurned the attractions of dozens of vibrant young men.

Two of the men at the bar were deep in conversation about the forthcoming GAA All Ireland final between counties Mayo and Fermanagh. Meath had one of the best records in the All Ireland championships in the past 30 years, although it had not done so well in recent years. In rural Ireland, especially among men and especially in pubs, being able to talk about *gaelic* football and hurling, being able to make good comments about matches and players, is part and parcel of making conversation, of being accepted and respected.

Being accepted and respected is also related to being educated, knowledgeable and informed, to knowing what is happening in the world whether it is local or global. This cultural capital can come from being well read, having some specialized knowledge, or simply being informed about what is going on in the world through the media or contact with people. As the two men were talking about the forthcoming GAA match, the two men beside them were talking to each other, and trying to engage the visiting English couple into conversation. One of the men referred to the dreadful weather and the flooding that had taken place in England the previous day. There had been dramatic pictures on television showing cars and trees being swept down the main street of a village in Cornwall. The English couple responded by referring to the hurricane that had hit Florida over the weekend. One of the local men said that he had heard that there was a possibility of New York being completely flooded. The Englishman said that this would be caused by a volcano occurring on one of the Canary Islands that would cause a big wave to build up across the Atlantic that would eventually crash onto the east coast of America. At the bar, one of the local men replied: "Oh sure, the way the world is going with wars and killing." His counter colleague continued: "It's terrible what is going on in Iraq."

The conversation became drowned with the arrival of two local men who had returned having gone out to smoke. Meanwhile there had been a switch in the conversation. The Englishwoman announced: "Dublin is full of foreigners. It's the same as London. When you are in Dublin you wouldn't think you're in Ireland. It's nicer here." Maybe this was picked up by the local men, maybe not. But there was a silence before one of the local men said: "Father Kenny died yesterday. He must have been nearly a hundred." The other man said: "A nice decent man." His friend replied: "He was a very nice man, that has to be said." It had been some years since Father Kenny had been in the parish having being promoted to Trim where he retired, eventually spending his days in a nursing home in Mullingar.

Then one of the local men turned to the Englishman. "How is the work over there in Birmingham and those places? I was in London, in Tottenham, for twelve years." There is a history of working-class men from places like Ballivor going over to work in building sites and factories in Britain. I could not hear the reply, but his friend intervened. "How long the Celtic Tiger will last, I don't know. I think it has escaped and won't be caught." His friend picked up the running on this and responded: "I don't know where the money is coming from. But it is a lot better than it was."

The Englishman said that he worked in property maintenance and that business is good. He was born in Edenderry (a small town in County Kildare), but he was brought up in London. His wife worked as a carer, looking after elderly people. One of the local men asked her how old she thought he was. She guessed 65 years. He told her that he was 61. He said that he used to go to the cattle market and that he knew a good deal about it, but he had retired now. The Englishwoman said that she thought you had to be 65 to retire. He told her that he had to give it up because of bad health.

The conversation took a turn towards Madonna. The Englishwoman asked, in a teasing manner, if the local men were going to her concert to be held in nearby Slane Castle at the end of the month. One man said no but that he believed the tickets were 100 euro each. The barmaid corrected him: "They're 88 euro." He said that the concert was being held on Sunday rather than Saturday. The barmaid told him that Saturday is Madonna's holy day.

The reason for choosing this incident is that in the same way that an analysis of one small village like Ballivor can help illuminate the way the local and the global mix, so, within Ballivor, there are small incidents that become vital clues into the way this mix takes place in everyday life. It is the way those involved easily and skillfully moved back and forth between the local and the global. The global MTV channel provided the stimulating, sexualized backdrop while the locals were deep in conversation about a recent football match. The locals tried to engage the tourists. They helped the visitors feel at home by making a connection with the weather outside and the weather in England. It was when the conversation was extended to global weather and the possibility of New York being flooded that the cosmopolitan knowledge of the visitors came to the fore. The downpour outside the pub was put within the context of bad weather around the world. The locals tried to save face by making a connection between the bad state of the weather and the bad state of the world generally. It is possible (doubtful, however) that in the sophisticated game of making conversation, the reference to the war in Iraq—given the British involvement—was a conscious rebuttal to the put-down about the ignorance of how New York could be flooded.

The Englishwoman switched the conversation back to global sameness and how nice it was to encounter local difference in Ballivor. Again, regardless of how deliberate it was, the local men went deep into the local with talk about the death of the former parish priest. This is conversational territory from which the visitors were necessarily excluded. But balance was restored and the visitors brought back in by one of the local men putting himself in an English context and asking how good life was there now. The reference to the frail nature of the Celtic Tiger economy not only introduced humor to heal any awkwardness but can also be seen as a form of self-deprecation—Irish economic might is nothing compared to that of the English.

The revelation that the Englishman was in fact Irish changed the direction of the conversation which immediately became personal. The conversation moved almost seamlessly from the global, to the international, to the local, and then to the personal. In order perhaps to overcome the embarrassment about the local man's age, the Englishwoman jokingly switched the conversation back to Madonna. This time it was the cosmopolitan cultural capital of the barmaid which came to the fore when she said that Madonna's religious beliefs prevent her from playing concerts on a Saturday.

When I mentioned this incident to Bríd Hiney she thought it was an indication of how globalization, particularly the arrival of the world into Ballivor through the media, had made cosmopolitans out of locals and, as a consequence, had made locals more socially equal to their Dublin counterparts. It used to be, she said, that when "Johnny" from Ballivor met someone from Dublin "the Dublin fellow sneered at him because he was talking about the spuds and the sticks maybe and that sort of thing you know, now Johnny from Ballivor meets your guy from Dublin and they discuss the floods in England and they discuss the hurricane in Florida."

BEING CATHOLIC

If one takes a long-term historical perspective, then, as in Ireland generally, the greatest cultural influence in Ballivor, is the Catholic Church. If one thinks of the Church as a transnational institution then with over 1 billion members and thousands of branches in countries all over the world, it easily outshines the influence of a corporation such as NEC. And, as in the rest of the country, there are outward signs that the people of Ballivor are still good Catholics. Attendance at Mass is good. The children in the local primary school are raised in the ethos, beliefs and practices of the Church. The parish priest may no longer have the same power and influence as his predecessors, but when I asked M.J. McGearty and Bríd Hiney who people would to go to if they were going to organize a local event, they both immediately said that Father Devine would have to be involved. Father Devine more than anyone else is at the center of local creolization, of bringing together the established villagers, the blow-ins and foreigners. Not only do they all come together in the local church for services but they participate in the many parish activities he organizes. And, of course, he is linked with the school, the other main center of social integration. But one wonders if Father Devine and with him the Catholic Church generally have as much influence in the way people see and understand themselves in Ballivor as was the case 20 or 30 years ago.

What is happening in Ballivor reflects what is happening to the Church generally in Ireland. The country has got rich, but the Church has not. The spiritual and moral influence of the

Church has declined enormously. This is most reflected in the decline in vocations. Forty years ago, an annual average of about 1,500 men and women joined the Church to become priests, nuns and brothers. Now it is less than 100.[11] And while the diocesan clergy have not fared as badly as religious orders, their numbers have declined enormously. When it comes to religious personnel, the Catholic Church in Ireland is not only getting old, it is dying off. And so when Father Devine took over as parish priest in Ballivor, he also had to take on the parish of Kildalkey. There are no longer enough priests to go around. The rapid rise in the population of Ballivor has not led to a rapid rise in the position and influence of the Church. What is happening to the Church in Ballivor is a bit like global culture. It now spreads over a far greater number of people but its influence is shallow. One suspects that as in the rest of the country, while the people still strongly identify with the Church, while they are happy to raise their children and send them to a Catholic school, and while they use the Church to celebrate rites of passage, they have become more consumed with themselves and working, commuting, shopping, being entertained and fulfilling their pleasures and desires. The Church is still the main cultural guardian in Ireland, particularly in terms of its influence over family and education, and yet, as we shall see below with the schoolchildren in Ballivor, its influence in family and everyday life seems largely absent.

One of the characteristics that drives global capitalism is the need for continual transformation. This is the catalyst behind economic growth. It is reflected in consumer society and it is reflected in the imperative for continual self-transformation. The *doxa*, or uncontested orthodoxy, of modernity is that things have to continually improve and this manifests in individuals in terms of transformation and improvement. In such circumstances one might expect that the Catholic Church would be a rock of stability and sameness. However, the Church too has to move with the times and this is reflected not just in transformations such as Vatican II, but in local responses to secularization. To bring people back into the Church, there is a need to do things differently; the Church should reach out to them and introduce fresh rituals that bring people together.

In the interregnum between Father Mollin's, retiring and Father Devine's taking over, Father Murphy acted as parish priest. In the Philippines, he had recognized the need to incorporate local traditions and customs into the mainstream rituals of the Church. Consequently, when he took over he introduced two new events: An annual outdoor Mass at the Mass Rock outside the village and, more daringly, a celebration of midsummer's night, out at the small landscaped copse at the end of the village on the Mullingar Road; about 80 to 100 people came.

Midsummer is a pagan tradition celebrating the importance of fire and light. I went along, fascinated to find out how global Catholic culture would be mixed in with local pagan customs. There were no overt Catholic or Christian symbols at the copse. Father Murphy began the celebration without introducing himself and without any traditional Catholic invocation. He talked about light and how our ancestors had always gathered together on the night of the longest day and how they had lit bonfires. These bonfires were lit in response to the main bonfire which was lit at the Hill of Tara, the sacred center of ancient Ireland which is in another part of the county. Father Murphy went on to explain how this was a celebration of the energy and light of the universe, a light and an energy that are within each one of us. The fire, he said, is a celebration of light, the summer season. The hearth fire has always been at the center of Irish homes. It was the center of family and social life. It was the place where strangers were welcome to come and take a seat. It is a reminder to us of the importance of sharing light and fire and welcoming strangers into our lives. He talked about the universal importance of fire and light, and about how the embers from the fire lit on midsummer's night were used to bless the home.

CHILD'S PLAY

As we have seen, global media easily penetrate into the heart of everyday life in Ballivor. The media provide a crucial knowledge and interpretation of what is going on in the world, a type of ontological security. And yet, at the same time, villagers are able to work their way around the media and mix its messages with local knowledge and information. But I was also interested in how the media has affected villagers, sense of self, belonging and identity.[12] To examine this, and to understand the way the global flow of culture mixed with local and national flows, I thought it would be revealing to look at the younger generation in Ballivor as they might be expected to be more exposed to popular western culture through television, popular music, computer games and magazines. In 2005, I was fortunate enough to persuade Willie Keegan, the principal of Ballivor Primary School, to allow me to meet with the sixth year class and their teacher Eunan Cassidy.

I asked the pupils who were mostly aged between 11 and 13 to write a short essay for about 30 minutes on "My World." I told them that this should be about themselves. It should be a short description of their everyday life and the world in which they lived. When this was finished I asked them to complete a short two-page questionnaire which dealt mainly with their lifestyle and hobbies, their favorite television programs, films, games, magazines, sports, food and so forth, the people they admired, the countries they had been to. The last two questions asked them if they considered themselves similar to or different from other Irish people, other people in Europe, and other people in the world. The final question asked them to name three things that they thought made Irish people different. There were 28 children in the class that day and I am very grateful for their participation. I have changed their names to protect their anonymity.

Most of the essays filled about three-quarters of a hand-written page. Most of the children interpreted "my world" as their everyday life and wrote about what they did each day or week. The lives of the children seemed to revolve around sport, entertainment, family and school life. I decided to pick one essay randomly to provide an overall sense of what the essays were like.

In my world I love horse riding, football, hurling, and swimming and nearly any other sports I play. In hurling I play for Killyon and in football I play for Ballivor. There is no hurling in Ballivor. I also love horse riding because I think it is very fun.

I like to eat in Fureys, the restaurant because their speciality is steaks and I love steaks because I love the flavour of them. On my Conformation [*sic*] we went to Fureys. I had soup for starters, steak and chips for main course and apple crumble for dessert. It was one of the nicest meals I ever had.

I like going off to shows because I really like the excitement.

My favourite film is *Hotel Rwanda*, it is sad in the middle of the film but it is happy in the end. My favourite programme is *Scrubs* because it is really funny.

What immediately comes across is how John sees his world in

terms of his immediate daily life, lived in the locality. Some of his lifestyle practices and personal tastes are synonymous with Western culture—eating out, going to shows, having a favorite film and television program—but his roots are local. What is most evident is his self-centeredness, his knowledge about what gives him pleasure and, most of all, his ability to announce all of this with such self-confidence. He vigorously pursues pleasures. He loves sport and engages in an eclectic mix. He seems to see himself primarily in terms of the different sports he plays. He shows a cosmopolitan sophistication not only by eating out but being able to announce his favorite restaurant and meal. John could be said to be a typical child of Western culture. He has been socialized into knowing what he likes. He has definite consumer preferences. He has a strong, definite sense of self. In the questionnaire John completed, he demonstrated more of his cosmopolitan cultural capital by saying that he had been to Austria, France and Spain. The people he most admires are all sportsmen. Two of them, Thierry Henry and Patrick Viera, are French and play soccer for the English club Arsenal. But the other person he most admires is Graham Geraghty, a well-known Meath county footballer. And, as always in the way the global mixes with the local, there is an anomaly. His favorite film is not some Hollywood blockbuster but rather a sophisticated story from modern Africa. Overall, of the 81 people the children most admired, 35 were from the world of sport. But what the essays and questionnaires revealed was how easily the local and global mix when it comes to sport.[13]

There was a pervasive preference and passion for playing *gaelic* football and hurling. When it comes to a sense of place, belonging and identity, these seem to be confirmed through physical engagement in the concrete, particular local sports. Take Keith:

We are in the play offs for the under 12 semi-finals against
Curragha. The last time we played them I was the captain and
we beat them. I play full-back because I am tall. Frank S
sometimes plays beside me. The other times Josh R plays there.
We have a very good back line. The forward line is excellent. We
have a big train in at full forward, his name is J.J. He scored over
four goals and eight points. I wouldn't want to get in his way.
Then we have a goal keeper, his name is Shane. He is always
eating sweets in the goal mouth. I think he is very good because
he is there when you want him to be. Today we have a match
and two serious weapons, one boy is as small as anything but
still stands tall. The other weapon is a girl who is very good at
football.

Keith may watch and engage in global media, but there is a
very strong sense of local identity from his essay. We get
another good insight from him into the importance of the
local in the lives of the children. Two other children mentioned this crucial semi-final match in their descriptions of
their world. The number of children who mentioned playing
soccer was quite small, particularly in comparison to the
number who watched it on television, or mentioned English
soccer clubs as their favorite team, and English soccer players
as among the people they most admired. But, again, it is the
easy way in which the local mixes with the global which is
most revealing. John put it simply: "For dinner I have spuds
and veg. and ham. Then I would go training for football and
hurling. In the Scottish league I support Celtic, and in the
Premier I support Arsenal and that's my life."

What was also interesting was the way in which these
children seemed to move seamlessly from playing local sports
to global computer games. This is how Ronnie described his
world:

In my world I like to play hurling on Saturday and Sunday all day. I like to watch The Simpsons on TV every evening that I can. I like playing San Andreas on the playstation as well as Need for Speed and Fifa 2005. My favourite hobbies are hurling and football. I like to play soccer with my friends in school I play football for Ballivor and I play hurling for Killyon.

The essays revealed how much the lives of the children center on family, community and school. There is a feeling that in many respects life for these children has not changed significantly from what their parents did at their age. It revolves around regular journeys: to school and back, to go to sports, to play, to meet friends, to go shopping. Everyday life is based on simple regular forms and routines. Many of the children wrote about what they did each day. For example, Carol wrote:

My favourite thing to do on a Monday is to see my friends after the weekend. On Tuesday is Tae kwon do. On Wednesday I go shopping. On Thursday I do Tae kwon do. On Friday I go to scouts. On Saturday I do horse-riding and Sunday I go swimming and spend time with my family. Ballivor is a great village. My favourite football team is Manchester United.

Again there seems to be a seamless mix between going over to a neighbor's house to help him out, coming home and helping at home and then playing computer games and listening to music. This is how Ollie describes part of his world:

After I help with his [a neighbor's] work I go to my house and then help my mother with the twin baby girls (Kate and Grace are their names). I then play my X box for an hour. Games such as Fifa

2005, Fifa Street, Ima manager 2005, Manchester United and others [difficult to decipher handwriting]. After that I go outside to play with my friends (Lee Doyle and Eoin Leech). That was my average day. I like to listen to all sorts of music such as hip hop (Exhibit, Nas, Twista, 2pac) dance music and rock, heavy metal, pop and others.

Television is a major dimension in the children's lives. Twenty-one of them mentioned watching television or watching a favorite program in their essays. Most of what they watch comes from global sources.[14] *The Simpsons* was undoubtedly the children's favorite program; 15 of them listed it in their questionnaires. Indeed when it came to declaring their favorite programs, national or home-made ones hardly got mentioned. Only 4 such programs were listed compared to 78 non-national programs. Similarly, when it came to films, the vast majority (54) mentioned Hollywood or British movies, while only 4 Irish films were mentioned. In terms of favorite singers and groups, 49 non-national ones were mentioned compared to only 3 national ones—11 of the 28 children said Eminem was their favorite singer.

When it came to travel it would appear that the children were quite cosmopolitan. Between them they had been to 14 different countries. The most frequently mentioned were England, Spain and France. But there was a division between the pupils. While 11 of the pupils said they had been to at least 3 countries, there were 7 children who not been outside Ireland and another 7 who had only been abroad once.

It is also important that however much global lifestyle, media messages and markets penetrate the minds and bodies of these young people, the daily concerns of their lives, what consumes them most perhaps, tended to be local and personal. Three of the children mentioned personal health problems, one of them had a serious heart ailment. Another three indicated that their parents had split up.

On the other hand, perhaps one of the main indicators of how much Ireland has changed and of the penetration of global cultural flows, was the absence of references to religion. Only one of the pupils mentioned religion—she said how she liked to go to Mass on Sundays. And in their questionnaires, when it came to describing what makes the Irish different, two people mentioned "different religion." But there was no indication from the essays or the questionnaires of religion playing any significant role in these children's lives.

There was, however, a concern for health and the environment. Ciara said that "today in the world there is lots of wars going on which I would like to stop because lots of people are dying for no reason. . . . In the world there is racism and killing which I would love to stop forever." Darina did not like the way some people go on picnics and "throw all their rubbish on the ground and then when you go there, there is a lot of rubbish around you." This concern was echoed by Katherine who complained about the litter people throw into rivers and on the ground. Liam said that one of the things he didn't like about his world was graffiti and pollution. Finally, Danny was concerned about smoking and drinking and while he was most concerned about how they would interfere with his own enjoyment of sport, he had a word of warning for others: "If you drink that will slow you down and if you smoke that will stop you from playing altogether. So a little word of advice do not smoke or drink."

In general, then, the children provide a good insight into how local, national and global flows of culture mix together in their daily lives. The essays and questionnaires reveal how the children move easily from playing *gaelic* football, hurling and camogie to playing computer games, how they consume a diet of global and national media, and how the people they admire could just as easily be local footballers as international soccer stars. In many respects, what the essays reveal, what we have come to see, is what many would regard as the obvious, unquestioned normalcy of contemporary childhood. They come across as bright young people who have been gently and subtly socialized into becoming consumers. They have also become very self-confident. As Cora, one of the children, described herself: "I am one of those people who don't care about what people think about me. People think I am a real outgoing person and are always saying how they would like to have all the courage I have."

These children are a mirror of the village and Irish culture. Very few of them mentioned the school as part of their world and none of them said anything about education and learning being central to their understanding of themselves and the world in which they live. The overwhelming feeling was that their identity and sense of self were rooted in family and community, particularly through sport, and that this sense of identity was easily mixed with global lifestyle and consumer choices primarily through the media. What the essays also reveal is how, perhaps like many other children all over the world, they are self-consumed. They come across as very rooted in the routines of everyday life. They mix the local—family, school and sport—with the consumption of global media and entertainment. They mix local stars and heroes with global ones. And yet there is something that seems to preside in its absence from the essays. There was no evidence of real poverty. The pupils in their essays and demeanor came across as happy, self-confident young boys and girls. And yet, even within this one small class, there was evidence of status if not social class divisions. In particular there was a division between the young well-to-do cosmopolitans who ate out regularly and who had been away on holidays and those who rarely went out and had never been abroad.

The primary school in Ballivor is bursting at the seams. The sudden and dramatic growth in blow-ins and foreigners has put an enormous strain on its resources. It will soon move to a new and bigger premise across the road. The school is no longer the enclave of established villagers. There are children from Nigeria and Eastern Europe as well as Dublin. The school principal, Willie Keegan, has to fly the Dublin as well as the Meath flag outside the school during the All Ireland football championships. But what will make it more difficult for Ballivor to maintain its difference will be the demise of local cultural guardians and its inability to produce people like M.J. McGearty. Children will not grow up in families in which there are stories about Ballivor and its history. Children will not go to school and be taught by people who grew up in the village. M.J. McGearty has the history of Ballivor in his hands but there is nobody to whom he can pass on the baton.

CONCLUSION

Like the rest of Irish society, Ballivor seems to be riding two horses, one of Catholic and the other of consumer capitalism. On the one hand it has been opened up through globalization, first directly through the arrival of NEC Ireland and then indirectly through the emergence of Dublin as another global city. On the other hand, it is struggling to maintain its traditional village culture. Whereas NEC had little impact on everyday life in the village—other than to increase the overall standard of living in the area—the development of extensive new housing estates—which also brought prosperity—has led to blow-ins outnumbering established villagers. What was once a small, sleepy village has, quite suddenly, been absorbed into the commuter belt of Dublin. The experience of Ballivor is little different from the many other villages in the surrounding counties of Dublin. The price of houses in Dublin has driven house-buyers further and further away from the city. The story of globalized Ireland is witnessed in the hundreds of villagers streaming out of the village in the early hours of the morning on their way to work in Dublin. They are caught in no man's land between Ballivor, the small corner of County Meath in which they live, and the greater Dublin area in which they work. It is a story of Ireland that is being acted out in hundreds of other villages across the east of Ireland.

There is, of course, nostalgia about the village life that the established villagers see disappearing before their eyes. There are still those whose sense of being in the world is firmly rooted in the village, they form a collective chain of memory that is able to link people to time and place. That world of fine difference between people, families, townlands and villages is being eroded. The local guardians of culture still stand proud against the tide of globalization that is sweeping through the village, but it seems that Ballivor has changed for ever. It is a tide that, generally, seems to have lifted most boats. Although the established villagers may talk with nostalgia about the bog, the cattle and the characters of the village, most of them remember the bad old days when people were forced to emigrate. Few want to return to those days. Globalization has brought many other cultural changes to Ballivor, most notably an influx of blow-ins. They will undoubtedly be a major part of the future of Ballivor as will foreigners. The established villagers are still an elite, but already there are signs of blow-ins beginning to make their mark in the village, particularly in the school and the local GAA club.

There seems to be an air of inevitability about the changes that are taking place in Ballivor. Established villagers, blow-ins and foreigners have gathered together in conditions not so much of their own choosing but that are the outcomes of global flows that have transformed Ireland's economy and society. It may not be possible or desirable to stand against the tide. If people want well-paid jobs, big comfortable houses, sleek new cars, the latest technologies, and regular holidays, if they want to fulfill their fantasies, pleasures and desires, then there is a price to be paid.

I began this book with a description of my parents and how deeply immersed they were in a Catholic habitus which disabled them emotionally and sexually. I was brought up in an ethical regime that emerged from a culture of death and self-sacrifice. There were crucifixes everywhere to remind us of Christ's suffering and death. The body was a source of awkwardness, guilt, shame and embarrassment. It was something to be hidden rather than admired and adorned. It was a society of guilt, secrecy, darkness and oppression. To have "bad" (read sexual) thoughts was a sin. To take pleasure in them was a mortal sin. Being concerned with oneself, particularly one's body, looks and beauty, was seen as the path to self-obsession. It was not just vain, it was profane. To look sexually attractive, to be erotic, to be sexually stimulated, to gaze at another longingly, were all seen as sinful. It was a deeply repressive society in which the sexually disobedient and deviant were humiliated, demoralized and often incarcerated. All of this led to peculiar sentimental relationships. There was love in my family, but it seemed to mirror the form of love that one would find in a seminary or convent. It was perhaps not unexpected that in such a habitus, Catholic parents like mine would have difficulty touching and hugging.

If the bonds that bind human groups are too strong they inhibit the development of individual difference. They inhibit members from talking about themselves, about their different tastes, preferences, orientations and desires. If a group systematically demands surrender and sacrifice of the individual for the greater cause of the group, then the group stymies its own development. I have argued that the bonds of Church, state, family and community were so strong, they had the effect of strangling individual difference and initiative. I have also argued that, more than anything else, it was these bonds that created the habitus that made the Irish different. It is not to say that there was not a similar disposition to family and community elsewhere, but that what made the Irish different was that this habitus lasted longer and reached deeper into people's mentalities and bodies than it did elsewhere. It produced a sense of self, a way of being in the world and relating to others that was different. It was this habitus of self-denial and surrender, linked to a repression of desire and the body, which were the vital ingredients in creating a vivid imagination, a peculiar sense of humor and a particular orientation to life and other people. The Irish still value the norms, habits and dispositions that developed from years of Catholic devotion. The social bonds that come from a tight-knit group still permeate social and cultural life. Symbolic capital and the honor and respect of others are still gained through being humble and self-deprecating and telling stories against oneself. At the same time, talking about oneself and, particularly, one's successes is becoming more acceptable. The skilful cultural actor learns how to balance these two. It is this presentation of self, the skilled way of combining practices from a traditional Irish Catholic habitus with those from a modern cosmopolitan global habitus, that is central to obtaining social, cultural and economic capital in Ireland. It is probably the most significant way in which the local and the global mix. It is a good example of creolization.

It is also important to remember that although there has been a distinct shift away from a Catholic to a consumer form of capitalism, Ireland is still a very Catholic country. Nine in ten people in the republic identify themselves as Roman Catholics. Attendance at Sunday Mass may no longer be universal as it was a generation ago, but Irish Catholics still have one of the highest levels of church attendance in the West. It may be that children are not as socialized into the same culture of guilt, fear and repressed self that I experienced when I was growing up, but there is still a strong level of identification with the Church. Children are taught the faith at home. This is cemented in school. They are still socialized into a Catholic habitus and sense of self. They still learn the art of humility and self-deprecation. Irish Catholics may not be as emotionally attached to the Church as in the past, but the idea of not bringing up their children as Catholics, of not marrying in Church, of not celebrating christenings, First Holy Communions and Confirmations, and of not being buried within the Church, is anathema to most. There is still a strong commitment to the family. Divorce became legal only in 1996 after a referendum when 51 percent voted in favor of the removal of the ban from the Constitution. Those who were against divorce said that it would open the floodgates and that it would destroy family life. It has not happened. There were 20,619 marriages in 2004 and only 3,347 divorces.[1]

There is, then, still a strong sense of Catholic identity and belonging. This is particularly evident in rural areas. A good example of this identity was when in September 2006, people protested outside the entrance to a new gas terminal in County Mayo which was being developed by the Shell Corporation. The *gardaí* had been trying to create a path so that workers could enter the terminal. In this instance, the weapon of the weak was prayer. As the *garda* superintendent tried to talk to the protestors, he was drowned out by a rising chorus of prayer. As the report in *The Irish Times* put it: "Some 100 protestors recited the Rosary from about 8 am onwards until Supt Joseph Gannon in charge of the Belmullet Garda district, instructed work crews to leave the area."[2]

What happened in Mayo is a metaphor for what is happening in Ireland. What was once isolated, insular and Catholic has been prised open. Western culture has been flowing freely into Ireland for the past 50 years. There were new ideas and knowledge, new ways of seeing and understanding, and new ways of being in the world. There were different messages about the nature of self and identity. Most of these messages came in through the media and the market. Most of them were embedded in consumerism. Most of them revolved around self-realization, self-satisfaction and self-indulgence. It used to be that these messages were received once in a while, mostly when people went to the movies. The real revolution in Irish culture came with the advent of mass media. The messages about the importance of self were relentless. The icons changed away from Christ, Our Lady and the saints, towards images of music and film stars. Personal identities became embedded in consumer choices—music, film, food and fashion. The Irish began to shake off the shackles of prudery and inhibition. They began to feel good about themselves. They began to take pleasure in their bodies. They could display themselves without being made to feel guilty and ashamed. They could demonstrate and talk about themselves, their feelings and emotions with greater ease. It was a new world, a world in which people like my parents were lost.

I have argued, then, that what made Ireland different was that over the past 150 years, it developed a very strong sense of sameness. This sameness was built on the strong bonds of family, community and religion which, because they demanded self-sacrifice and denial, gave rise to a different sense of self. This sameness, identity and belonging were what, on the global stage, made the Irish different. They were reflected in the language, music and sport that Irish people took with them around the world. The cultural strategies the Irish developed became caught up in global flows. Often they then became enmeshed in other forms in other cultures and, later, became exported back into Ireland. In more recent years, the inward flows of global culture have intensified through technology, mass media, travel and immigration. Irish people are learning to mix and match cultural forms. Irish culture is becoming hybridized and creolized. The Irish are becoming more cosmopolitan. The result is that many of the cultural forms and practices that made the Irish different are not just surviving but thriving. But, increasingly, the survival of Irish cultural forms is linked to, if not dependent on, their becoming commercialized and commodified. Irishness is becoming a series of cultural representations that are pro-duced and consumed not as part of an inherited, ascribed social identity but as part of a chosen personal identity. It is not just Irish people at home and abroad who embrace being Irish, but people who may have little or no roots or links but who simply like being Irish, who embody an Irish lifestyle that is part of their ongoing construction of individual dif-ference. It is an identity coat that they like to wear, perhaps not all the time, but in certain places, at certain times, with certain people. Being Irish is becoming mixed with a multitude of other cultural representations, practices and lifestyles. The varieties of Irishness are increasing. At the same time, how-ever, the way cosmopolitans adapt, present and perform their Irishness and their other identities is becoming standardized. The result is that the contrast between the Irish and the rest of the West is being reduced. National differences have become packaged and commodified to be included in the ongoing construction of personal identities and sense of self.

There is an important link between individual difference and national difference. As much as there is no core or essence to any individual—there is no true self—there is no true, essential core to being Irish. People construct themselves as individuals in the same way as nations construct themselves as imagined communities. There are as many ways of constructing oneself as there are ways of being Irish. It was never necessary to have Irish blood to be Irish, to be born in Ireland, to speak Irish, to be white, to be Catholic. There are strong Protestants in the North of Ireland who are as much Irish as I am. What keeps a sense of being Irish alive, and what will keep it alive in an increasingly globalized culture, is the number of people and the different ways in which people—not just in Ireland but around the world—use Irish cultural representations as a way of constructing their personal identity.

IRISH CULTURAL CAPITAL

The Catholic Church, the state, the GAA, along with many other institutions, organizations and individuals—including the media and the market—have been central to maintaining the distinctiveness of the Irish habitus. They are the cultural guardians who maintain the practices from which Irish difference emerges. Unless embodying the beliefs and practices of the Catholic Church, speaking the Irish language, playing *gaelic* games, and listening to and playing Irish music, remain important sources of cultural capital, then what is different about being Irish will be rapidly eroded. It is because embodying Irish cultural representations is still an important form of cultural capital, not just in Ireland but across the world, that Irish difference is maintained. Indeed it may well be that descendants of the Irish diaspora are more Irish than those at home. There is greater need to maintain a sense of identity and belonging, and there are greater benefits to being Irish. But the questions remain. How long will being Catholic and embodying Irish cultural representations be central to Irish people's sense of identity and belonging? How long will they be an important dimension of cultural capital? And, more significantly, in a world in which everyday life is rapidly becoming similar, in which people are more self-consumed, does being Irish and embodying Irish cultural representations have any real significance?

In some respects what is happening in Ireland is reflected in what is happening in Ballivor. With the exception of the Catholic Church and the GAA, what was once unique about Ballivor is slowly fading away. The more the cultural guardians of Ballivor die away, the more it becomes swamped by blow-ins who have little or no interest in the history of the village and its people. The more people treat the village as a means to an end rather than an end in it itself, the more Ballivor will sink beneath the surface of Greater Dublin. If one was to use the children of Ballivor as a monitor of cultural difference, then besides family and community life—and the extent to which they embody a Catholic habitus—the main thing that keeps Ballivor different from other villages in the West may be the GAA.

UNQUESTIONED ORTHODOXIES

The opening up of Irish society and culture to global flows has led to a switch in ethical regimes, to a change in the nature of social bonds, and to new senses of self. The younger generation has been liberated from the shackles of fear, guilt and shame which stalked Catholic Ireland. But is it liberation or another, more subtle, more deeply penetrative form of domination and control? Have the Irish simply switched from a Catholic to a consumer form of colonization? Is an ethical regime of self-obsession and self-indulgence more liberating and more sustainable, than an ethical regime of self-emptying and self-denial?

This leads us back to Bourdieu's demand for resistance against the unbridled forces of radical capitalism, profit maximization and the insidious threat of the market. This leads to two important and related questions. In moving from Catholic capitalism to consumer capitalism, have the Irish become more immoral and unethical? Is the world not just a capitalist system of international production and consumption but, also, a moral system based on hedonistic liberal individualism? Second, in becoming a society of individuals, have the Irish become less sympathetic, caring, supportive and responsible for each other? Have the social bonds that bind families, groups and communities been weakened? Are inequality and injustice the necessary consequences of economic growth and a society of individuals? For the wealth of the nation to increase, is it necessary for the gap between rich and poor to grow? If individuals are to resist globalization, then one of the questions they have to address is whether they are living ethical lives. It is not just a question of changing the structures of the world capitalist system, of challenging and resisting the forces of neo-liberalism and the market, it is also a question of whether we can be saved by the force of reason that will develop a new ethic of global responsibility that enables people to realize they have enough, to concentrate on developing social bonds rather than individual fulfillment, and to respect and cherish rather than destroy the environment.

It is hard to think outside the box. It is hard to go beyond the unquestioned orthodoxies in which we live. There are people who question the need for economic growth, the need for things to get bigger and better. But they are a small minority. Culture, the environment and reason may matter to people, but economic well-being matters more. It was not long ago that Ireland was in the depths of economic repression with high levels of unemployment and emigration. Now the economy is strong, there is less unemployment, and emigration is not a necessity. There are more jobs than there are Irish people to fill them. And so we have hundreds of thousands of people coming to live and work here. Ireland is slowly becoming a cosmopolitan melting pot.

The unquestioned orthodoxy of the West is not just the right, not just the need, but the moral imperative of every individual to pursue life, liberty and happiness. This has become a truth that most people in the West hold to be self-evident. This belief in individualism is increasingly becoming the core value in Irish society. The Irish believe in themselves. They have become self-reliant, self-confident, self-assertive. They have also become self-indulgent. They look after number 1. They believe they are worth it. But, of course, self-indulgence and continual self-transformation are essential to the maintenance and development of the Irish economy. If people stop indulging themselves, the economy could collapse. Liberal-individualism is also what holds the world capitalist system together. It has become the unquestioned orthodoxy of global culture. It is what transforms all locals into cosmopolitans.

Self-belief and self-indulgence have been central to the success of the Irish economy. They have led to a substantial increase in the general standard of living. But self-belief and self-indulgence may have also made the Irish more selfish. The Irish may have become rich, but there is not much evidence that Irish society has become more equal and caring. The insistence on a low level of taxes means less money to spend on health and social welfare. It also means that the gap between the rich and poor has not diminished significantly. The poor may not have gotten poorer, but the rich have certainly became richer. Despite having one of the highest levels of Gross Domestic Product per capita, it is estimated that in 2004 one in five Irish people were at-risk-of-poverty. If there were no social welfare payments, it is estimated that the proportion would be two in five.[3]

Elliot and Lemert conclude their book *The New Individualism* by arguing that the way to survive in a world full of increasing risks is for individuals to become more aggressive. They insist that aggression is an essential part of our biological instinct for survival and that in a world shaped by structures, forces and risks that are way beyond our control, the solution is for everyone to pursue their self-interest aggressively. However, they conclude by telling us that this aggressive individualism is only effective when it is combined with the "drives for attachment to others."[4] It would certainly be the best of both worlds if being more aggressive about self-realization led to stronger social bonds and to people being more sensitive, caring and responsible for each other. You can be both selfish and loving.

This is similar to the argument developed by Appiah. In a truly and fully cosmopolitan world people have the right to go their own way, but they recognize and appreciate this right not just for themselves but for others. In an ideal cosmopolitan world people take an interest in human differences and this would be combined with a genuine interest and concern for humankind. What is key here is that cosmopolitans accept that we have obligations for people "beyond those to whom we are related by ties of kith and kin, and even the more formal ties of a shared citizen."[5] This brings us back to the problem of bonding. The more the pool of human beings becomes the same, the more everyday life in the world capitalist system becomes the same, the greater the need for individual, local and national cultural differences to be created and maintained. But not only are these differences no longer as significant, they are diminishing. And as the pool of sameness gets bigger, the bonds that hold people together get looser. The individual is left pursuing difference in a sea of sameness. Strong individual difference comes from being members of different social groups who have significantly different ways of being in the world and who survive through individuals sacrificing the right to go their own way.

It is the rigorous pursuit of self, of individual difference, that makes cosmopolitans the same. It is the same difference. But it may well be that real, strong sustainable difference only comes from being part of a family, group or community in which individuals regularly and consistently, surrender, sacrifice and lose themselves in the wider social whole. To live in a family may be the same as to live in a culture. It is a matter of developing and maintaining social bonds, of self-surrender rather than self-realization, of being the same rather than being different. It may be that without this sense of belonging and bonding it is not possible to develop the emotional stability on which sustainable individual difference can be maintained.

Endnotes

ONE

1. See, for example, Robert Holton. (2005). *Making Globalization*. London: Palgrave Macmillan; Mike Savage, Gaynor Bagnall and Brian Longhurst. (2005). *Globalization and Belonging*. London: Sage; Steven Flusty. (2004). *De-Coca-Colinization: Making the Globe from the Inside Out*. London: Routledge.

2. Much of this book pertains to the Republic of Ireland. An interesting question, not addressed in this book, is the extent to which culture and everyday life in Northern Ireland—the six counties in the north-east of the island that remained part of the United Kingdom when the island was divided politically in 1922—is the same as or different from the Republic.

3. The focus on the practices of everyday life originated within French structuralism. See Henri Lefebvre. (1991). *The Critique of Everyday Life*, Volume 1. London: Verso; Michel de Certeau. (1984). *The Practice of Everyday Life*. Berkeley: University of California Press. For a rich deep description of contemporary everyday life in working-class France, see Pierre Bourdieu *et al.* (1999). *The Weight of the World: Social Suffering in Contemporary Society*. Cambridge: Polity Press.

4. This notion of habitus is derived from Pierre Bourdieu. (1990). *The Logic of Practice*. Cambridge: Polity Press, 50–65.

5. See Anthony Elliot and Charles Lemert. (2006). *The New Individualism: The Emotional Costs of Globalization*. London: Routledge.

6. Bourdieu, *The Logic of Practice*, 53.

7. Bourdieu uses the analogy of fish in water to describe his concept of habitus, "the durable and transposable systems of schemata of perception, appreciation, and action that result from the institution of the social in the body. . . ." He reminds us that

during socialization we inherit the lifestyle, class, religion and general way of being of our parents, and that this is not just a mental outlook but something that is physically embodied. It becomes part of who we are, our identity and sense of self. It becomes second nature to us. It seems to me that the Catholic habitus into which my mother was socialized was so strong that not only did it become second nature to her, but that it dominated or perhaps even alienated her from first nature, to such an extent that being physical was physically awkward. Pierre Bourdieu and Löic Wacquant. (1992). *Invitation to Reflexive Sociology*. Cambridge: Polity Press, 127.

8. Nancy Scheper-Hughes. (2001). *Saints, Scholars and Schizophrenics: Mental Illness in Rural Ireland*, 20th anniversary edn. Berkeley: University of California Press.

9. Tom Inglis. (1998). *Moral Monopoly: The Rise and Fall of the Catholic Church in Modern Ireland*. Dublin: University College Dublin Press.

10. Tom Inglis. (1998). *Lessons in Irish Sexuality*. Dublin: University College Dublin Press.

11. Michael Carroll. (1999). *Irish Pilgrimage: Holy Wells and Popular Catholic Devotion*. Baltimore, MD: Johns Hopkins University Press.

12. Tom Inglis. (2005). "Origins and Legacies of Irish Prudery: Sexuality and Social Control in Modern Ireland" *Eire/Ireland* 40(3&4): 9–37.

13. This is discussed in more detail in Chapter Four. See A. Greeley. (1996). "The Catholic Imagination" *Doctrine and Life* 46: 195–204.

14. Emile Durkheim. (1976). *The Elementary Forms of the Religious Life*. London: Allen & Unwin.

15. Richard Jenkins. (1996). *Social Identity*. London: Routledge.

16. R.F. Foster. (1988). *Modern Ireland 1600–1972*. London: Penguin, 323, 345, 355.

17. Quoted in *Irish Catholic Directory*, 1928: 596, 1 August 1927.

18. The Economist, *The World in 2005*, 86.

19. Economic Intelligence Unit, *The World in 2005*, 91–98.

20. *The Irish Times*, 12 October 2006.

21. Denis O'Hearn. (2001). *The Atlantic Economy: Britain, the US and Ireland*. Manchester: Manchester University Press, 176.

22. *The Irish Times*, 5 March 2005.

23. George Ritzer. (1999). *Enchanting a Disenchanted World*. Thousand Oaks, CA: Pine Forge Press, 75.

24. *The Irish Times*, 5 March 2005.

25. George Ritzer. (2000). *The McDonaldization of Society*. London and Thousand Oaks, CA: Pine Forge Press.

26. Roland Robertson. (1992). *Globalization: Social Theory and Global Culture*. London: Sage, 27.
27. R. Robertson. (1995). "Glocalization: Time-Space and Homogeneity–Heterogeneity" pp. 25–44 in M. Featherstone, S. Lash and R. Robertson (eds.) *Global Modernities*. London: Sage, 28.
28. This is central to the argument of Elliot and Lemert's *New Individualism*.
29. Pierre Bourdieu. (1986). *Distinction*. London: Routledge & Kegan Paul.

TWO

1. See Roland Robertson's extended discussion of the ongoing shifts between universalism and particularism. Roland Robertson. (1992). *Globalization: Social Theory and Global Culture*. London: Sage, 97–114.
2. For a more detailed discussion of the growth and development of Irish cultural nationalism, see John Hutchinson. (1987). *The Dynamics of Cultural Nationalism: The Gaelic Revival and the Creation of the Irish Nation State*. London: Allen & Unwin; Jim Mac Laughlin. (2001). *Reimagining the Nation State: The Contested Terrains of Nation-Building*. London: Pluto.
3. Robert Holton. (2005). *Making Globalization*. London: Palgrave Macmillan, 14–15.
4. Anthony Giddens. (1990). *The Consequences of Modernity*. Stanford, CA: Stanford University Press, 21.
5. Thomas Friedman. (2005). *The World is Flat: A Brief History of the Globalized World in the 21st Century*. London: Penguin, 45.
6. Robertson, *Globalization*, 27.
7. Immanuel Wallerstein. (1974). *The Modern World System*. New York: Academic Books. Immanuel Wallerstein. (1979). *The Capitalist World-Economy*. Cambridge: Cambridge University Press. Immanuel Wallerstein. (1980). *The Modern World System II: Mercantalism and the Consolidation of the European World Economy*. New York: Academic Press.
8. Following Bourdieu, *doxa* can be understood as a realm of orthodox belief which is outside the realm of debate. Pierre Bourdieu. (1977). *Outline of a Theory of Practice*. Cambridge: Cambridge University Press, 168.
9. See Manuel Castells. (1997). *The End of the Millennium*. Oxford: Blackwell; Scott Lash and John Urry. (1994). *Economies of Signs and*

Spaces. London: Sage; Zygmunt Bauman. (1998). *Globalization: The Human Consequences*. Oxford: Blackwell.

10. Holton, *Making Globalization*.

11. Michael Burawoy et al. (2000). *Global Ethnography: Forces, Connections and Imaginations in a Postmodern World*. Berkeley: University of California Press; P. Berger and S. Huntington (eds.) *Many Globalizations: Cultural Diversity in the Contemporary World*. Oxford: Oxford University Press; Mike Savage, Gaynor Bagnall and Brian Longhurst. (2005). *Globalization and Belonging*. London: Sage; Steven Flusty. (2004). *De-Coca-Colinization: Making the Globe from the Inside Out*. London: Routledge.

12. Arjun Appadurai. (1996). *Modernity at Large: Cultural Dimensions of Globalization*. Minneapolis: University of Minnesota Press; A. Appadurai. (1990). "Disjuncture and Difference in the Global Cultural Economy" pp. 293–310 in Mike Featherstone (ed.) *Global Culture: Nationalism, Globalization and Modernity*. London: Sage; A. Appadurai. (2003). "Grassroots Globalization and the Research Imagination" pp. 1–21 in A. Appadurai (ed.) *Globalization*. Durham, NC: Duke University Press.

13. Ulf Hannerz. (1996). *Transnational Connections: Culture, People, Places*. London: Routledge; Ulf Hannerz. (1992). *Cultural Complexity: Studies in the Social Organization of Meaning*. New York: Columbia University Press; Ulf Hannerz. (1990). "Cosmopolitans and Locals in World Culture" pp. 237–251 in Featherstone (ed.) *Global Culture*.

14. I. Wallerstein. (1991). "The National and the Universal: Can There Be Such a Thing as World Culture" pp. 91–105 in A. King (ed.) *Culture, Globalization and the World-System*. London: Macmillan; Christopher Chase-Dunn. (1989). *Global Formation: Structures of the World Economy*. Oxford: Basil Blackwell; Phillip McMichael. (1996). *Development and Social Change: A Global Perspective*. Thousand Oaks, CA: Pine Forge Press.

15. Wallerstein argues that the concept of culture is a nineteenth-century invention of social science that was used to counterbalance the emphasis on politics and economics. I. Wallerstein. (1990). "Culture is the World-System: A Reply to Boyne" pp. 63–65 in Featherstone (ed.) *Global Culture* (65).

16. I. Wallerstein. (1990). "Culture as the Ideological Battleground of the Modern World-System" pp. 31–55 in Featherstone (ed.) *Global Culture* (38).

17. Wallerstein, "The National and the Universal," 105.

18. Robertson, *Globalization*, 90.

19. Robertson, *Globalization*, 91–94.

20. Appadurai sets out to examine the disjunctures in the global economy between economy, culture and politics by looking at the relationship among five dimensions of global cultural flows which he terms (a) ethnoscapes, (b) mediascapes, (c) technoscapes, (d) financescapes, (e) ideoscapes. Appadurai, *Modernity*, 33. Castells also uses the notion of flows and refers to flows of capital, information, technology, organizational interaction, images, sounds and symbols. Manuel Castells. (1996). *The Rise of the Network Society*. Oxford: Blackwell, 412. John Urry refers to flows of people, information, money and images. John Urry. (2000). *Sociology Beyond Societies: Mobilities for the Twenty-first Century*. London: Routledge.

21. Appadurai, *Modernity*, 34–37.

22. Appadurai, *Modernity*, 36.

23. Of course it was Weber who emphasized the important connection between culture and economics, specifically the development of ascetic Protestantism and the rise of the type of risk venture capitalism in the West which, as he said, was "a line of development having *universal* significance and value." Max Weber. (1958). "Author's Introduction" pp. 13–31 in *The Protestant Ethic and the Spirit of Capitalism*. New York: Charles Scribner's Sons, 13. But the culture of Protestantism did not burst on the medieval scene. Weber emphasized "the numerous close relationships between the asceticism of Western monasticism and the ascetic conduct of Protestantism." Weber, *The Protestant Ethic and the Spirit of Capitalism*, 254. The significance of the Reformation was that "now every Christian had to be a monk all his life." Weber, *The Protestant Ethic*, 120. Weber insisted that the "great historical significance of Western monasticism" was that it developed "a systematic method of rational conduct." He argued that "it was precisely in the Occident that *labor* emerges as the distinctive mark of Christian monasticism, and as an instrument of both hygiene and asceticism." Max Weber. (1978). *Economy and Society*, ed. G. Roth and C. Wittich. Berkeley: University of California Press, 555. The contribution of the Rules of St Benedict, the monks of Cluny, the Cistercians and, most particularly the Jesuits, was they "attempted to subject man to the supremacy of a purposeful will, to bring his actions under constant self-control with a careful consideration of their ethical consequences." Weber, *The Protestant Ethic*, 118–119. The reason for going carefully through this argument, is that there is

a strong connection between the monastic Orders and type of monasticism referred to by Weber, and the type of monasticism developed in Ireland from the sixth century and exported throughout Europe over the following centuries. In other words, in understanding globalization, we have to appreciate that the ideas that give rise to specific interactions that lead to the emergence of the world capitalist systems had some of their origins in Ireland centuries previously.

24. For more detailed descriptions and discussions of hybridization and creolization, see J. Nederveen Pieterse. (1995). "Globalization as Hybridization" pp. 45–68 in M. Featherstone, S. Lash and R. Robertson (eds.) *Global Modernities*. London: Sage; Hannerz, *Transnational Connections*, 65–78.

25. R. Robertson. (1995). "Glocalization: Time-Space and Homogeneity–Heterogeneity" pp. 25–44 in Featherstone, Lash and Robertson (eds.) *Global Modernities*.

26. Friedman, "Being in the World" in *The World is Flat*; P. Berger. (2002). "Introduction: The Cultural Dynamics of Globalization" pp. 1–16 in Berger and Huntington (eds.) *Many Globalizations*, 10.

27. Hannerz, *Transnational Connections*, 25–28.

28. Appadurai, *Modernity*, 31, 33.

29. Savage *et al.*, *Globalization and Belonging*; Flusty, *De-Coca-Colinization*.

30. E. Hobsbawm and T. Ranger (eds.). (1983). *The Invention of Tradition*. Cambridge: Cambridge University Press; Benedict Anderson. (1983). *Imagined Communities*. London: Verso.

31. Appadurai, *Modernity*, 181, 184.

32. Hannerz, *Transnational Connections*, 74.

33. For a good description of some of Ireland's pre-eminent cultural entrepreneurs see Fintan O'Toole. (1997). *The Ex-Isle of Erin*. Dublin: New Island Books.

34. Hannerz, *Transnational Connections*, 103.

35. Ciarán Carson. (1986). *Traditional Irish Music*. Belfast: Appletree.

36. Bauman, *Globalization*; Press; Hannerz, "Cosmopolitans and Locals;" Friedman, "Being in the World."

37. Flusty, *De-Coca-Colinization*, 32.

38. Hannerz, *Transnational Connections*, 239–244.

39. Berger, "Introduction."

40. Hannerz, *Transnational Connections*, 246; R.K. Merton. (1957). *Social Theory and Social Structure*. Glencoe, IL: Free Press.

41. Adrian Peace. (2001). *A World of Fine Difference: The Social Architecture of a Modern Irish Village*. Dublin: University College Dublin Press, 74.

42. Pierre Bourdieu. (1986). *Distinction: A Social Critique of the Judgement of Taste*. London: Routledge & Kegan Paul; P. Bourdieu. (1986). "The Forms of Capital" pp. 241–258 in J. Richardson (ed.) *Handbook of Theory and Research for the Sociology of Education*. New York: Greenwood Press.

43. Émile Durkheim. (1976). *The Elementary Forms of the Religious Life*. London: Allen & Unwin; Émile Durkheim and Marcel Mauss. (1969). *Primitive Classification*, 2nd edn. London: Cohen & West.

44. Durkheim, *The Elementary Forms*, 376–388.

45. Anderson, *Imagined Communities*.

46. Durkheim, *The Elementary Forms*, 378.

47. "For above all else, a faith is warmth, life, enthusiasm, the exaltation of the whole mental life, the raising of the above himself. Now how could he add to the energies he possesses without going outside himself?" Durkheim, *The Elementary Forms*, 425.

48. Durkheim, *The Elementary Forms*, 102.

49. See Lemert's "Ferdinand de Saussure and Why the Social Contract is a Cultural Arbitrary" pp. 81–86 in Charles Lemert. (2006). *Durkheim's Ghosts: Cultural Logics and Social Things*. Cambridge: Cambridge University Press. For a good discussion on group boundaries and the social organization of difference and the symbolic construction of sameness, see Richard Jenkins. (1996). *Social Identity*. London: Routledge, 90–118. The problem for cosmopolitans, postmodernists and critically reflective cultural actors is that while they can experience and appreciate different cultures, they cannot become completely submerged in a culture.

50. For a more detailed discussion of this division, see T. Inglis. (2007). "The Religious Field in Contemporary Ireland, Being Religious and Symbolic Domination" pp. 111–134 in L. Harte and Y. Whelan (eds.) *Ireland Beyond Boundaries: Mapping Irish Studies in the Twenty-first Century*. London: Pluto.

51. Robertson, *Globalization*, 100, 102.

52. Robertson, *Globalization*, 104, 113.

53. Robertson, *Globalization*, 103.

54. This discussion of decreasing contrasts and increasing variety relies on Elias. See Norbert Elias. (2000). *The Civilising Process*, revised edn. Oxford: Blackwell, 365–382. See also Stephen Mennell. (1992). *Norbert Elias: An Introduction*. Oxford: Blackwell, 243–246.

55. Robertson, *Globalization*, 183.

56. Robertson, *Globalization*, 27.

57. Anderson, *Imagined Communities*.

58. A.D. Smith. (1990). "Towards a Global Culture?" pp. 172–192 in Featherstone (ed.) *Global Culture*, 179–180.

59. Danièle Hervieu-Léger. (2000). *Religion as a Chain of Memory*. Cambridge: Polity Press.

60. Mac Laughlin, *Reimagining the Nation-State*, 242–271.

61. Marshall McLuhan. (1964). *Understanding Media: The Extensions of Man*. London: Routledge & Kegan Paul.

62. http://www.hvk.org/hvk/articles/1097/0026 [downloaded 8 January 2005].

63. Pierre Bourdieu. (1998). *Acts of Resistance: Against the New Myths of Our Time*. Cambridge: Polity Press; Pierre Bourdieu. (2003). *Firing Back: Against the Tyranny of the Market 2*. New York: The New Press.

64. Bourdieu, *Firing Back*, 84, 86.

65. Bourdieu, *Acts of Resistance*, 34, 39.

66. Bourdieu, *Acts of Resistance*, 34–37.

67. Bourdieu, *Acts of Resistance*, 43.

68. Bourdieu, *Firing Back*, 71.

69. Bourdieu, *Acts of Resistance*, 76–77.

70. Holton insists that the question at the heart of globalization is how it works. Holton, *Making Globalization*, 2.

71. The same can be said for French structuralists such as Baudrillard, de Certeau and Lefebvre and those working within the Frankfurt School tradition such as Adorno, Marcuse and Habermas. Both theoretical traditions have a conception of individuals being manipulated by structures of which they are not aware. Regardless of whether this is actually the case, there is a need to understand the logic of consumerism for the consumer. See Anthony Elliot and Charles Lemert. (2006). *The New Individualism: The Emotional Costs of Globalization*. London: Routledge, 54–60.

72. *Guardian*, 21 September 2004.

THREE

1. http://www.imagesofireland.net/johnfkennedy.html

2. Mary Hickman. (2005). "Migration and Diaspora" pp. 117–136 in J. Cleary and C. Connolly (eds.) *The Cambridge Companion to Modern Irish Culture*. Cambridge: Cambridge University Press.

3. Tom Inglis. (1998). *Moral Monopoly: The Rise and Fall of the Catholic Church in Modern Ireland*, 2nd edn. Dublin: University College Dublin Press; Charles Salazar. (2006). *Anthropology & Sexual Morality: A Theoretical Investigation*. New York: Berghahn Books.

4. Kerby A. Miller. (1985). *Emigrants and Exiles: Ireland and the Irish Exodus to North America.* Oxford: Oxford University Press, 556.

5. David Fitzpatrick. (1994). *Oceans of Consolation: Personal Accounts of Irish Migration to Australia.* Cork: Cork University Press.

6. Graham Davis. (2000). "The Irish in Britain, 1815–1939" pp. 19–36 in A. Beilenberg (ed.) *The Irish Diaspora.* Harlow: Longman, 21.

7. Miller, *Emigrants and Exiles,* 291.

8. Davis, "The Irish in Britain."

9. Cormac Ó Gráda. (1973). "A Note on Nineteenth Century Irish Emigration Statistics" *Population Studies* 29: 143–149.

10. Miller, *Emigrants and Exiles,* 560.

11. Luke Gibbons. (1996). *Transformations in Irish Culture.* Cork: Cork University Press, 175.

12. Andrew Greeley. (1988). "The Success and Assimilation of Irish Protestants and Irish Catholics in the United States" SSR [Society for the Study of Reproduction] 72(4): 229–235.

13. Andrew Greeley. (1988). *The Irish Americans: The Rise to Money and Power.* New York: Warner Books.

14. D.H. Akenson. (1993). *The Irish Diaspora.* Belfast: Institute of Irish Studies, Queen's University, 6.

15. Mary Hickman. (2002). " 'Locating' the Irish Diaspora," *Irish Journal of Sociology* 11(2): 14.

16. Akenson, *The Irish Diaspora,* 6.

17. Jim Mac Laughlin. (1994). *Ireland: The Emigrant Nursery and the World Economy.* Cork: Cork University Press, 23–30.

18. Hickman, "Locating," 22.

19. Jim Mac Laughlin. (2000). "Changing Attitudes to 'New Wave' Emigration? Structuralism versus Voluntarism in the Study of Irish Emigration" pp. 317–330 in Beilenberg (ed.) *The Irish Diaspora,* 324.

20. Ulf Hannerz. (1996). *Transnational Connections: Culture, People, Places.* London: Routledge, 17.

21. Mac Laughlin, "Changing Attitudes," 329; Fintan O'Toole, *The Irish Times,* 19 January 1994.

22. www.ireland.com/newspaper/special/2003/mcaleese/index.htm

23. Daniel Murphy. (2000). *A History of Irish Emigrant and Missionary Education.* Dublin: Four Courts Press, 526.

24. Edmund Hogan. (1980). *The Irish Missionary Movement: A Historical Survey 1830–1980.* Dublin: Gill & Macmillan, 8.

25. Murphy, *A History of Irish,* 527.

26. Hogan, *The Irish Missionary*, 2.
27. Akenson, *The Irish Diaspora*, 147.
28. Hogan, *The Irish Missionary*, 8.
29. Mike Cronin and Daryl Adair. (2002). *The Wearing of the Green: A History of St Patrick's Day*. London: Routledge, 9.
30. Cronin and Adair, *The Wearing of the Green*, 252.
31. Thomas Wilson and Hastings Donnan. (2006). *The Anthropology of Ireland*. Oxford: Berg, 108–112.
32. *Irish Independent*, 19 March 2005.
33. http://www.finfacts.com
34. Matt Ramstedt and Ann Hope. (2005). *The Irish Drinking Culture: Drinking and Drinking-related Harm, a European Comparison*. Dublin: Irish Health Promotion Unit.
35. *Irish Independent*, 26 November 2004.
36. E. Slater. (2000). "When the Local goes Global" pp. 247–258 in M. Peillon and E. Slater (eds.) *Memories of the Present*. Dublin: Ireland.
37. http://www.guinness.com
38. M. McGovern. (2002). "The 'Craic' Market: Irish Theme Bars and the Commodification of Irishness in Contemporary Britain" *Irish Journal of Sociology* 11(2): 77–98.
39. Richard Stivers. (2000). *Hair of the Dog: Irish Drinking and Its American Stereotype*. New York: Continuum, 92.
40. Stivers, *Hair of the Dog*, 190.
41. This form of ritual hard drinking, particularly among men, is obviously not confined to the Irish. The question is whether, like many other aspects of Irish culture, the Irish did it more extremely, more often.
42. For a more detailed description and analysis of *Riverdance* in the context of traditional Irish dancing, see Helena Wulff (in press) *Dancing at the Crossroads: Memory and Mobility in Ireland*. Oxford: Berghahn Books. See also, Wilson and Donnan, *Anthropology of Ireland*, 92–98.
43. http://www.ey.com/global/content.nsf/Ireland_EOY_E/winners-Riverdance
44. Quoted in Fintan O'Toole. (1997). *The Ex-Isle of Erin: Images of a Global Ireland*. Dublin: New Island Books, 146.
45. O'Toole, *Ex-Isle of Erin*, 145, 147.
46. O'Toole, *Ex-Isle of Erin*, 152.
47. B. O'Connor. (1998). "Riverdance" pp. 51–62 in M. Peillon and E. Slater (eds.) *Encounters with Modern Ireland*. Dublin: IPA, 52.
48. J. Sherlock. (1999). "Globalisation, Western Culture and River-dance" pp. 205–218 in A. Brah, M. Hickman and M. Mac an

Ghaill (eds.) *Thinking Identities: Ethnicity, Racism and Culture*. London: Macmillan.

49. V. Azarya. (2004). "Globalization and International Tourism in Developing Countries: Marginality as a Commercial Commodity" *Current Sociology* 52(6): 940–967; Clem Tisdell. (2001). *Tourism, Economics, the Environment and Development*. Cheltenham: Edward Elgar; R. Wood. (1997). "Tourism and the State: Ethnic Options and Constructions of Otherness" pp. 1–34 in M. Picard and R. Wood (eds.) *Tourism, Ethnicity and the State in Asian and Pacific Societies*. Honolulu: University of Hawaii Press.

50. John Urry. (1990). *The Tourist Gaze: Leisure and Travel in Contemporary Societies*. London: Sage.

51. http://www.cso.ie/statistics/HouseholdTravel.htm

52. S. Flanagan and C. Conlon (eds.). (1999). *The Business of Tourism: Urban-led Growth?* Dublin: Blackhall.

53. Fáilte Ireland Report by Millard Brown IMS, Visitors Attitude Survey 2004, Dublin, 2004.

54. Fáilte Ireland, 2004, iii.

55. This is a paraphrase and elaboration of William James's notion that the individual has as many selves as people who recognize him or her. See Anthony Elliot and Charles Lemert. (2006). *The New Individualism: The Emotional Costs of Globalization*. London: Routledge, 33.

56. http://www.cso.ie/statistics/HouseholdTravel.htm

57. http://www.bbc.co.uk/2/hi/uk_news/2137729.stm

58. http://www.immigrantcouncil.ie/stats.pdf

59. Central Statistics Office. (2004). *Population and Labour Force Projection 2006–2036*. Dublin: Government Publications, 17.

60. However, most of the huge influx of immigrants up to 2000 were returning Irish or from the United Kingdom. Only 10 percent were asylum refugees.

61. Central Statistics Office. (2004). *Census of Population 2002 Religion*, Volume 12. Dublin: Government Publications, table 4a.

62. M. Corcoran. (2006). "Ethno-city" pp. 181–192 in M. Corcoran and M. Peillon (eds.) *Uncertain Ireland: A Sociological Chronicle, 2003–2004*. Dublin: IPA, 181–182.

63. Piaras MacÉinrí and Paddy Walley. (2003). *Labour Migration into Ireland*. Dublin: Immigrant Council of Ireland, 23–24.

64. Micheál MacGréil. (1996). *Prejudice in Ireland Revisited*. Maynooth: Survey and Research Unit, St. Patrick's College, 67, 151.

65. http://www.cso.ie/census/documents/vol4_entire.pdf

66. *The Irish Times*, 15 September 2005.

67. *The Irish Times*, 10 August 2006. These are the numbers who registered to work. However, the number still resident in Ireland is likely to be much smaller as many may have returned to their home country.

68. MacÉinrí and Walley, *Labour Migration*, 24.

69. Chichi Aniagolu. (1997). "Being Black in Ireland" pp. 43–52 in E. Crowley and J. Mac Laughlin (eds.) *Under the Belly of the Celtic Tiger: Class, Race, Identity and Culture in the Global Ireland*. Dublin: Irish Reporter, 51.

70. *The Irish Times*, 23 January 2006.

71. http://www.knowracism.ie/dynamiccontent/43Presentation

72. M. Breen, A. Haynes and E. Devereux. (2006). "Citizens, Loopholes and Maternity Tourists: Media Frames in the Citizenship Referendum" pp. 59–70 in Corcoran and Peillon (eds.) *Uncertain Ireland*.

73. John Waters, *The Irish Times*, 28 March 2005. However, as well as government strategies, the decline may be due to fewer asylum seekers and refugees coming to Ireland.

74. *Sunday Tribune*, 27 March 2005.

75. *The Irish Times*, 26 March 2005.

76. In March 2005, there was considerable coverage given in the media to the story about 35 young Nigerians who had been deported back home and, in particular, the story of Olunkunle Elukanlo who had come to Ireland when he was 14 and, after a long struggle of resistance, was sent back to Nigeria that month. An editorial in *The Irish Times* (17 March 2005) on St Patrick's Day noted that St Patrick was an immigrant into Ireland and that a notable theme in the reconfiguration of his legacy had been Ireland's diasporic identity as a migratory nation. Such a legacy, the editorial announced, makes it "all the more reprehensible that 35 Nigerian nationals should have been deported, apparently summarily, on the eve of the national holiday." The editorial argued that "such an unworthy betrayal of St. Patrick's legacy should prompt a fight back against this callous policy."

77. For a more detailed analysis of the Travellers in Ireland, see Bryan Fanning. (2002). *Racism and Social Change in Ireland*. Manchester: Manchester University Press; Jean Helleiner. (2000). *Irish Travellers: Racism and the Politics of Culture*. Toronto: University of Toronto Press.

78. http://www.census.gov/Press-Release/www/releases/archives/facts_for_features /001687.html The overall number

of people around the world claiming Irish ancestry has been estimated at 70 million. http://www.irelandroots.com/roots4.htm

79. http://www.world-tourism.org/facts/eng/pdf/indicators/Top25_ita.pdf The world leader was Macao (China) with 2,869 followed in second place by Hong Kong with 318.

80. http://www.eurodad.org/uploadstore/cms/docs/European AidReport.pdf

81. http://en.wikipedia.org/wiki/Development_aid#2004_ODA_figures *The Irish Times*, 1 November 2006.

FOUR

1. Benedict Anderson. (1983). *Imagined Communities*. London: Verso.

2. Jim Mac Laughlin. (2001). *Reimagining the Nation State: The Contested Terrains of Nation-Building*. London: Pluto, 6–7.

3. Mac Laughlin, *Reimagining*, 129; for a detailed discussion of the role of the print media in nation building see 186–209.

4. Mac Laughlin, *Reimagining*, 238.

5. Roland Robertson. (1992). *Globalization: Social Theory and Global Culture*. London: Sage, 97–114.

6. Liam de Paor. (1986). *The Peoples of Ireland: From Prehistory to Modern Times*. Notre Dame, IN: Notre Dame University Press, 11.

7. Gordon Childe. (1958). *The Prehistory of European Society*. Harmondsworth: Penguin, 127.

8. de Paor, *Peoples of Ireland*, 39.

9. Anthony Elliot and Charles Lemert. (2006). *The New Individualism: The Emotional Costs of Globalization*. London: Routledge.

10. Foucault traces the origins of these practices back to medieval Christianity. However, the Irish monks were among the first to develop detailed penitentials in the fifth century. See Michel Foucault. (1980). *The History of Sexuality*, Vol. 1. New York: Vintage, 116; Hugh Connolly. (1995). *The Irish Penitentials*. Dublin: Four Courts Press; John Ó'Ríordáin. (1980). *Irish Catholics: Tradition and Transition*. Dublin: Veritas.

11. Tom Inglis. (1998). *Moral Monopoly: The Rise and Fall of the Catholic Church in Modern Ireland*. Dublin: University College Dublin Press, 129–30.

12. Michel Foucault. (1987). *The Use of Pleasure*. Harmondsworth: Penguin, 138.

13. Jean Baudrillard. (1998). *The Consumer Society: Myths and Structures*. London: Sage, 136.

14. See Joseph Ruane and Jennifer Todd. (1996). *The Dynamics of the*

Conflict in Northern Ireland: Power, Conflict and Emancipation. Cambridge: Cambridge University Press; Colin Coulter. (1999). Contemporary Northern Irish Society: An Introduction. London: Pluto Press; John McGarry and Brendan O'Leary. (2004). The Northern Ireland Conflict: Consociational Engagements. Oxford: Oxford University Press.

15. de Paor, Peoples of Ireland, 176.

16. Michael Carroll. (1999). Irish Pilgrimage: Holy Wells and Popular Catholic Devotion. Baltimore: Johns Hopkins University Press.

17. Declan Kiberd. (1995). Inventing Ireland: The Literature of the Modern Irish Nation. London: Jonathan Cape, 151.

18. Diarmuid Ferriter. (2004). The Transformation of Ireland 1900–2000. London: Profile, 99; Helen O'Murchú and Máirtín O'Murchú. (1999). Irish Facing the Future. Dublin: Irish Committee of the European Bureau for Lesser Used Languages, 2.

19. J.J. Lee. (1989). Ireland 1912–85: Politics and Society. Cambridge: Cambridge University Press, 662–666.

20. Anderson, Imagined Communities, 122; Kiberd, Inventing Ireland, 137.

21. Ferriter, Transformation of Ireland, 350.

22. www.tg4.ie/bearla/index.htm

23. http://www.rte.ie/tv/theafternoonshow/story/ 1040595.html

24. Census Office. (2004). Census of Ireland 2002, Vol. 11. Dublin: Government Publications.

25. Kiberd, Inventing Ireland, 569.

26. MORI. (2004).

27. Thomas Davis. (2003). "The Irish and their Nation: A Survey of Recent Attitudes" The Global Review of Ethnopolitics 2.2: 17–36(23).

28. Gearóid Ó'Thuathaigh. (2005). "Language, Ideology and National Identity" pp. 42–58 in J. Cleary and C. Connolly (eds.) The Cambridge Companion to Modern Irish Culture. Cambridge: Cambridge University Press, 57.

29. The Irish Times, 15 March 2004.

30. Norbert Elias and Eric Dunning. (1986). Quest for Excitement: Sport and Leisure in the Civilising Process. Oxford: Blackwell.

31. Mike Cronin. (1999). Sport and Nationalism in Ireland: Gaelic Games, Soccer and Irish Identity since 1884. Dublin: Four Courts Press, 106–107.

32. Marcus de Búrca. (1999). The GAA: A History, 2nd edn. Dublin: Gill & Macmillan; W.F. Mandel. (1987). The Gaelic Athletic Association & Irish Nationalist Politics 1884–1924. Dublin: Gill & Macmillan. Cronin, Sport and Nationalism in Ireland.

33. Quoted in Cronin, *Sport and Nationalism in Ireland*, 91.
34. Liam Delaney and Tony Fahey. (2005). *Social and Economic Value of Sport in Ireland*. Dublin: ESRI, 35, 42, 27.
35. http:///www.gaa.ie
36. Richard Doak. (1998). "(De)constructing Irishness in the 1990s—The Gaelic Athletic Association and Cultural Nationalist Discourse Reconsidered" *Irish Journal of Sociology* 8: 25–48.
37. Tom Humphries. (1996). *Green Fields: Gaelic Sport in Ireland*. London: Weidenfeld & Nicolson, 9.
38. Cronin, *Sport and Nationalism*, 113.
39. Ciarán Carson. (1986). *Traditional Irish Music*. Belfast: Appletree, 9.
40. Carson, *Traditional Irish Music*, 20.
41. Carson, *Traditional Irish Music*, 21–22.
42. *The Irish Times*, 23 March 2005.
43. Fintan Vallely. (1999). *Traditional Irish Music Database*.
44. *The Irish Times*, 30 August 2004.
45. F. Vallely. (1997). "The Migrant, the Tourist, the Voyeur, the Leprechaun . . ." pp. 107–115 in T. Smith and M. Ó'Súilleabháin (eds.) *Blas: The Local Accent in Irish Traditional Music*. Limerick: Irish World Music Center, 111–112.
46. John Whyte. (1971). *Church and State in Modern Ireland, 1923–1970*, 1st edn. Dublin: Gill & Macmillan, 362–363.
47. J. Toner. (1953). "The Local Loveliness" pp. 17–21 in *Rural Ireland: The Official Handbook of Muintir na Tíre*, quoted in Séan L'Estrange. (2004). *Catholicism and Capitalist Social Order in Ireland, 1907–1973—An Historical Institutionalist Analysis*. PhD thesis. Queen's University Belfast, 162.
48. http://www.politics.ie/wiki/index.php?title=Fianna_F%C3%A1il_Policy_to_D%C3%A1il_%C3%89ireann_Speech.
49. Quoted in M. Moyinhan (ed.). (1980). *Speeches and Statements of Éamon de Valera*. Dublin: Gill & Macmillan, 466.
50. Roy Foster. (1988). *Modern Ireland 1600–1972*. Harmondsworth: Penguin, 528.
51. Lee, *Ireland 1912–1985*, 241, 334.
52. *Sunday Independent*, 14 October 2001.
53. This notion of social bonds and individual difference is derived from Scheff. See Thomas Scheff. (1997). *Emotions, the Social Bond, and Human Reality: Part/Whole Analysis*. Cambridge: Cambridge University Press, 98–114; Thomas Scheff. (1990). *Microsociology*. Chicago: Chicago University Press, 79; Thomas Scheff. (1994). *Bloody Revenge: Emotions, Nationalism and War*. Boulder, CO: Westview Press, 49–50.
54. For a more detailed discussion of the embodiment of Catholic culture, see T. Inglis. (2003). "Catholic Church, Religious

Capital and Symbolic Domination" pp. 44–70 in M. Böss and E. Maher (eds.) *Engaging Modernity: Readings of Irish Politics, Culture and Literature at the Turn of the Century*. Dublin: Veritas.

55. A. Greeley. (1996). "The Catholic Imagination and Ireland" *Doctrine and Life* 46: 194–204 (199).

FIVE

1. See, for example, George Ritzer. (1993). *The McDonaldization of Society*. Newbury Park, CA: Pine Forge Press; Benjamin Barber. (1996). *Jihad vs. McWorld: How Globalization and Tribalism Are Reshaping the World*. New York: Ballantine Books. Samuel Huntington. (1996). *The Clash of Civilizations and the Remaking of the World Order*. New York: Simon & Schuster; Frederick Buell. (1994). *National Culture and the New Global System*. Baltimore, MD: Johns Hopkins University Press; Tyler Cohen. (2002). *Creative Destruction: How Globalization Is Changing the World's Cultures*. Princeton, NJ: Princeton University Press.

2. Fintan O'Toole. (1997). *The Ex-Isle of Erin: Images of a Global Ireland*. Dublin: New Island Books, 147.

3. Cohen, *Creative Destruction*, 102–127. A.D. Smith. (1990). "Towards a Global Culture?" pp. 172–192 in M. Featherstone (ed.) *Global Culture: Nationalism, Globalization and Modernity*. London: Sage, 177.

4. Theodore Levitt. (1983). "Globalization of Markets" *Harvard Business Review* May/June: 92–102 (96).

5. Istávan Kónya and Hiroshi Ohashi "International Consumption Patterns among High Income Countries: Evidence from the OECD Data": http://www.e.u-tokyo.ac.jp/cemano/research/DP/documents/coe-f–66.pdf [down loaded 10 September 2006]

6. Thomas Friedman. (2000). *The Lexus and the Olive Tree*. New York: Anchor Books, 278–279.

7. Smith, "Towards a Global Culture?" 176.

8. Ben Highmore. (2002). *Everyday Life and Cultural Theory*. London: Routledge; Michael Gardiner. (2000). *Critiques of Everyday Life*. London: Routledge.

9. Henri Lefebvre. (1991). *The Critique of Everyday Life*. London: Verso, 30–31.

10. Serge Latouche. (1996). *The Westernization of the World: Significance, Scope and Limits of the Drive Towards Global Uniformity*. Cambridge: Cambridge University Press, 38–41.

11. Anthony Elliot and Charles Lemert. (2006). *The New Individualism: The Emotional Costs of Globalization*. London: Routledge.

12. Most of the books written about Ireland as a globalized society have concentrated on economic globalization and, in particular, the emergence of the Celtic Tiger economy during the 1990s. The most recent and comprehensive study is Michael O'Sullivan. (2006). *Ireland and the Global Question*. Cork: Cork University Press. For a broad, comparative, long-term historical perspective see Denis O'Hearn. (2001). *The Atlantic Economy: Britain, the US and Ireland*. Manchester: Manchester University Press; Denis O'Hearn. (1998). *Inside the Celtic Tiger: The Irish Economy and the Asian Model*. London: Pluto. For a more socialist commentary, see Kieran Allen. (2000). *The Celtic Tiger? The Myth of Social Partnership in Ireland*. Manchester: Manchester University Press. For a more mainstream analysis see Ray McSharry and Padraic White. (2001). *The Making of the Celtic Tiger: The Inside Story of Ireland's Boom Economy*. Cork: Mercier Press. For a comprehensive analysis of Irish society and economic performance see Brian Nolan, Phillip O'Connell and Chris Whelan (eds.). (2000). *Bust to Boom? The Irish Experience of Growth and Inequality*. Dublin: IPA.

13. Mark Cassidy. (2004). "Productivity in Ireland: Trends and Issues" Central Bank, Quarterly Bulletin, Spring: 83–105.

14. Ulrick Beck. (1992). *Risk Society: Towards a New Modernity*. London: Sage; Cassidy, "Productivity in Ireland," 87, 86.

15. James Wickham. (2000). *Changing Times: Working Time in Ireland 1983–2000*. Dublin: Employment Research Center, Trinity College, 2.

16. European Foundation for the Improvement of Working and Living Conditions, 2005: http://www.eiro.eurofound.ie/2005/03/update/tn0503104u.html

17. Forfás. (2005). News: http://www.forfas.ie/news.asp?page_id=358

18. Harry Braverman. (1988). *Labor and Monopoly Capital: 25th Anniversary Edition*. New York: Monthly Review Press, 59–85.

19. Douglas McGregor. (1960). *The Human Side of Enterprise*. New York: McGraw-Hill.

20. O'Sullivan, *Ireland and the Global Question*, 68.

21. S. O'Riain. (2000). "Net-Working for a Living: Irish Software Developers in the Global Workplace" pp. 175–202 in M. Burawoy *et al. Global Ethnography: Forces, Connections, and Imaginations in a Postmodern World*. Berkeley: University of California Press.

22. O'Riain, "Net-Working," 184.
23. O'Riain, "Net-Working," 191.
24. O'Riain, "Net-Working," 200.
25. Michel Foucault. (1979). *Discipline & Punish: The Birth of the Prison*. New York: Vintage Books.
26. Norbert Elias. (2000). *The Civilising Process*, revised edn. Oxford: Blackwell, 365–382.
27. Jacques Ellul. (1967). *The Technological Society*. New York: Vintage.
28. Cas Wouters. (1992). "On Status Competition and Emotion Management: The Study of Emotions as a New Field" *Theory, Culture and Society* 9(1): 229–235.
29. Austin Hughes and David Duffy. (2006). "In Too Deep?: Preliminary Findings of a Survey-based Assessment of the Burden of Personal Debt in Ireland." Dublin: IIB-ESRI, 3.
30. Minitel. (2001). Special Report on Irish Lifestyles: 13.
31. http://www.cso.ie/statistics/newdwellings.htm
32. Frank McDonald and James Nix. (2005). *Chaos at the Crossroads*. Kinsale: Gandon Books, 17.
33. http://www.cso.ie/census/2006_preliminaryreport.htm
34. http://www.cso.ie/releasespublications/documents/other_releases/2004/progress/measuringirelandsprogress.pdf
35. McDonald and Nix, *Chaos at the Crossroads*, 22.
36. *Sunday Business Post*, 11 December 2005.
37. Kieran Keohane and Carmen Kuhling. (2004). *Collision Culture: Transformations in Everyday Life in Ireland*. Dublin: Liffey Press.
38. M. Cronin. (2002) "Speed Limits: Ireland, Globalisation and the War against Time" pp. 54–66 in P. Kirby, L. Gibbons and M. Cronin (eds.) *Reinventing Ireland: Culture: Society and the Global Economy*. London: Pluto Press, 60.
39. http://www.nra.ie/RoadSafety/Research/YoungDriver Accidents 2000
40. *The Irish Times*, 23 October 2006.
41. http://www.finfacts.com/irelandbusinessnews/publish/article_10006275 .shtml
42. Minitel. (2001). Special Report on Irish Lifestyles: 57.
43. David Morley. (1992). *Television, Audiences and Cultural Studies*. London: Routledge.
44. R. Allen. (1996). "As the World Turns: Television Soap Operas and Global Media Culture" pp. 110–130 in E. McAnany and K. Wilkinson (eds.) *Mass Media and Free Trade: NAFTA and Cultural Industries*. Austin: University of Texas Press.

45. Arjun Appadurai. (1996). *Modernity at Large: Cultural Dimensions of Globalization*. Minneapolis: University of Minnesota Press, 82.

46. John Tomlinson. (1999). *Globalization and Culture*. Cambridge: Polity, 86.

47. John Urry. (1995). *Consuming Places*. London: Routledge, 123.

48. For one of the earliest and best analyses of consuming difference, see Jean Baudrillard. (1998). *The Consumer Society: Myths and Structures*. London: Sage, 87–98.

49. Barbara Adam. (1994). *Time and Social Theory*. Cambridge: Polity.

50. E.P. Thompson. (1967). "Time, Work-Discipline and Industrial Capitalism" *Past and Present* 38: 56–97; Anthony Giddens. (1990). *The Consequences of Modernity*. Stanford, CA: Stanford University Press, 112.

51. Appadurai, *Modernity at Large*, 82.

52. Elias, *The Civilising Process*. For an overall description and analysis of Elias's theory, see Stephen Mennell. (1992). *Norbert Elias: An Introduction*. Oxford: Blackwell, esp. 200–224.

53. P. Berger. (2002). "Introduction: The Cultural Dynamics of Globalization" pp. 1–16 in P. Berger and S. Huntington (eds.) *Many Globalizations: Cultural Diversity in the Contemporary World*. Oxford: Oxford University Press, 4.

54. Latouche, *The Westernization of the World*, 41.

55. Gerard Madden. (1990). *Holy Island: Jewel of the Lough*. Tuamgraney, Co. Clare: East Clare Heritage.

56. Baudrillard, *Consumer Society*, 129.

57. Tom Inglis. (1998). "From Sexual Repression to Liberation?" pp. 99–104 in M. Peillon and E. Slater (eds.) *Encounters with Modern Ireland*. Dublin: Institute of Public Administration.

58. Tom Inglis. (1998). *Lessons in Irish Sexuality*. Dublin: University College Dublin Press.

59. http://www.cso.ie/newsevents/vstats_q1_04.htm

60. Richard Layte, Hannah McGee, Amanda Quail, Kay Rundle, Claire Donnelly, Fiona Mulcahy and Colette Leigh. (2006). *The Irish Study of Sexual Health and Relationships*. Dublin: ESRI.

61. Layte *et al.*, *Irish Study of Sexual Health*, 125.

62. Layte *et al.*, *Irish Study of Sexual Health*, 159, 170.

63. Layte *et al.*, *Irish Study of Sexual Health*, 82.

64. A description of Barbie quoted in *The Economist*, Vol. 365, 21 December 2002. For a more detailed description and analysis of the culture of Barbie, see Mary Rogers. (1999). *Barbie Culture*. London: Sage.

65. Writing originally in 1970, Baudrillard was probably the first to

draw attention to the implications the sexed doll had for civilization; Baudrillard, *Consumer Society*, 149.

66. Kevin Rockett. (2004). *Irish Film Censorship: A Cultural Journey from Silent Cinema to Internet Pornography*. Dublin: Four Courts Press, 138.

67. http://www.womensaid.ie/pages/WHAT/findings.htm

68. http://loosewire.typepad.com/blog/2003/10/news_wanna_get_.html

69. http://www.silconrepublic.com/news/news.nv?storyid=single3417. The findings of this study were rejected by the IE Domain Registry and by siliconrepublic—Ireland's Technology News Service.

70. Tony Fahey, Bernadette Hayes and Richard Sinnott. (2005). *Conflict and Consensus: A Study of Values and Attitudes in the Republic of Ireland and Northern Ireland*. Dublin: IPA, 30–56.

71. Darrin McMahon. (2006). *The Pursuit of Happiness: A History from the Greeks to the Present*. Harmondsworth: Allen Lane; Mark Kingwall. (1998). *In Pursuit of Happiness: Better Living from Plato to Prozac*. New York: Crown.

72. Margaret Fine-Davis, Mary McCarthy, Grace Edge and Ciara O'Dwyer. (2005). *Work-life Balance and Social Inclusion in Ireland: Results of a Nationwide Survey*. Dublin: Trinity College, 116–117.

73. Fine-Davis *et al.*, *Work-life Balance*, 112–113, 109, 55.

74. Economist Intelligence Unit 2005 "The World in 2005" *The Economist*: 86.

75. Tomlinson, *Globalization and Culture*, 3–10.

76. William F. Ogburn. (1964). *Social Change with Respect to Culture and Original Nature*. Gloucester, MA: Peter Smith.

77. Pierre Bourdieu. (1977). *Outline of a Theory of Practice*. Cambridge: Cambridge University Press, 78–79.

78. Economist Intelligence Unit "World in 2005": 86.

SIX

1. The concept of established villagers comes from Elias and Scotson's distinction between the established and the outsiders in their study of the suburban community of an English city in the 1950s. See Norbert Elias and John Scotson. (1994). *The Established and the Outsiders: A Sociological Enquiry into Community Problems*. London: Sage.

2. This borrows from the title of Peace's book; Adrian Peace. (2001). *A World of Fine Difference: The Social Architecture of a Modern Irish Village*. Dublin: University College Dublin Press. Other good

studies of Irish villages are Hugh Brody. (1974). *Inniskillane: Change and Decline in the West of Ireland.* Harmondsworth: Penguin; Chris Eipper. (1986). *The Ruling Trinity: A Community Study of Church, State and Business in Ireland.* Aldershot: Gower.

3. My examination of Ballivor was also an attempt to transcend Clifford's distinction between local and traveling cultures and the traditional association within anthropology of the village being the epitome of culture into which one is rooted and away from which one travels. J. Clifford. (1992). "Travelling Cultures" pp. 96–116 in L. Grossberg, C. Nelson and P. Treichler (eds.) *Cultural Studies.* London: Routledge.

4. Transnational companies started coming to Ireland in the 1970s. They have brought wealth and prosperity. They are the backbone of the Celtic Tiger. Once they go, the Tiger could be permanently paralyzed. Ireland has little in common with the Asian Tiger economies. It does not have the same networks of financing, science and technology. Nor does it have the same physical infrastructure or high levels of research and development. Finally, it is not backed by the same form of authoritarian states found in the Asian Tiger economies. Once Eastern European companies develop the same educated workforce, the same low levels of corporate and personal tax, and the same form of stable government, the transnational companies may pack up their factories and leave. See Dennis O'Hearn. (1998). *Inside the Celtic Tiger: The Irish Economy and the Asian Model.* London: Pluto; Michael O'Sullivan. (2006). *Ireland and the Global Question.* Cork: Cork University Press, 95–96.

5. http://www.nec.co.jp/press/en/0605/1101.html

6. *The Irish Times*, 22 February 2006.

7. *Sunday Tribune*, 17 September 2006.

8. The survey was conducted by Next Era Calling, a voluntary group of former staff and management, along with local community representatives and business owners, set up after NEC closed. This was not a sample survey and there is no indication of its reliability or validity. http://www.nexteracalling.com/skills.html

9. Elias and Scotson, *Established and Outsiders*, 81.

10. http://www.rollercoaster.ie/boards/mc.asp?ID=48097&G=26&forumdb=5

11. Tom Inglis. (1998). *Moral Monopoly: The Rise and Fall of the Catholic Church in Modern Ireland*, 2nd edn. Dublin: University College Dublin Press, 212.

12. See Mike Savage, Gaynor Bagnall and Brian Longhurst 2005 *Globalization and Belonging*. London: Sage, 155.

13. Sport was one of the most important things in these young people's lives. Out of the 28 pupils, 21 said they played a sport and all of these mentioned *gaelic* football, hurling and camogie (women's hurling), which were the most frequently named. There was also a wide range of other sports: soccer, athletics, swimming, basketball, table tennis, badminton, motorbike riding, lacrosse, horse riding, Tae Kwan Do.

14. When they were asked in the questionnaire about their favorite television channels, 52 mentioned non-national channels compared to 24 who mentioned Irish channels. Of course, it must be remembered that there are effectively only four national channels compared to numerous global channels. Nevertheless, 12 of the children mentioned Sky Television first.

SEVEN

1. http://www.cso.ie/releasespublications/documents/statistical yearbook/2006

2. *The Irish Times*, 27 September 2006. The notion of weapons of the weak comes from Scott. James C. Scott. (1990). *Domination and the Arts of Resistance*. New Haven, CT: Yale University Press.

3. http://www.cso.ie/releasespublications/documents/statistical yearbook/2006 The measure of at-risk-of-poverty involves calculating the national median income and then identifying those whose income is less than 60 percent of this.

4. Anthony Elliot and Charles Lemert. (2006). *The New Individualism: The Emotional Costs of Globalization*. London: Routledge, 196.

5. Kwame A. Appiah. (2006). *Cosmopolitanism: Ethics in a World of Strangers*. London: Penguin, xv.

Index

147, 162, 167–72, 193, 200; and
cargo cults 210; 213–5, 235; in
Ireland 281n
Tracey, David 153
Travellers 110
tsumani 75–6, 112

U

United States *see* American
Urry, John 265n
USTech 172

V

Valleley, Fintan 143

W

Wallerstein, Immanuel 264n

Weber, Max 265n
West Briton 128
Whyte, John 145
Wilson, Thomas 97
Wombole Software 171
work and productivity 169–72; and
family life 172; and emotions
175
world capitalist system 6–7, 13, 26,
28, 31, 34, 45, 46–8, 51, 57,
65, 72, 81–3, 119, 122, 159,
165, 168, 221, 256–9; and
happiness 190; unquestioned
orthodoxy 175, 257; resistance
221

Y

Yamashiro, Kenji 218